Criteria for Writers

Criteria for Writers

DANIEL BROWN
San José State University

BILL BURNETTE
San José State University

HOLT, RINEHART AND WINSTON
New York Chicago San Francisco Philadelphia
Montreal Toronto London Sydney
Tokyo Mexico City Rio de Janeiro Madrid

Copyright Acknowledgments

Heifferon, Nancy, "On Fear of Spiders" and related pre-writing notes. Reprinted with permission.

Baer, Cindy, "A Mud Theory of One Writer's Beginnings" and related pre-writing notes. Reprinted with permission.

Hanabusa, Wendy Ichimaru, "The Lessons of Yesterday." Reprinted with permission.

Vergillo, Michael, "The Narley Stuff." Reprinted with permission.

Tran, Tuan, "Travar, Young American." Reprinted with permission.

Leibenberg, Pamela, "The First Year." Reprinted with permission.

Smail, Karen, "Two Weeks One Summer." Reprinted with permission.

Yohn, David, "Ghosts." Reprinted with permission.

George, Wayne, "Work and the Silicon Valley Individual." Reprinted with permission.

Panek, Carol, "The Bird Courage." Reprinted with permission.

Lynch, Kathleen, "Small Change." Reprinted with permission.

Eggleston, Perry, Assignment Response: (Two letters on one topic). Reprinted with permission.

Lindseth Leif, "The Emeryville Crescent." Reprinted with permission.

Hanabusa, Wendy Ichimaru, "Verses of Promise." Reprinted with permission.

Lynch, Kathleen, "Seeing Ourselves." Reprinted with permission.

Leonard, David, "Lasers in the Modern Hospital." Reprinted with permission.

Anderson, Paul J., "That's Mr. Dill to You, Buddy!" Reprinted with permission.

Cover photo "Book with Pen" by M K Morgan.

Library of Congress Cataloging-in-Publication Data

Brown, Daniel, 1951–
    Criteria for writers.

    Includes index.
    1. English language—Rhetoric.   I. Burnette, Bill.
II. Title.
PE1408.B854   1986   808'.042   86-9932

ISBN 0-03-006173-3

Copyright ©1987 by CBS College Publishing
Address correspondence to:
383 Madison Avenue
New York, N. Y. 10017
All rights reserved
Printed in the United States of America
Published simultaneously in Canada
7 8 9 0 090 9 8 7 6 5 4 3 2 1

CBS COLLEGE PUBLISHING
Holt, Rinehart and Winston
The Dryden Press
Saunders College Publishing.

There are some things which cannot be learned quickly, and time, which is all we have, must be paid heavily for their acquiring. They are the very simplest things, and because it takes a man's life to know them, the little new that each man gets from life is very costly and the only heritage he has to leave.

Ernest Hemingway

For Lewis J. Brown
who taught the very simplest things

To Students and Instructors

The first discipline is the realization that there is a discipline—that all art begins and ends with discipline—that any art is first and foremost a craft. We have gone far enough on the road to self-indulgence now to know that. The man who announces to the world that he is going to "do his thing" is like the amateur on the high diving platform who flings himself into the void shouting at the judges that he is going to do whatever comes naturally. He will land on his ass. Naturally.

Archibald MacLeish

I am the best and sharpest critic of my own work.

Anne Frank

Books of this sort usually have a two-part preface, one part called "To the Student," the other "To the Instructor." The division implies that students and their instructors inhabit separate communities with different goals and different requirements. Unfortunately, to some extent this is true: Instructors have a variety of things in mind that little concern students—how their courses fit into the curriculum, how much material must be covered during the term, how learning will be tested and performance evaluated and records kept. Students, for their part, have their own concerns—how to fit the work for the course into an already hectic life, how to cope with (or perhaps conceal) their anxieties, how to confront a topic they may think is boring or intimidating or both, and of course how to keep up that important GPA.

But we've chosen in this preface to address students and instructors together, as a group, because we want to underscore the most basic premise of this textbook: that a class, like an athletic team, is a single unit, and instructor and students, like coach and players, in spite of their different responsibilities and interests, have a single, common goal—performance.

Apparent as this seems, it may be the most often-forgotten truth in the whole process of education. The classroom is too often a place of alienation and distrust, a place in which the normal relationship between instructors and students is an adversarial one, a grim struggle of opposing forces.

The struggle is over grades, of course. In grading, more than in any other aspect of classroom interaction, instructors and students are frequently at cross purposes. For instructors, grading is an impersonal, objective process, a weighing of the students' work against established criteria. But students in a writing class may see grading as anything but impersonal. They have put a lot of themselves on the line in writing an essay—not just their skills but their thoughts, their feelings, and their good intentions as well. Asking them to be impersonal about their grades is quite unrealistic. Too often the result is alienation between instructors and students; too often suspicion lurks beneath the surface like a sand bar on which everyone's best efforts run aground.

Because of grading, the relationship between writing instructors and writing students isn't, as it should be, the same relationship that exists between coaches and their players. Instructors should pass on the insights that experience has provided, suggest techniques that beginning writers might not otherwise uncover in their own explorations, and above all encourage and support and urge the students on to their best efforts the way that baseball managers slap their players on the back as they leave the dugout to take the field in a close game.

Imagine, if you will, a baseball game in which the managers must act as umpires as well. Imagine Billy Martin, that notorious kicker of dirt onto umpires' shoes, standing behind home plate and calling his own players out. Intellectually, they might still believe that he had their best interests at heart, but emotionally they would find it hard to feel that the slaps on the back and the dugout speeches of encouragement had been sincere. They would feel, and rightly so, that Martin owed a greater allegiance to the rules than to his players. So it is in the classroom—as long as instructors must be umpires, they will have trouble being effective coaches.

We've written this text to accomplish three important purposes: to explain to students how instructors distinguish between effective and ineffective writing, a process that can seem mysterious and even capricious to student writers; to give instructors and students a common vocabulary with which to discuss the students' efforts; and, most important, to take the burden of being umpires off of instructors. We hope to make this text the umpire and leave instructors free to be helpers, advisors, friends, and coaches. We hope to stand behind the plate and make the judgment calls, and we hope that instructors—if our calls don't do justice to their students' writing—will storm out of the dugout and kick dirt on our shoes, proving once and for all where their allegiance lies. This, we expect, will remove a major distraction from the classroom and will allow the entire class to work as a team.

We've divided the kinds of judgments we must make into four broad categories: Content, Organization, Style, and Mechanics. We discuss each of these concerns in detail in a separate chapter, using both student and professional writing to demonstrate the ways in which specific evaluative criteria can be fulfilled and providing short exercises to allow practice in fulfilling them. At the ends of Chapters 3, 4, and 5, we have assembled collections of full-length essays, written by our students, illustrating the success they have had by being their own best critics. We do not mean to hold these up as specimens of perfect student essays, for they are not. But in each there is much that works well, much that can be pointed to, examined, discussed, admired, and perhaps even imitated.

The book goes beyond judging finished essays, though, for writing goes beyond the classroom. The back slapping and encouraging words stop at the dugout steps, and, like athletes, writing students must eventually go out and perform more or less on their own. To that end, *Criteria for Writers* begins by discussing writing as a process, in Chapters 1 and 2. Here our purpose is to demonstrate the ways in which a knowledge of the evaluative criteria can act as a guide throughout the process, ultimately making writing students their own coaches and umpires, allowing them to be the arbiters of their own work while it is in progress, enabling them to eliminate their own weaknesses and build on their own strengths before the finished product is submitted to a reader. In each of these first two chapters, we follow the evolution of a single essay through a series of stages to show how an awareness of the process and an awareness of judging criteria must come together in the end and be one.

In short, *Criteria for Writers* brings out into the open the judgments instructors make when evaluating writing so that student writers can make these judgments on their own when writing. We suggest that at least the first when five chapters be read quickly, in the first few weeks of the term, and then perhaps reviewed and consulted later as the class wrestles with the complexities of producing its own writing.

Acknowledgments

We owe much to many who helped us to conceive of and write this book. We want to thank all of them: chief among them the students who allowed us to publish their writing so that others could learn from their successes and failures; Scott Rice, who taught one of us 93.2% of what is in the style chapter; Cindy Baer, Sharon Brown, and Nancy Heifferon, who offered their writing, their ideas, their criticisms, and their faith, again; the staff at Holt, Rinehart and Winston—most especially Tom Hogan—who encouraged us to do our own thing; and these colleagues from around the country, who provided much sage advice:

Victoria Aarons, Trinity University;
Commodore Craft, Thornton Community College;
Susanna Mason Defever, St. Clair County Community College;
Charles Duke, Utah State University;
Elizabeth Fifer, Lehigh University;
Lyle Morgan, Pittsburgh State University; and
John O'Connor, George Mason University.

Contents

Chapter Five

Style   131

Chapter Six

Mechanics   186

A User's Guide to Mechanics   219

Index   221

Chapter One

The Writing Process: A Fermentation of Ideas

Imagine that before you sits a glass of wine, deep and ruby red. You hold it up to the light and turn it, slowly. You wonder: Is it a mellow Pinot noir from California's Napa Valley, or Red Thunder jug wine from some far less romantic place? A true Epicurean, you decide to test it, evaluate it against known criteria. You inhale the spicy aroma; roll the liquid across your palate; examine the bouquet, the clarity, the body, and the color; and finally pronounce the wine first-rate, a robust Pinot noir.

But again you wonder: How can such a wine come to be? How is it that one batch of Pinot noir grapes crushed, pressed, and fermented produces a bottle to be opened on your graduation day, while another produces something closer to vinegar? Why does one winemaker's product fulfill all of the evaluative criteria you bring to it as a taster, while another fulfills none?

The answer, of course, is in what happens between the time the grapes mature on the vine and the time the bottle is finally opened. The process that leads to the product decides everything, has everything to do with whether or not, in the end, the wine meets the taster's criteria of taste and texture, color and clarity. Wine does not ordinarily spring forth full-bodied and beautiful of its own accord. It is the vintner's familiarity with the wine-making process, with the steps and options available along the way, combined with his sure knowledge of the criteria he hopes to fulfill in the product, that makes the final difference between *vin ordinaire* and something to savor.

The writing criteria discussed in this book represent tools that you and your instructor can use together to judge the quality of your written work. These criteria will be most useful to you while the writing is still being done—during the process of composing—not after you've turned the paper

1

in. It stands to reason, then, that before you worry too much about the criteria you aim to meet in your finished writing, you should understand the process other writers typically go through in order to produce an effective product.

"Typically" is a key word here, for no two writers follow exactly the same process, even when they write on the same topic and for the same audience. Even an individual writer may vary his or her writing process—either radically or subtly—as different contingencies arise and different problems must be solved. Moreover, writers who generally go through the same steps often find that these steps do not always follow in the same order and cannot always be neatly separated from one another. For instance, one writer may find that selecting a main idea to write about, a step that generally comes before writing a full draft, is sometimes easier and more profitable after a first draft is completed. Another may still be gathering new ideas to discuss, a step that usually takes place very early in the process, as he or she revises what was intended to be the next-to-final draft of an essay.

Nevertheless, all writers do carry out certain activities in one way or another during the writing process, and these activities do ordinarily occur in a more or less predictable sequence. To be familiar with both—to know the steps and the order in which they are most likely to occur—is a crucial starting point for anyone who would write more effectively and easily. In this chapter, I mean to discuss those steps, divided into the phases that I typically go through when I write. I offer them as advice from one who has been where you are going, not as a prescription for success. Ultimately, every writer needs to develop his or her own version of the process.

The Preparing Phase: A Clean Well-Lighted Place

Probably the first thing you'll need to consider—before you compose anything, whether a research paper or a short, personal essay—is when, where, and with what you'll write.

In many ways, when there is writing to be done I'm always writing. Much of my writing takes place quietly, beneath the surface of my consciousness, or nearly beneath it, while I sit and drink coffee at McDonald's or mow the lawn in the back yard. Little snippets of information lock together, phrases form and get stored away, images suggest themselves, a thesis gets reworked. In fact, most of the early stages of my own writing process occur this way—not in a sustained period of exertion as I hunch over paper, but in fragments of thought scattered through my daily routine.

Of course, a time does come when one must sit down and actually write, pull everything together and forge the links that will make one piece of writing out of many separate ideas. I've discovered, as does anyone who writes often, that there are both times and places where the writing will happen more or less easily, and others where it won't happen at all, no matter what. I can write—that is form thoughts on paper—either early in the morning or late at night, but almost never in between times. Other writers I know can only write for a few hours in the afternoon. Still others *can* write whenever they must, but are much more comfortable working at some particular time of day. So one of the first things you, as a novice writer, should do is to consider when you are most likely to feel like writing, and when least, and then plan to have pen and paper handy during your most productive hours.

Place is important, too. Some writers work easily in unlikely places— scrunched up in the back seat of a city bus or straddling a bench in a crowded cafeteria. But few of us are so able to tune out background noise; most of us need a relatively quiet and well-lit place in order to turn our attention fully to the task at hand. For me that place is at my old, oak desk by the window. Wherever you feel most comfortable writing, whether in a hay loft or at a library desk, I suggest you get into the habit of going there when work must be done. You'll find that the place itself soon makes you feel more like writing.

Finally, there is the matter of props. Most people seem to write more easily if they are content with the things that surround them as they write, and especially with the implements they actually use to do the writing—a pen that feels right in the hand, a pad of paper that reflects the right amount of light, an old, familiar coffee mug, warm in the hand. You may compose best on a portable typewriter, or on a certain kind of scratch pad. You may like the crisp feel of a #2 pencil cutting across paper, or the smooth, cool touch of a personal computer's keyboard. You may also discover that certain tools work better for you at different stages of the process. As with finding a time and a place for writing, finding the right props becomes easier with experience, and more important as you take your writing more seriously.

The Assessing Stage: Who? What? Why?

In one sense, writing is a kind of problem solving. A blank page always provokes a host of questions: What's my topic? How long should this paper be? What can I say? What *should* I say? Whom am I addressing? What am I trying to accomplish? What should I sound like? How long will I be able to work?

Writing involves working out the solutions to these questions and others like them. None can be fully answered until the writing is finished. But very early in the process, perhaps as soon as you've found a time and a place to work, you should begin to frame the basic questions that you will need to resolve as you work toward a finished product. Among these, three should be of particular concern right from the beginning:

Whom are you writing to?
What will you write about?
Why are you writing?

The first question is particularly difficult to answer in a composition class. When you write a letter to your kid sister, you know who's on the receiving end of your words, and so many of your other problems are immediately solved. You know what kind of language is appropriate for her, you know what her basic likes and dislikes are, you know what subjects will interest or bore her. But in academic writing you seldom know so much about your readers. Most probably, they will be instructors whom you see two or three times a week across a classroom; in general, they will seem to be much more knowledgeable than you about the topics you'll be writing about. How then to address them?

The answer is that you probably shouldn't. Instead of writing to an un-known quantity like your instructor, try writing to an imagined reader, an ideal reader of your own making. If you're writing an argument about the Equal Rights Amendment, write to an intelligent, perceptive open-minded person who just happens to believe precisely the opposite of what you believe. If you're writing about your experiences in a wilderness survival program, imagine someone who is interested to hear about your experi-ences but who knows nothing about survival in the wilderness. Even in the earliest stages of a writing project, experienced writers begin to think this way, imagining what their best readers might be like, what they might need to know, how they might react to each idea or fact. Don't make your imag-ined reader too easy a mark, though. Make him or her intelligent enough and tough enough to draw out your best efforts. Then as you begin to gather and select your information you won't be working alone; your reader will be watching over your shoulder, offering hints, whispering suggestions, muttering complaints, and patting you on the back as you sift through your ideas and wrestle with your material.

If you find it hard to fashion an ideal reader out of pure air, look around at your relatives, friends, and classmates—people whom you like and re-spect—and pick one of them or several of them to act as an imagined audience for your performance. The place to begin writing is not in putting words on paper but in finding someone to write to—someone who wants and needs to see your words.

The second problem, the question of what to write about, may or may not be solvable so early in the process. If your instructor has provided you with a clear issue, or a narrow topic to focus on, you need only follow where he or she has lead. Often, though, you will need to *analyze* an as-signment to see just what it asks of you. In such cases, read whatever instructions you have very carefully, underlining the key terms, circling the verbs that tell you what to do—"compare," "discuss," "persuade," and so on. Try rephrasing the assignment as a question or questions to be answered by your writing. If, for instance, you are told to discuss the relationship between two poems, ask yourself: What makes these poems alike? What makes them different? What among their similarities and differences seems most significant? If you are asked to propose a law you would like to see enacted in your community, ask yourself: What problems are going unaddressed in this town? What bothers me about life here? What has happened here or in the news that seemed unjust to me? When was the last time I got angry watching the news? Usually, translating an assignment into a question or questions will lead you to a specific topic. If it doesn't, if questions and careful study of the assignment don't yield a clear focus for your paper, you may need to move further into the process, exploring the subject and gathering more material before you try to settle on a topic.

Even when you know whom you want to address and what you want to discuss, one fundamental question remains: Why are you writing? In one sense, of course, in a writing class, you are probably writing to fulfill an assignment, get some practice, and earn a good grade. Those are good reasons in themselves, but they are also, ultimately, not very important to anyone but yourself; and writing that is important only to the writer shouldn't go any further than the writer's desk. When writing succeeds in satisfying readers, it does so because it gives them something they need, want, expect, or are pleasantly surprised to find. Your readers may come to your pages in search of many things—hard facts, amusement, explanations, escape, proofs, inspiration, a good argument—but they will always come in hope of finding something worth the effort of reading.

If you want them to find what they are looking for, you may need to rephrase the last question: Instead of just asking, "Why am I writing?" ask more specifically, "What do my readers want or need from me here?" If the answer is "information," start looking for facts. If the answer is "explanations," consider what will help your readers to understand the topic as you do. If the answer is "proof," take a stand you can back up and assemble the evidence and reasoning that have led you to embrace that position. If the answer is "entertainment," recall incidents that have amused you, describe something that moves you, tell a joke, play with words, let your wit shine, have fun.

Although their needs vary widely with circumstances, I think you'll find that all readers, in one way or another, read in search of some combination of those four basic elements: information, explanations, arguments, and entertainment. As you move through the writing process, if you're not sure which they want at a particular point, pause and listen to them. Grow quiet, call them up in your imagination, consult them, ask their advice—above all, attend to what they're muttering in your ear. Usually, they'll tell you what they want, what to do next.

Assessing does not end here. In fact, it only begins here. The writing process—from start to finish—involves asking, attempting to answer, re-asking, and re-answering the kinds of questions I've discussed here. Perhaps the best one can really hope for at the beginning of the process is to raise good questions. The process itself will gradually reveal good answers.

The Gathering Phase: Resources from Within and Without

No matter how fine a writing environment you create for yourself and how well you assess the basic problems you will face, you're likely to find that you are in for a struggle when you first sit down to put something on paper. If your topic is new to you, you may feel that you have nothing to say. If you have been thinking about your topic for a while, words, images, and ideas that have been churning about in your head may not be inclined to spill gracefully out onto a page. The biggest, scariest, most enduring problem all writers face is finding out what they want to say.

Fortunately, much research and quite a bit of common sense thinking have been going on lately concerning what exactly experienced writers do to get past this problem. As a result, many specific techniques have come to light. Below are some that have worked for me and for writers I know. Before touching on them, though, let me make two more general suggestions. One is that you conduct your search for writing material on two fronts: the world within you—the untapped reserves of your memory, your imagination, and your subconscious—and the world around you—the veritable sea of information in which you swim everyday. The other is that, whether you look within or without for information to write about, you should be as acquisitive as possible. Greedy even. Jot down *anything* that has *anything* to do with your topic; you'll have plenty of time later to toss out marginal or downright irrelevant material.

LOOKING WITHIN: ACTIVITIES

First consider a series of techniques for exploring what you may already know about a given topic—which is probably much more than you will at first suspect. Each of these techniques has worked for some writers; probably none will work for all. None is going to provide you with a finished essay, but one or more may well leave you with a sufficiently rich stockpile of ideas to build an essay out of.

Freewriting: Simply look at your topic, put your pen to paper, tell yourself that, no matter what, you are going to keep writing for a set period of time (say ten minutes) and go. The only rule is that your pen can't stop moving until the time is up. Because you have to keep your pen moving, your subconscious will begin to search for things to say about the topic, things you would not otherwise be able to recall. By the end of the time limit, you will have discovered much of what you know and feel about the topic. Especially if you keep a regular journal of freewriting for your composition class, you should have more than enough to write about when essays come due.

Clustering: Find a large, preferably blank, piece of paper. Put a word or phrase representing your topic, or a potential topic, in the center of the page. Draw a circle around the central word and then begin to free associate, jotting down *whatever* words or phrases occur to you as you look at that central word. Then jot down *whatever* occurs to you as you look at the new words, and continue in the same way—moving outward from the middle word, drawing bubbles around each new word and letting each suggest still others to you. Work quickly and without worrying about whether you will actually use the ideas that occur to you. Again you will discover what your subconscious already knows and feels about the subject at hand. You may want to do some freewriting immediately after making a cluster, while your mind is still abuzz with ideas. A sample cluster appears in Figure 1-1.

Turkey-tracking: This technique is much like clustering, except that here you start at the top of the page and work downward. Free associate as in clustering, but try to break the subject in each bubble down into smaller, more specific subtopics as you descend, pushing into finer and finer details as you fill up the page. Turkey-tracking has the advantage of encouraging you to form hierarchies of thought, revealing how one idea or fact supports another. In fact, a turkey-track produces what is in essence a free-form outline, and you may want to transform a turkey-track into a more structured and conventional outline before writing. You'll find a sample turkey-track in Figure 1-2.

Questioning: This is a trick journalists and others who have to write often and under deadline pressure sometimes find helpful. Write the questions "Who?", "What?", "When?", "Where?", and "How?" across the top of separate pages of note paper. Then bombard your topic with as many variations on each of these questions as you can think of. Recast each question in any form that can be applied to your topic. When asking "How?" questions about a proposed antismoking regulation on your campus, for instance, you might ask: How would it be implemented? How much would it cost? How would it affect people's rights? How did the demand for it arise? How can someone support or oppose it? As they occur to you, write down answers for each question, moving back and forth among your questions and your pages as new possibilities for questions and answers arise.

Conversing: Find a friend or a relative whose intelligence you respect and simply begin talking about your topic with him or her. The idea here is not to learn what the other person knows so much as it is to find out what *you* know. The activity of talking, of having to form words, will stimulate your imagination and give you access to what you already know. Jot down some notes during the conversation and do some freewriting or clustering immediately afterward.

LOOKING WITHOUT: PLACES

As rich a source of ideas as your interior world is, there will be times, especially in more formal kinds of college writing, when you need to look outside of yourself for more material to work with. Fortunately, we live in what has come to be called, with good reason, the information age. You probably already have a pretty good sense that your culture is awash in hard knowledge, much more than you or I will ever make our own. But the problem, when you confront a writing assignment, is where to find the information that will actually help you. So what follows here is a very partial list of places to look for facts and ideas. Keep in mind again, as when looking at inward sources, that your goal in this phase should be to accumulate as much information as you can.

The library: The hub of any school is its library, and it's sad that so few students find their way to it until late in their college careers. You'll find few better friends at college than your reference librarian; and you'll never again be short of things to write about once you learn to maneuver your way from the card catalogue, to the stacks, to the check-out desk. Enough said.

The living room: Not all research is done in a library, though, nor with anything so formal as a library book. The magazines on your coffee table are chock-full of interesting stories about contemporary issues. The newspaper at your door touches on a thousand topics. Your parents or spouse or roommates carry lifetimes of experience and knowledge around with them. Even the television set—especially when it's tuned to the news or to a public station—can reveal abundant possibilities for writing. With a notepad in your hand, and the basic skills of reading, conversing, and listening at your command, any one of these sources can provide you with the raw material for a dozen essays.

The classroom: For practical reasons, colleges tend to compartmentalize learning. Your school is probably divided into departments: History, English, Biology, and the like. Within each department, you probably take courses in still more particular subjects: microbiology, modern European history, and so on. All this creates the impression that history has nothing to do with economics, economics nothing to do with anthropology, anthropology nothing to do with biology. This, of course, is nonsense. As a writer looking for information, you can tear down the artificial barriers between the various kinds of knowledge you are acquiring in college. So long as you give due credit to your sources, notebooks and textbooks from past and present classes can yield rich stores of legitimate information for use in your English compositions.

The neighborhood: "Books are for the scholar's idle times" wrote Emerson. He knew what soon becomes clear to most writers—that the world around us, the physical, touchable, tangible world, is the richest pool of information and inspiration to be found. Books only report what others have already found there. As a writer, you will want to cultivate your powers of observation, learning to look at what surrounds you as if you had never seen it before, looking for the significance in everyday occurrences and familiar places. If you have a paper to write for an anthropology course on social interactions between women and men, you will find that your neighborhood is full of women and men interacting socially. If your English instructor wants an essay discussing the relevance a particular incident holds for all of us, you'll find that such incidents happen every day, to everyone you know. Talk to your grocer, who lost his store to higher interest rates, or to your landlord, who's raised your rent because of higher interest rates. The stuff of writing is all around you.

"ON FEAR OF SPIDERS": AN EXAMPLE OF GATHERING

In Figure 1-1 are the notes and scribblings a friend of mine, Nancy Heifferon, made as she gathered material for a short, personal experience essay. Working mostly from within, tapping her memory, Nancy began with an incident jotted down in a short journal entry and then produced a cluster based on that incident. As we look at the later phases of the writing process, we will follow her essay to its completion.

Last night, while I was dressing my baby for bed, a spider startled me by running across the bed. As usual, I felt creepy and called my husband to get rid of it. My fear of spiders could be a subject for writing.

Figure 1-1. A Journal Entry and Cluster for "Fear of Spiders."

The Selecting Phase: A Search for Relevance

Some of the material you come up with in the gathering phase may be thoroughly interesting but nevertheless irrelevant to what you hope to accomplish in your impending piece of writing. If you find yourself in this situation, you might do two things. First, count your blessings, for it's a far kinder fate to have too many ideas than to have too few. Second, learn to be ruthless.

No fact, idea, image, allusion, or phrase belongs in an essay if it is not manifestly related to the main idea, the thesis, of that essay. That's where the ruthlessness comes in. No matter how pretty the phrase, intriguing the idea, startling the fact, if it doesn't contribute to developing the thesis in some way it will have to be thrown out—or perhaps saved for another essay.

So it's a good idea to form at least a tentative statement of your main idea early, before going very far into the writing process; this thesis statement will be your primary guide to selecting what does and doesn't belong in the paper. Looking at the collection of facts and ideas you've assembled so far, consider what holds them together. What, ultimately, is the significance of the data you have found? What single idea about what precise topic will you use this information to develop?

In asking and answering such questions, you may find several possible main ideas, multiple hypotheses that you will need to test for validity before you know which is the best potential thesis. When this is the case—when you see several directions in which an essay might go—write down all the possible thesis statements. Then, like a rancher holding eggs up to a candle to check them for fertility, you can hold each thesis up next to the material you have gathered, testing each to see which you can best support, which might develop into the strongest and most interesting essay.

Once you have chosen a tentative thesis and written it down, you can begin to fiddle with its wording, making it clearer and more to the point. (You'll find a much more thorough discussion of how to form and recognize a good thesis statement in Chapter Three.) Even if you decide not to state your thesis outright in the finished essay, you need a working thesis now to serve as a touchstone for what to include in the essay.

If relevance to your thesis is the first criterion you use to select material, interest to your audience must come in a close second. Consider again whatever assessment you have made of your readers' needs. Look at the facts and ideas you have assembled so far from their point of view. One of the harder lessons in learning to write well is realizing that not everything that interests you will necessarily interest your readers. I am especially aware of this now, writing this chapter. My thesis here is that you need to be familiar with the basic stages of the writing process if you are to write essays that will fulfill the evaluative criteria making up the rest of this book. But I have too much information sitting before me on my desk. I could write a whole book just about the writing process—dividing it into many more phases, going into much more detail about each phase. That would interest me, but it would be a different kind of book, and it wouldn't provide you with what will most help you here. For now you need simply to get an overview of the most essential steps in the process; and so I find myself having to limit what I include, ruthlessly.

"ON FEAR OF SPIDERS": AN EXAMPLE OF SELECTING

Figure 1-2 shows more of Nancy Heifferon's prewriting. Notice that she's used a turkey-track based on her previous cluster, not to generate new material so much as to begin to select incidents and focus on a more particular theme. Then, using the turkey track as a guide, she has listed possible thesis statements, marking with an asterisk the one in which she finds the most promise for an essay.

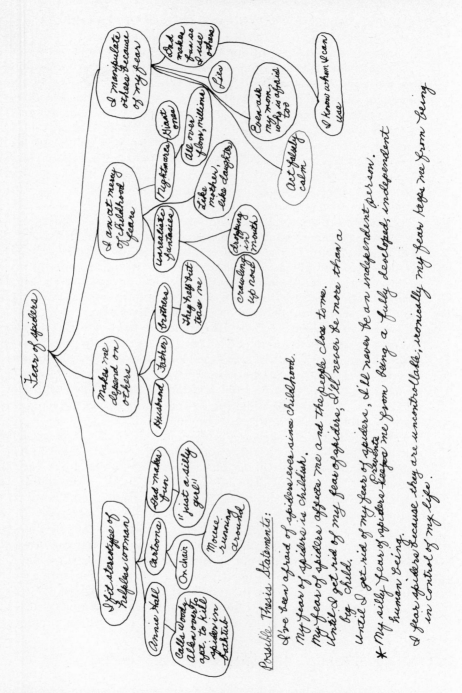

Figure 1-2. A Turkey-Track and Possible Thesis Statements for "Fear of Spiders."

The Arranging Phase: A Continuous Thread of Revelation

As important as a sense of audience is in the assessing, gathering, and selecting phases, it becomes even more so throughout the remainder of the process. Your ideas should follow one another, not as they happen to occur to you as you write, but in a deliberate progression that unfolds those ideas to your particular readers—in what Eudora Welty calls a "continuous thread of revelation." To spin such a thread, you will need to know both whom you are addressing and what sort of overall structure will best help them to see your meaning. Ideas—even very good ones—thrown down carelessly upon a piece of paper do not an essay make; they make something more akin to wheat mush, something grey, thick, and slushy. An essay, I think, ought never to resemble wheat mush in any way.

To choose a plan of organization for a particular piece of writing, begin by looking closely at what you have before you in your prewriting notes. You may well find that an order is inherent in the material you have selected. If you are going to retell an event, for instance, you will probably want to arrange incidents in the order in which they occurred, leading your readers from incident to incident. If you want to discuss the virtues of two political systems, you have in your material the makings of a comparison and contrast scheme, and you can guide the readers back and forth between two sides of the topic. If you have an argument to present, you may discover that an analysis of opposing viewpoints leads naturally into a list of your own proofs, that you can move your readers from the wrong side of the issue to the right. Usually, a structure already lies waiting for you; the trick is to uncover it, to let it lead you, and to avoid the temptation to slap an artificial form on it.

Once you've found whatever internal order holds your ideas together, you will probably want to make some sort of scratch outline to help you visualize it and to keep you on track as you write. Ideas of what an outline should look like vary widely among writers. Some prefer rigidly formal structures with Roman numerals followed by capital letters and so on. I usually find a looser, less formal listing of ideas in the sequence in which I want to discuss them to be just as effective and less constraining on my imagination. Some of my students prefer to write from a turkey-track. You'll need to experiment to find out which approach works best for you. What's sure, though, is that you'll need some sort of device for sorting out your ideas and showing yourself the relationships among them before you start drafting an essay. If you start to write without knowing more or less where you are going, you can pretty much count on never getting there.

"ON FEAR OF SPIDERS": AN EXAMPLE OF ARRANGING

In the scratch outline in Figure 1-3, Nancy Heifferon has begun by writing down the thesis she chose in the selecting phase. Next, she has arranged the points she wishes to discuss in an order that provides her, and her readers, with an orderly progression of ideas leading from her personal experiences to a thesis of more general significance for all of us. Notice that she is still forming, adding, and deleting ideas at this stage. The writing process is not a lock-step formula; its phases often overlap and intermingle to the profit of the writer.

Outline

Thesis: My silly fear of spiders prevents me from being a fully developed and independent human being.

I haven't ~~grown up~~ matured beyond my unfounded childhood fears.
 — Wouldn't go to bathroom, thought spiders were all over floor
 — Afraid one will fall in my mouth
 — Nightmares then & now
 — Hordes of spiders taking revenge for torture

When I ~~get upset and call for~~ shriek for help, I am ~~acting like~~ nothing but a ridiculous stereotype of a helpless woman.
 — cartoon of woman on chair
 — Annie Hall
 — movie clichés

Because of my hysterical fear, I would rather depend on others than take care of myself.
 — My brothers / tease me, make me beg
 — My husband / not as willing now after years of marriage

Like most people who depend on others, I resort to sneaky methods of manipulation.
 — Bribe my brothers
 — Creative lies to get my husband to do it
      "I'm holding baby"

As long as I am at the mercy of this ~~silly~~ foolish fear, I will ~~be~~ remain a child forever.
   in one way,
   , manipulation
 — ~~Fear~~ = incompleteness
 — Authentic people don't use others

Figure 1-3. A Scratch Outline for "Fear of Spiders."

The Drafting Phase: The Thing Itself

Maybe the best thing I can say about drafting an essay—it's certainly the most honest thing—is that it doesn't always happen the way it's supposed to. When I've thought long and hard about my topic and worked productively through the earlier stages of the process, I always seem to expect that I'll be able to sit down and simply watch a full-blown essay leap into being before my contented eyes. It happens sometimes, but seldom. Much more often, I will have surrounded myself with heaps of yellow paper crumpled into forlorn little wads before I can finally sit back and look at a full draft of an essay, several sweaty hours later.

To be sure, the fuller and more productive the early stages, the easier the actual writing becomes in the later stages of writing. But it never really becomes entirely easy. You may be able to take some consolation in the truth of what Richard Sheridan, the eighteenth-century dramatist, said:

> Easy writing's cursed hard reading.

Beyond that, though, about the best one can do is to learn a few tricks for coping with the difficult task of composing thoughts on paper. Below are some of the tricks I use; as you will see, some of them are the same techniques I suggested for generating thoughts earlier in the process.

- I go back to that comfortable writing spot—my old, oak desk—find my most familiar writing tools, and latch onto my warm coffee mug.

- I do a little freewriting, glancing now and then at my outline, simply to get my hand, eye, and mind all in gear.

- If I can't get one part of the writing going, I shift to another. No rule says I have to write the first paragraph first.

- I call a friend and talk over my paper with him or her, perhaps reading my outline; then, I dash back to my desk while the right neurons are still firing in my brain.

- I try to envision my reader or readers and begin to talk inwardly with them, asking them what they need and want to know about the subject.

- If all else fails, I simply clear my mind and stare out the window at the hills, deliberately not thinking about my writing. Perversely, this is often when an image or phrase that starts me writing comes creeping stealthily to mind.

One thing I never do is worry about mechanical correctness or neatness while drafting. I know that I'll be revising and then editing the essay later, and that there will be a chance then to catch spelling errors and repair faulty sentences. I don't want anything so superficial as an exaggerated concern with misplaced apostrophes to stand now between me and my intended meaning. In drafting, all I really want to think about is what I have to say and to whom I want to say it.

The Revising Phase: The Pause That Refreshes

I like revising. It's my favorite part of the writing process, the part that I feel most comfortable with and get the deepest satisfaction from. Yet revision is probably the most frequently ignored and misunderstood part of the process. Too many people, by far, confuse it with editing. The difference is this: While editing simply involves finding and correcting errors, revising involves reconsidering every aspect of a paper, including its content.

Actually you probably will have done substantial revising before you ever produce a rough draft. You will have added and deleted ideas, moved parts around, and found new directions all through the process. (In the next chapter, you'll find an example of how one writer has paused repeatedly to judge her evolving essay and reassess her decisions.) But at some point you will also need to sit down with a full rough draft and turn all your attention to revising, giving yourself a second chance at everything you've done so far. I find that idea of a second chance very liberating.

To revise well, you will need to have done two things even before you approach your rough draft. First, let as much time as possible pass between finishing a draft and beginning to revise. Time will give you a distance from your own words; the distance, in turn, will allow you to see possibilities that you would never have seen in the throes of first composing the paper. Second, bring back your imagined readers yet again. This time, though, do more than just hold a conversation with them or listen to their advice. *Become* them as you review the draft. Try to see the writing entirely through their eyes now. Write down the kinds of comments they might make on the draft itself if they were reading it to you. React to it as if you had never fully seen it before; that is how your real readers will surely react.

Because I judge a paper on four basic criteria—the same criteria of content, organization, style, and mechanics discussed in the following chapters—I encourage my students to look at their rough drafts in "layers," each layer corresponding to one of these four categories of criteria. I do the same thing with my own rough drafts, marking the paper four separate times with four different kinds of comments to guide me when I rewrite.

I find that the advantage to revising with detailed criteria in mind, whether I do so repeatedly during the process or wait until a full draft is on my desk, is that I need only worry about one layer at a time, so I can see much more to revise in each. Revising with such specific criteria clearly in mind gives me a chance to pause and reassess—to kick off my walking shoes, stretch out my legs, and take a look at where I am.

"ON FEAR OF SPIDERS": AN EXAMPLE OF REVISING

Figure 1-4 is the first typed draft of "On Fear of Spiders," with Nancy Heifferon's comments for revision written in the margins. Please read the essay all the way through so that you'll be able to see how she changed the essay between this draft and the final one. You'll find that in this first draft she is really just reaching out for ideas, still trying to find a direction. But in her written comments you'll see that she is beginning to find out more clearly what she thinks about her topic. Not content with striking out a word here or there, she is questioning her first impressions, searching for a broader significance, adding examples, reformulating ideas.

FIRST DRAFT
FEAR OF SPIDERS

A boring intro. need to make it more specific, more active.

I could describe a real incident to get attention

Men in my life have always made fun of me because of my squeamishness about spiders. My father, my old boyfriends, and now my husband have all treated me like a child whenever I have turned to them for as-sistance. As hard as this fear is for me to over-come, I ought to try because these men have shown me an important truth about myself. My silly fear of spiders keeps me from being a fully developed and independent human being.

Is this my thesis?

I am as frightened of spiders today as I was when I was seven. I haven't matured a day beyond my un-founded childhood fears. When I was seven, I wouldn't get up from bed to go to the bathroom be-cause I imagined the floor covered with millions of hairy spiders, crawling all over each other. Now I worry that one will fall from the ceiling into my open mouth while I am sleeping. Spiders dart irra-tionally through my nightmares now as they did then, giant ones, mutant ones, malevolent ones. And I still suspect that outraged hordes of tarantulas will seek revenge on me because my brothers plucked off the legs of their helpless cousins years ago.

This needs more specifics. Bring in:
① Raiders of the Lost Ark?
② Maureen O'Sullivan & Johnny Weissmuller
③ Maureen O'Hara & John Wayne

But if they come for me, I'll try to go quietly. When I shriek to be saved from spiders, I am nothing but a ridiculous stereotype of a helpless woman. I know what I must look like—a cartoon woman standing on a chair, clutching her skirt, and screaming be-cause a mouse is loose in the room. In the movie An-nie Hall, Dianne Keaton calls Woody Allen all the way over to her apartment to get rid of a spider in her bathtub. The scene was funny, but it (is) a movie cliche—a woman throwing herself into the arms of a big, strong man to save her from some harmless beast.

Represents? is based on? Plays on?

A spider is certainly harmless, but, because of my hysterical fear, I would rather look like the fool and depend on others than take care of myself. My *maybe this is really my thesis. And in this way I grant power over me to whomever I depend on*

I could add examples — other women I know and their fears.

too brief. It ends too abruptly. Extend to include feminism and the broader issue.

brothers used to dispose of spiders for me; they would do it because they could poke fun at me first and make me beg. Now I depend on my husband, but he takes his time about it, and he can't always resist teasing me either. However, I prefer humiliation to taking spiders into my own hands.

Like most people who depend so much on others, I resort to sneaky methods of manipulation to get my way. I know on whom I can count. My father always called me a silly girl; he never would humor me in my fear. But my brothers, when they weren't in the mood to tease me, could be bribed. My husband used to slay a spider out of love, but, after five years of marriage, appeals to his affection for me don't always work. I have to be more creative—''Jerry, I'm busy holding the baby; will you get this spider so it won't scare Emily?'' I have discovered that the more casual and unconcerned I sound, the more likely I am to get someone to take care of the problem for me.

However, I am not proud of my subterfuge. It is a sign of incompleteness. I have always believed that truly authentic and independent people do not use others. And as long as I am at the mercy of this foolish fear, I will remain, in one way, a child forever.

How does this fit in with my feminism?

What would Phyllis Schlafley say?

We all have our "spiders" to kill.

The Editing Phase: A Moral Matter

This is going to sound a little like a sermon, a little preachy, but that's because, to me, editing is a moral matter. "Moral" is a strong and often carelessly used word, and I hope I am not using it carelessly here. I use it not because editing concerns the difference between the right spelling and the wrong, or good grammar and bad, though both are true. I say editing is a moral matter because the quality of their editing determines whether or not writers sabotage their own best efforts, something I've often done myself and I see my students doing every day. I think it's downright wrong to work long and hard at developing an engaging essay and then ruin it by failing to make the writing itself correct.

If you'd scrimped and saved to buy a brand new, cherry-red Ferrari, and spent a hot afternoon washing and waxing it, you'd probably want to buff the wax at the end of the process. To drive such a car around covered with opaque Turtle Wax would rob you of the very effect you intended to create. Something like this applies to editing and proofreading an essay: the buffing and polishing assure that your efforts will be shown off to their best advantage. Of course, an absence of errors does not in itself make for a good essay, report, or poem. But if your writing contains a single idea of which you are proud, then even a single conspicuous error will detract more than you ought to accept.

Unedited or poorly edited writing has two negative effects on readers. First, it's simply hard to comprehend a paper in which spelling, grammar, punctuation, or usage errors obscure the writer's message. Each error puts a new burden of effort on the readers, who are bound to resent the extra work. Second, sloppy mechanics make a clear and unambiguous statement about the writer's attitude. They say flat out that here is a writer who doesn't care enough about the topic or the audience to make things right.

That's the end of the sermon—now some practical advice. Effective editing, like effective revising, is best done after time has passed. If you've revised your essay in the four "layers" suggested in the last phase, you will already have looked at the mechanics in your paper at least once. But let your final draft rest again, at least overnight, before editing it one last time for correctness. As in revising, you'll see more through fresher eyes.

It also helps to know what you are looking for. The skills discussed in the "Mechanics" section (Chapter Six of this book) are those that college students most often have trouble mastering. You'll find a "user's guide" for that section on pp. 219–220. If you keep the book nearby when you edit your papers, and consult the guide and the pages it leads you to when you are uncertain about an issue of correctness, you should be able to edit more effectively. You probably don't make all the errors discussed there, though. Most of us don't really make very many different kinds of errors in writing; we just keep making the same ones over and over again. One of the most valuable things you can do to become your own best editor is to supplement the discussion in Chapter Six with a personal checklist of the skills *you* most often have trouble with. Simply keep an on-going list of things you want to watch for as you edit your papers. Use your instructor's commentary on corrected papers as a guide to what you will include.

"ON FEAR OF SPIDERS": AN EXAMPLE ESSAY

Nancy Heifferon's finished essay is, as you will see, a far different—and a much more interesting—thing than her rough draft. Where before she seemed to be groping for a direction to take, here she has found one; and especially in the three new paragraphs she has added at the end, she has found a way to bring her readers face to face with her thesis. After you've read "On Fear of Spiders," you may want to flip back through the various stages of its evolution in this chapter to get a better sense of how the writing process shaped Nancy's final product. And after you've read the rest of this book, you may want to come back to her essay one more time to see how well it fulfills all four of the evaluative criteria outlined in the subsequent chapters.

On Fear of Spiders
Nancy Heifferon

"Jerry. Jerry, come here please," I called, trying to keep the anxiety from rising in my voice. "Come here and get rid of this spider, please."

"Why can't you do it yourself?" My husband laughed it off.

Of course, I had no answer. There is no reason that a thirty-three-year-old woman with a career and two children can't squash a spider or, better yet, ignore it. Reason has nothing to do with it. Everytime I catch, out of the corner of my eye, the sharp black scurrying on white walls, I want to run screaming from the room. And it is not, as my husband thinks, entirely a laughing matter. My silly fear of spiders keeps me from being a fully developed and independent human being.

I am as frightened of spiders today as I was when I was seven. I haven't matured a day beyond my unfounded childhood fears. When I was seven, I wouldn't get up from bed to go to the bathroom because I imagined the floor covered with millions of hairy spiders, crawling all over each other. Now I worry that one will fall from the ceiling into my open mouth while I am sleeping. Spiders dart irrationally through my nightmares now as they did then—giant ones, mutant ones, malevolent ones. And I still suspect that outraged hordes of tarantulas will seek revenge on me because my brothers plucked off the legs of their helpless cousins years ago.

But if they come for me, I'll try to go quietly. When I shriek to be saved from spiders, I am nothing but a ridiculous stereotype of a helpless woman. I know what I must look like—a cartoon woman standing on a chair, clutching her skirt and screaming because a mouse is loose in the room. In the movie *Annie Hall*, Dianne Keaton calls Woody Allen all the way over to her apartment to get rid of a spider in her bathtub. The scene is funny, but it plays on the movie cliché of a woman throwing herself into the arms of a big, strong man to save her from some harmless beast—Maureen O'Sullivan into the arms of Johnny Weismuller, Maureen O'Hara into the arms of John Wayne. As a variation on the theme of "calm man rescues helpless woman," in *Raiders of the Lost Ark* Harrison Ford forgets his own terror of snakes to save the hysterical heroine—a woman ostensibly tough enough to own a bar in an uncivilized outpost.

A spider, unlike a pitful of vipers, is certainly harmless, but, because of my hysterical fear, I would rather, like Dianne Keaton, look the fool and depend on others than take care of myself. My brothers used to dispose of spiders for me; they would do it because they could poke fun at me first and make me beg. I would even suffer my father's derision of "you're just a silly girl" if I could find no one else to turn to. Now I depend on my husband, but he takes his time about it, and he can't always resist teasing me either. However, I prefer humiliation to taking spiders into my own hands.

Like most people who depend so much on others, I resort to sneaky methods of manipulation to get my way. I know on whom I can count. My father would seldom humor me in my fear. But my brothers, when they weren't in the mood to tease me, could be bribed. My husband used to slay a spider out of love, but, after five years of marriage, appeals to his affection for me don't always work. I have to be more creative—"Jerry, I'm busy holding the baby; will you get this spider so it won't scare Emily?" I have discovered that the more casual and unconcerned I sound, the more likely I am to get someone to take care of the problem for me.

However, I am not proud of my subterfuge. It is a sign of incompleteness. I have always believed that truly authentic and independent people do not use others. So, as long as I am at the mercy of this foolish fear, I will remain, in one way, a child forever.

Certainly, I am not the only person to be stunted in this way. My husband insists that he trembles at the sight of blood and can't bear to see loved ones in pain; therefore, when emergencies strike, I am the one who takes our children to the doctor and soothes them while their wounds are stitched. A dear friend, confident in her career, hides when her doorbell rings during the day, and, when her phone rings in the evening, she lets her husband answer it as often as he will, all because she fears encounters with missionaries, salesmen, and solicitors. Another friend shudders at the thought of auto mechanics. She talks me into going with her to the garage and then whispers so that I end up interpreting for the mechanic.

In fact, most of us, given the slimmest chance, will rely on others to take care of our unpleasant tasks. But when we do, we grant others a power over us, a power they may easily use against us. They know our weaknesses, they know their strengths. Women who flippantly claim they want men to open doors and to stand in busses for them, who find Phyllis Schlafly an eloquent spokesperson, whether they recognize it or not, give up something for the privileges, something like respect. Probably the most important sacrifice any of us make when we depend on others to do unpleasant things for us is the opportunity to surmount a difficulty and to learn about ourselves, in other words to grow. Feminists, too, when we rail at men for oppressing us, must temper our bitterness with some understanding that we have often ceded control over our lives in exchange for the dirty work that men will do for us.

I do not mean that there are not significant wrongs to be righted; law suits to be pressed; programs to be funded; laws to be passed, changed, or implemented; amendments to be ratified. I only mean that I, for one, have many of my own spiders yet to kill.

EXERCISES

1. A. Write the phrase "A place for writing" in the middle of a piece of paper. Circle the phrase and begin to form a cluster around it. Thinking about where, and also when and with what, you feel most comfortable writing, generate as many specific details as you can about your ideal writing environment. Try to fill up the page with details.

B. Looking back to your cluster as a source of information, and adding anything else that comes to mind as you work, freewrite to create a description of your ideal writing environment. Be prepared to read your response to your classmates and to discuss how your idea of a good spot for writing resembles or differs from theirs.

2. A. Search your local newspaper for an article (or editorial or opinion column) that interests you. Try to find a piece that evokes a strong emotional response from you—anger, sympathy, joy, etc. Clip the article out and reread it carefully. Then, with the clipping in front of you, freewrite for at least 15 minutes about your reaction to the contents of the article.

B. Looking over your freewriting, write down at least three complete statements expressing opinions you hold about the topic discussed in the article.

C. Mark with an asterisk (*) the one statement that you feel you could best write an essay to support.

D. Submit to your instructor: the newspaper clipping, your freewriting, and your opinion statements.

3. A. Find among the quotations listed below an idea with which you agree or disagree. Using whatever prewriting techniques you find most helpful to generate support, write a full, rough draft of a short essay expressing your agreement or disagreement with the idea. When you have finished, put the draft aside at least overnight.

A friend in power is a friend lost.

Henry Adams

The easiest person to deceive is one's own self.

Edward Bulwer Lytton

Atomic warfare is bad enough; biological warfare would be worse; but there is something that is worse than either. . . it is subjection to an alien oppressor.

Elmer Davis

There is no such thing as a moral or an immoral book. Books are well written, or badly written. That is all.

Oscar Wilde

A human being is not, in any proper sense, a human being until he is educated.

Horace Mann

B. Return to your draft, and read it as if you had never seen it before. On a separate piece of paper, write down the following headings, and under each make as many specific, accurate evaluations as possible—both positive and negative—about that "layer" of the draft: Content (How true, interesting, and complete is what you've said?), Organization (How well have you arranged the parts for the readers?), Style (How effectively have you chosen your words and constructed your sentences?), and Mechanics (How correct are the spelling, punctuation, and grammar?).

C. Turn in both the draft and your evaluation sheet and let your instructor add his or her own comments to the evaluation before you revise the draft and turn in a final version for grading.

Chapter Two

"What Is It That You Want?"

Chapter One discussed writing as a process. By extension, then, an essay for a writing class is the end result of that process—a satisfactory, polished piece of finished writing. But if you're like most students I've met, even though you want to create that finished product successfully, you're not sure what it's supposed to look like when you're done with it. Students I've tried to teach seem to know fairly well what the instructors of their other classes want from them: their geometry instructors want them to be able to calculate the volume of a truncated cone; their history instructors want them to know what caused the French Revolution and what the general significance of that event is; their chemistry instructors want them to know what elements constitute magnesium phosphate and what bonds link those elements together. All this is readily apparent, but when I first began to teach writing, the goals of my English composition classes—like, I noticed, the goals of many of my colleagues' writing classes—were often not so easily deduced, and the question I heard most often from students was "What is it that you want?"

The Question of Good Writing

In the broadest general terms, of course, the answer to this question is simple: your English instructors want you to write well. But all this does is raise the subsequent question "What is good writing?" Answering this question is difficult, for writing is a varied and complex activity. There are many different kinds of writing, done for different purposes on different occasions, and often two pieces of writing that are both acknowledged as "good" bear little resemblance to one another. Consider the following passages:

25

A Letter to Lord Chesterfield

My Lord

I have been lately informed by the proprietor of The World that two Papers in which my Dictionary is recommended to the Public were written by your Lordship. To be so distinguished is an honour which, being very little accustomed to favours from the Great, I know not well how to receive, or in what terms to acknowledge.

When upon some slight encouragement I first visited your Lordship I was overpowered like the rest of Mankind by the enchantment of your adress, and could not forbear to wish that I might boast myself Le Vainqueur du Vainqueur de laTerre, that I might obtain that regard for which I saw the world contending, but I found my attendance so little incouraged, that neither pride nor modesty would suffer me to continue it. When I had once adressed your Lordship in public, I had exhausted all the art of pleasing which a retired and uncourtly Scholar can possess. I had done all that I could, and no Man is well pleased to have his all neglected, be it ever so little.

Seven years, My Lord, have now past since I waited in your outward Rooms or was repulsed from your Door, during which time I have been pushing on my work through difficulties of which It is useless to complain, and have brought it at last to the verge of Publication without one Act of assistance, one word of encouragement, or one smile of favour. Such treatment I did not expect, for I never had a Patron before.

The Shepard in Virgil grew at last acquainted with Love, and found him a Native of the Rocks. Is not a Patron, My Lord, one who looks with unconcern on a Man struggling for Life in the water and when he has reached ground encumbers him with help. The notice which you have been pleased to take of my Labours, had it been early, had been kind; but it has been delayed till I am indifferent and cannot enjoy it, till I am solitary and cannot impart it, till I am known and do not want it.

I hope it is no very cinical asperity not to confess obligation where no benefit has been received, or to be unwilling that the Public should consider me as owing that to a Patron, which Providence has enabled me to do for myself.

Having carried on my work thus far with so little obligation to any Favourer of Learning, I shall not be disappointed though I should conclude it, if less be possible, with less, for I have been long wakened from that Dream of hope, in which I once boasted myself with so much exultation, My lord Your Lordship's Most humble Most Obedient Servant,

Samuel Johnson

Sonnet I

Nuns fret not at their convent's narrow
  room;
And hermits are contented with their
  cells;
And students with their pensive citadels;
Maids at the wheel, the weaver at his
  loom,
Sit blithe and happy; bees that soar for
  bloom,
High as the highest Peak of Furness-fells,
Will murmur by the hour in foxglove
  bells:
In truth the prison, unto which we doom
Ourselves, no prison is: and hence for me,
In sundry moods, 'twas pastime to be
  bound
Within the Sonnet's scanty plot of ground;
Pleased if some Souls (for such there needs
  must be)
Who have felt the weight of too much
  liberty,
Should find brief solace there, as I have
  found.

William Wordsworth

From *The Right Stuff*

   In the training film the flight deck was a grand piece of gray geometry, perilous, to be sure, but an amazing abstract shape as one looks down upon it on the screen. And yet once the newcomer's two feet were on it . . . *Geometry*—my God, man, this is a . . . skillet! It *heaved*, it moved up and down underneath his feet, it pitched up, it pitched down, it rolled to port (this great beast *rolled!*) and it rolled to starboard, as the ship moved into the wind and, therefore, into the waves, and the wind kept sweeping across, sixty feet up in the air out in the open sea, and there were no railings whatsoever. This was a *skillet*—a frying pan!—a short-order grill!— not gray but black, smeared with skid marks from one end to the other and glistening with pools of hydraulic fluid and the occasional jet-fuel slick, all of it still hot, sticky, greasy, runny, virulent from God knows what traumas—still ablaze!—consumed in detonations, explosions, flames, combustion, roars, shrieks, whines, blasts, horrible shudders, fracturing impacts, as little men in screaming red and yellow and purple and green shirts with black Mickey Mouse helmets over their ears skittered about on the surface as if for their very lives (you've said it now!), hooking fighter planes onto the catapult shuttles so that they can explode their after-burners and be slung off the deck in a red-mad fury with a *kaboom*! that pounds through the entire deck—a procedure that seems absolutely con-trolled, orderly, sublime, however, compared to what he is about to watch as aircraft return to the ship for what is known in the engineering stoi-cisms of the military as "recovery and arrest."

Tom Wolfe

Here are three very different pieces of writing—different forms written in different ages for different purposes. The first is an irate letter to an eigh-teenth-century patron of the arts who has provided no support but wants to take credit for the writer's work. The second is a sonnet published around the turn of the nineteenth century. The third is a very contemporary de-scription of a pilot trainee's first experience with the deck of an aircraft carrier. And yet diverse as these three pieces are, all three are that per-plexing thing that English teachers call "good writing." Little wonder that you might not be sure what you are being asked to produce in a writing class.

Using Criteria to Identify Good Writing

On the other hand, diverse though they are, the three passages do have traits in common, and to a reader who has consistent criteria with which to judge them, it seems neither arbitrary nor capricious to identify all of them as good. It is the purpose of this text to establish and explain such criteria, and to that end, the book is divided into four general sections, "Content," "Organization," "Style," and "Mechanics." By using these four broad categories, I can analyze the three pieces of writing presented here and see why, different though they are, I would call them all "good."

ANALYZING CONTENT

Briefly defined, "content" refers to the ideas in a piece of writing. Are they significant? Are they interesting? Are they thoroughly explored?

Samuel Johnson's letter: The letter interests me immediately because it is part of a quarrel or conflict, and conflict is interesting. In it Johnson tells a story, a story of a little man, done an injustice by an important man. I find it significant because it touches a universal human chord in me. Like most people, I like to see the underdog win one now and then, and in this story, the little guy has published his work and achieved reknown and can afford to show his scorn for his would-be benefactor. There are other universal elements here too. Lord Chesterfield proves to be a fair-weather friend, and I've known one or two of those; and there is, too, something of what the French call *esprit d'escalier*, or the spirit of the stairs, by which they mean all the perfect retaliatory remarks people think up after it is too late to deliver them. But Johnson delivers his comeback here, and I can relish it with him because of all the times I wish I had done the same. As for working the idea out in its entirety, Johnson tells the whole story here, even though the letter is brief; I know what his relationship to Chesterfield is, why he is angry with him, and why he can afford the luxury of telling him off.

Wordsworth's poem: There is an element of conflict here too, inherent in the phrasing of the ideas. Wordsworth says some contradictory things in this poem—that prisons are not prisons and that too much liberty is a burden to bear. These are paradoxes, self-contained contradictions, and they make intriguing little intellectual puzzles that capture my interest. There is an element of the universal here too, although at first glance, since the poem is about writing sonnets, readers who aren't poets might think the poem has nothing to do with them. Close examination, however, reveals a theme more universal than just talk of poetic technique: in talking about the limited form of the sonnet, Wordsworth is talking about the restrictions of self-discipline in general, the willing relinquishment of freedom by focusing on an exacting task. In fact, the poem makes me think of Mary Lou Retton, the olympic gymnast, and other young athletes who sacrifice normal lives for a limited excellence. Wordsworth illustrates the universality of the theme by presenting diverse examples—nuns, hermits, students, even honey bees. And through the presentation of these examples, even though the sonnet is a "scanty plot of ground," the poet develops the idea enough for me to understand it.

Wolfe's description: Conflict makes this interesting too—the conflict between the relatively tame appearance of the carrier deck from a distance and the frightening reality of it close up. But is there any universal significance here? Will you or I ever land a jet fighter on a heaving carrier deck? Perhaps not, but I know I've gotten involved in activities only to find out that they were much more intimidating close up than they seemed from a distance (writing classes I took, for instance), so I can empathize with the pilots as they step out on the deck, and I'll wager you can too. As for working the idea out, Wolfe presents enough vivid detail here so that I get the point, on an emotional as well as an intellectual level.

ANALYZING ORGANIZATION

Organization is the shape of a piece of writing. Does it hang together around a central idea? Does it have a recognizable beginning, middle, and end? Do the parts proceed in a logical order that rises out of the subject matter itself?

Johnson's letter: Personal correspondence is often chatty and rambling, but Johnson's letter to Chesterfield isn't; he has a purpose in mind, and he sticks to it. He wants to take his patron to task for his shabby conduct, and everything he mentions contributes to that end—he's let his purpose select his content. Having done so, he lets the sequence of events help him organize his letter. He uses Chesterfield's reviews of his dictionary as an introductory gambit, and after that presents events as they occurred, beginning with his first encounter with Lord Chesterfield and ending with the rejection of his attention, an appropriate pattern of organization for the story he tells. He concludes with the pointed rejection of any further attention, so the letter has a definite sense of beginning, middle, and end.

Wordsworth's poem: Wordsworth chooses a very strict form—the Petrarchan sonnet, which has 14 lines that must follow a set rhyme scheme and rhythm. This rigidly prescribed form requires that the first eight lines present an idea and that there be a turn in thought of some sort, a refutation or a solution perhaps, in the last six. Wordsworth works within the form, presenting his examples in the first eight lines, and explaining them in the last six. But while he follows the form, he does not let it push him around—he deviates from the set rhyme scheme, and you could argue that his turn in thought occurs in the eighth rather than the ninth line. But that suits me fine: lockstep following of a form, even an effective form, is seldom good organization. The main thing to note here, though, is that everything revolves around the statement made in the the eighth and ninth lines—that is the "thesis" of the poem, and Wordsworth sticks to it.

Wolfe's description: This has less of a sense of beginning, middle, end than the other two because it is part of a larger piece of writing—an excerpt from a chapter in a novel. Nonetheless, it is tightly organized around the beginning pilot's dominant impression of the carrier deck—frightening as hell. That dominant impression governs Wolfe's selection of detail, and he presents nothing that does not further that impression. But the control that the dominant impression exerts goes beyond selection and arrangement; the choice of words and the shape of the sentences too are governed by Wolfe's desire to make his readers experience the flight deck as the trainee does. You can't stick to a main idea much more tightly than this.

ANALYZING STYLE

Language presents options, and style involves choosing among those options to achieve a controlled effect. The question, then, is, have the choices been soundly made? Do they suit the subject, the occasion, and the audience?

Johnson's letter: Johnson's purpose is to vent his emotion, and to portray himself as a virtuous and injured party. The choices he makes are effective. He creates images of himself that move the reader, images of Johnson standing hat in hand outside his Lordship's door, the comical but telling image created by the metaphor of the drowning man reaching shore through his own efforts and then being encumbered by his would-be rescuer. Tone and voice, created largely by strong parallel structures such as "... without one act of assistance, one word of encouragement, or one smile of favour" are appropriate too, the tone angry with a hint of restraint, the voice that of a righteous and indignant man.

Wordsworth's poem: Poets are, of course, experts in style, and their choices among language options will be particularly apt. Wordsworth's point is to argue in favor of the sonnet as a form, and the best way for him to make his case is to make the form work. The rhyme and the meter create a strong rhythm, working hand in hand with parallelism (Nuns fret not at their convent's narrow room; /And hermits are contented with their cells; /And students with their pensive citadels.), trapping the readers pleasantly within the confines of the form. Within those narrow confines, word choice is vivid, as witness verbs such as "soar," "bound," "murmur," and "doom." There are strong images, too, the image of the bee in the foxglove bell a particularly evocative one. Tone and voice are calm, wise, and introspective, suggesting a man content within his self-imposed restrictions. And of course the poet uses figures to go beyond the literal capability of language, naming discipline a prison, calling the sonnet a plot of ground and thereby suggesting that with careful tending life might spring forth from it—an effective blending of form and subject.

Wolfe's description: Here form matches subject too, phrases like "... all of it still hot, sticky, greasy, runny, virulent from God knows what traumas—still ablaze!—consumed in detonations, explosions, flames, combustions, roars, shrieks, whines, blasts, horrible shudders, fracturing impacts ..." mirroring the seeming chaos of the carrier deck. Figurative language turns the deck into a short-order grill (suggesting that the men on it are about to be fried) and gives planes the capability of feeling red-mad fury. Word choice is as vivid as the poet's, perhaps more so: "smeared," "glistening," "consumed," "skittered." Tone and voice put the reader in the point of view of the new pilot, not that of an objective observer, helping accomplish Wolfe's purpose, which is to cause the reader to experience rather than merely see the carrier deck.

ANALYZING MECHANICS

In this book the term "mechanics" is used to encompass various aspects of grammar, syntax, and punctuation. For most beginning writers, the central question about mechanics is "Are there errors here that detract from my purpose?" For the more experienced writer, it becomes "How can the mechanics of the language *further* my purpose?"

Johnson's letter: Some aspects of Johnson's letter might seem ungrammatical to you—"cinical" for cynical, for instance. But remember that he wrote in a different time, and the language had not become as rigidly standardized as it is now. In fact, Johnson himself wrote the first English dictionary, which is the source of his conflict with Lord Chesterfield. Since it would have been extraordinarily embarrassing for him to make an error while crowing about his prowess as a dictionary writer, I assume he minded his Ps and Qs carefully.

Wordsworth's poem: Poetry always looks grammatically odd because of the rearranged word order poets use to control meter and rhyme. Unusual as the word order seems, though, the poem is grammatically correct in every respect, and had Wordsworth not been something of a grammarian, he couldn't have created the rhythm and rhyme as well as he did. He even finds punctuation a boon rather than a hindrance in following the sonnet form, using semicolons to separate his examples in the first eight lines and both signaling his turn of thought and bracketing his "thesis" for emphasis with colons.

Wolfe's description: Wolfe's passage is peculiar, emphatic, and yet, like Wordsworth's poem, grammatically correct. Only a fine knowledge of the mechanics of the language could permit such creative manipulation of structures, and only someone familiar with the effects of the smallest of our language symbols could get the emphasis and dramatic effect out of dashes, ellipses, and other punctuation marks that Wolfe does.

   This analysis by categories uncovers the similarities within the diverse forms: All three pieces of writing contain some element of interesting conflict; all contain universally applicable ideas; all hang together around a main idea; all use such devices as parallelism, imagery, and figurative language to advance the writer's purpose; all show a keen awareness of the mechanical conventions of the times in which they were written; and so on. Hence, different though they are, all can be termed "good."

Using Criteria to Produce Good Writing

But what I've just done is an exercise in judging, useful in showing what a good finished product is, but not the most beneficial application of criteria. It's what we teachers do when we evaluate a final draft of an essay, and as you probably know, at that point, while our comments might provide guidance for future efforts, what they do mainly is to make you feel good or bad about your work. But criteria can be applied more constructively, and from your point of view as a writer, the criteria discussed in this book should be seen as your own guide to consult thoughout the process described in Chapter One.

The following essay, presented in various stages of its development, was written by someone in a unique position to understand both what teachers want and what students go through trying to provide it. After several years of teaching freshman composition, Cindy Baer entered the graduate program in English at the University of Washington, and as a teaching assistant there found herself once again on the other end of the red pencil, required by her supervisor to write an essay about her own beginnings as a writer. As a student of literature, she has used the criteria to analyze poetry and fiction, and as a composition teacher she has used them to judge student writing. But here, as a writer, she uses them *during* the writing process, guiding her own efforts with them as she moves toward the finished product.

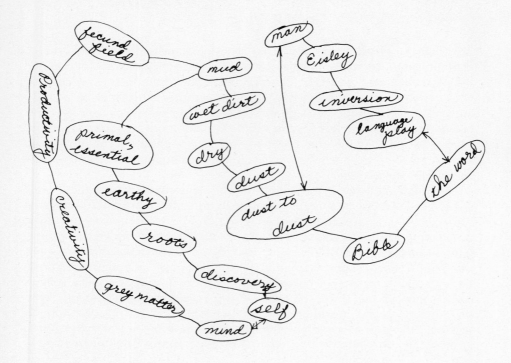

There is something primal something essential about mud. It's probably not a mistake that both our religious & our scientific wonderers have come up with mud theories of creativity — dust to dust from the Bible and man was mud and mud was man from scientist/writer Loren Eisley — incidentally one of my favorite examples of linguistic play in the classroom as I teach writing as I teach language, as I try to get students to see what I may have sensed before I understood — that playing in words is a lot like playing in mud, feeling the primal exhiliration of creativity as I break new ground, as I run my fingers through the fecund soil of my mind where I am literally growing.

Figure 2-1. Cluster/Vignette.

WRITER'S COMMENTS ON CLUSTER/VIGNETTE

Content: I like the surprise of the comparison—mud & words, writing. Originally the image of playing in the mud seemed to intrude on my thinking about being a writer, but as I explore it now, I see that it is integral to it. This is my origin. My evolution as a writer begins here. Perhaps I can work from that angle—developing as writer using the tension of surprise to make that biographical sketch interesting. I don't have much detail yet. That's a problem I will have to work out through more collecting.

Organization: A "working thesis" is all I have here: I began my career as a writer playing in the mud, but I do have the tension to guide me in my development of the paper. I will want to keep that tension central to the pattern of the paper as I demonstrate my thesis. I see both sequence and contrast here then. So as I develop the biography the threads will be both time (sequential development) and contrast (my development as opposed to what one might think of as underlying that sequence or informing it.) I need to find a good introductory idea to set up the contrast before I begin the sequential development, I think, so that that "informing" will take place.

Style: I like the voice in this vignette. As usual I use lots of appositives, always renaming everything as I go. I think the accretiveness of this works here, though: as it moves more deeply into the image it also grows, mirroring the ideas it expresses. The explosion of metaphor at the end was fun and I think the energy of that works, too. This may be a good place to end—as it brings me up to my present role as a writer, teacher.

A Creative Theory

Evolution : ~~A Personal Theory~~ A ~~Theory~~ of ~~One~~ Writer's
Beginnings

Begin — reference to Eu. Welty's book — the moon
passage

    my beginnings were not so poetic —
        I began by playing in the
        mud at age 3

    ~~Narrative~~ Anecdote — playing in mud — Chinese torture telling I'm a pig that fits

Need
To collect
More
Here   backyard in P.A. field
    Transition — creativity, ans trays, cakes dad had to eat
        that create same   seek activity them
            feeling in school
                Numbers.   words
                ~~Both~~ didn't do it. ~~English~~ did
                    ↓
    Anecdote — playing in words

            Mr. Wright's Fundamentals
                of Writing Class
            writing a ¶ on a picture
                    ↓
                found out things about
                    myself I didn't know

        got in touch   my strength as a
            w/my   writer to
            intuitive   create images &
            writer   ~~to move an~~ rhythms that
        my creative   audience
            self I felt   &
        like I was back   to move myself
        in the mud again

            ↳ a growing
                esp. for me

    uprooted from the pot of my PA
        backyard. ~~put into~~ planted into the seemingly
    foreign soil of school where I
    found I had my own roots
Conclusion — There is something primal...

Figure 2-2. Sketch/Outline.

WRITER'S COMMENTS ON SKETCH/OUTLINE

Content: I still need more details to create the initial feeling I had when playing in the mud—some detail that will show the energy of creating for *me* that I experienced there. What was the first thing I created?> *The day I got in trouble* for it, the first day in fact. The same problem is apparent in the writing class anecdote—I'll have to go back into memory to really make that part vivid. It's important.

Organization: I think the opener will set up that contrast I wanted nicely and lead into the anecdote about playing in the mud smoothly. But the transition between the playing in mud anecdote and the writing class anecdote is still fuzzy, getting clearer toward the end in the image of the *pots* and *transplanting*. I'll have to work that out in the writing, I guess. At any rate, the leap in time here will take some work. Maybe there's not as much *sequence* here as I first thought. More comparison/contrast. I still like the "There is something primal . . ." as a conclusion.

Style: Try to get the same energy that you have in the last paragraph into the anecdotes.

> There's a beautiful passage in Eudora Welty's <u>One Writer's Beginning</u> in which she describes the influence of the moon on her writing. I guess my beginnings as a writer are not so auspicious as that — (as nor will my career as a writer be as auspicious as hers, I'm sure) — my beginning was not so poetic — mine began with mud, not grapes, with texture not images. According to Chinese astrology I'm a pig — maybe that explains it. Anyway, my writing career began in the muddy field just beyond the grassy boundary of our property in York, P. a.

Figure 2-3. False Start.

WRITER'S COMMENTS ON FALSE START

Style: I don't like the way this is going—too many awkwardnesses—the parenthetical phrasing is a contortion painful enough for me, more painful I'm sure for the reader. The pig thing is cute, but do I want "cute" or "flip" here? The *anyway* suggests just how far off track that gets me.

Content: Get hold of the quote itself—the brief reference isn't getting the idea across.

Draft #1

Cindy Baer
October 25,1985

rework this title:
this isn't very
engaging

A Mud Theory of One Writer's Beginnings

this sentence
is hard to
get through

In Eudora Welty's book <u>One Writer's Beginnings</u>, she *underline title*
talks about becoming aware through her senses of the
word, recognizing the connection a word has with
what it means. What follows is one of the most beautiful passages in the book—the moon passage:

At around age six, perhaps, I was standing by myself in our front yard waiting for supper, just at
that hour in a late summer day when the sun is already below the horizon and the risen full moon in
the visible sky stops being chalky and begins to
take on light. There comes the moment, and I saw
it then, when the moon goes from flat to round.
For the first time it met my eyes as a globe. The
word ''moon'' came to my mouth as though fed to me
out of a silver spoon. Held in my mouth the moon
became a word. It had the roundness of a Concord
grape Grandpa took off his vine and gave me to
suck out of its skin and swallow whole, in Ohio.
(p. 10)

I like this—
the rhythms,
the contrasts
have an
energy of
their own

My own beginnings as a writer were hardly as poetic *Does*
or romantic as Welty's—my career began in the mud of *dash*
a Pennsylvania corn field, not the skies of the West *make*
Virginia back country; with texture rather than *sentence*
sound or images; in the palm of my hand rather than *too long?*
the fullness of my mouth. But the effect was the
same, I think: like Welty, I was attracted by the
power of words, their energy, their vitality, and by
the possibilities of harnessing that energy for myself, my own creation.

At around age six, I guess, it first hit me—my *Conclusion*
fascination with mud. I've read since then that all *comes*
kids are at some point attracted to the stuff; *back to*
there's something primal, something essential about *this,*
it that mothers with their Tide and Clorox will *offers a*
never understand, or perhaps just don't remember. At *tie back*
any rate, my writing career began in the muddy field *to the*
of corn just beyond the grass boundary of our neatly *beginning*
here.

I like this
tie back to
the passage

trimmed lawn. It began as the usual childhood mischief after a summer thunder storm, the kind which
brings thunder that peels the paint of walls, shakes
the whole earth and even the thick apple tree in the
back yard, the kind that vibrates up from your shoes
to your ringing ears and leaves the whole landscape
charged with its energy and you with it. It was
after just such a storm that I discovered the mud.
There was the usual period of testing, first one tip
of the index finger and a quick glance over the
shoulder at the kitchen window where Mom might be
watching; then a little dab on the end of the fingertip, rubbing it into the palm of the other hand
and peeking over the shoulder once more. The mud of
a Pennsylvania corn field after a summer rain is
smooth and thick and rich, dark and deep and
lovely—and warm. As I sunk deeper into the field,
from finger tip to elbow, I just explored its texture, rubbing it in my hands, letting it ooze
through my fingers as I squeezed it, forgetting
about Mom altogether.

This was also the period in my life I remember
fantasizing that the Mom at the kitchen window was
not my real Mom—my real Mom had been kidnapped and
was being held prisoner in the attic; this was a
wicked substitute, some fiend or witch put here to
torment my soul and fill me with rage and sinful
hate. That day she was the devil himself. But as I
stalked to my room, hands in pockets, I found comfort in the smooth, thick darkness I harbored there.
And in my room I made my first mud creation. I don't
remember what it was exactly but it was a shape, a
shape I made out of mud that soothed my rage, became
it, embodied it. Whether it was round like the comfort I sought and remembered or jagged like my
thoughts, what I remember of it is not the thing itself, but its creation—the feeling of pouring out
myself onto some outside matter and shaping it into
my form, giving it my life.

I cannot say when exactly I made the connection
between my mud creations and language creations. But
I do remember that eventually my mud creations became a way of communicating, too. Once Mom resigned
herself to my fascination, I had the pleasure of
making gifts and presenting them to adult audiences
who received them with delight—Dad would gobble up

show this shaping in more detail

again—the memory is more vivid than the writing. add detail.

this sentence is difficult to get through

This is an important idea, an important part of the whole experience. I need to show here!

my mud cookies and pies and cakes; Mr. Campbell
would actually use one of my ashtrays, the one Dad
let me harden on the grill. At some point, mud became a medium for shaping an audience in the same
way I had originally shaped the mud itself, and of
course language had the same power—I could perhaps
sense that in the language of the books that so
moved me as Sister Dorita or Mrs. Overbaugh, or Mom
read them to me, though I was not adept at using it
until much later.

My first success as a writer came in my sophomore
year of high school in Mr. Wright's Fundamentals of
Writing class. We were told to describe a picture of
an old man that was in our text—just one paragraph.
I struggled with that one paragraph. I had long ago
given up mud creations, but I still knew that feeling of intense connection with shapeless matter as I
breathed life into it that marked those earlier
creations. And I just didn't feel that connection
here. At midnight I gave up and resigned myself to
bed and an embarrassing scene with Mr. Wright in the
morning. But at twelve-fifteen the light was back
on—words were oozing up in my head and mentally I
squeezed them through my fingers—a smooth, dark,
rich, warm flow of words. I could feel the energy of
the language in the same way I felt the energy of
the mud that first day in my bedroom. And when Mr.
Wright and the class received my creation with delight, I knew I could shape an audience with language, too.

There is something primal, something essential
about mud. It's probably not a mistake that both our
religious and our scientific wonderers have come up
with mud theories of creation—the Biblical ''dust to
dust'' and the evolutionary ''Man was mud and mud
was man'' from scientist-writer Loren Eisley—
incidentally one of my favorite examples of language
play in the classroom as I teach writing, as I try
to get students to feel what I may have sensed before I understood—that playing in words is a lot
like playing in mud, feeling the primal exhilaration
of creativity as I break new ground, as I run my
fingers through the fecund soil of my mind where I
take root, where I am literally growing. Mud may not
be as auspicious a beginning as is communion with
the moon—we don't often associate artistic creation

connection here is not smooth.

I like this—recalls the mud experience effectively

I still like this as a conclusion

There is room here, I think, to step back and make more of the Earth/Heaven idea. I think I can expand this to make a more universal comment

with Earth but with the Heavens. Still, I think I found the same essential connection in the muddy cornfield of my Pennsylvania home as Welty found in the moonlit skies of the West Virginia backcountry. *about the origins of language & creativity.*

C.B.

WRITER'S COMMENTS ON FIRST DRAFT

Content: The personal significance here is clear—these are my origins. And the surprise of the connection is in itself interesting. But is there also universal significance in my experience? To some extent, I think there is—in the contrast between Welty's heavenward gaze and my earthy one I think there is a whole cultural bias about the nature & origin of creativity. I can explore this to enrich the content here. There are a number of points where detail is sorely lacking. I need to try to make the writing as vivid as the memory throughout. I should aim for the texture of the second paragraph throughout.

Organization: The lead & conclusion work pretty well, I think, though the conclusion may be expanded some. There is a clear progression of ideas here and I think the chronology works well. I do need to work on the transition to the language section. I'm still stuck here.

Style: I think the voice is consistent, with just enough variation to avoid monotony (i.e. the Clorox idea and the devil idea interject a little humor.) There are a couple of sentences that need to be reworked—my usual tendency toward verbosity here.

Mechanics: Check final draft for comma splices and subject verb agreement—these sometimes slip by you at first.

A Mud Theory of One Writer's Beginnings
Cindy Baer

In *One Writer's Beginnings*, Eudora Welty describes her sensory awakening to words, recognizing through her senses the connection a word has with what it means. What follows is one of the most beautiful passages in the book—the moon passage:

> At around age six, perhaps, I was standing by myself in our front yard waiting for supper, just at that hour in a late summer day when the sun is already below the horizon and the risen full moon in the visible sky stops being chalky and

begins to take on light. There comes the moment, and I saw it then, when the moon goes from flat to round. For the first time it met my eyes as a globe. The word "moon" came to my mouth as though fed to me out of a silver spoon. Held in my mouth the moon became a word. It had the roundness of a Concord grape Grandpa took off his vine and gave me to suck out of its skin and swallow whole, in Ohio. (p. 10)

My own beginnings as a writer were hardly as poetic or romantic as Welty's—my career began in the mud of a Pennsylvania corn field, not the skies of the West Virginia back country; with texture rather than sound or images; in the palm of my hand rather than the fullness of my mouth. But the effect was the same, I think: like Welty, I was attracted by the power of words, their energy, their vitality, and by the possibilities of harnessing that energy for myself, my own creation.

At around age six, I guess, it first hit me—my fascination with mud. I've read since then that all kids are at some point attracted to the stuff; there's something primal, something essential about it that mothers with their Tide and Clorox will never understand, or perhaps just don't remember. At any rate, my writing career began in the muddy field of corn just beyond the grass boundary of our neatly trimmed lawn. It began as the usual childhood mischief after a summer thunder storm, the kind which brings thunder that peels the paint off walls, shakes the whole earth and even the thick apple tree in the back yard, the kind that vibrates up from your shoes to your ringing ears and leaves the whole landscape charged with its energy—and you with it. It was after just such a storm that I discovered the mud. There was the usual period of testing, first one tip of the index finger and a quick glance over the shoulder at the kitchen window where Mom might be watching; then a little dab on the end of the fingertip, rubbing it into the palm of the other hand and peeking over the shoulder once more. But the mud of a Pennsylvania corn field after a summer rain is smooth and thick and rich, dark and deep and lovely—and warm. It invites a kind of oblivion, a slow sinking into its depths. And at six I had hardly enough conscience to resist its primal pull. As I sank deeper into the field, from finger tip to elbow, I explored its texture, rubbing it in my hands, letting it ooze through my fingers as I squeezed it, forgetting about Mom altogether—and the smarting sting of her wrath.

This was also the period in my life I remember fantasizing that the Mom at the kitchen window was not my real Mom—my real Mom had been kidnapped and was being held prisoner in the attic; this was a wicked substitute, some fiend or witch put here to torment my soul and fill me with rage and sinful hate. That day she was the devil himself. Surprising me just as I was about to lose myself completely in the mud, her voice thundered through to my muddy consciousness, and I stood frozen in my guilt. But as I stalked to my room sulkily, hands in pockets, I found comfort in the smooth, thick darkness I harbored there. And in my room I made my first mud creation. I don't remember what it was exactly but it was a shape, a shape I made out of mud that soothed my rage, became it, embodied it. Whether it was round like the comfort I sought and remembered or jagged like my thoughts, what I remember of it is not the thing itself, but its creation—the feeling of pouring out myself onto some outside matter and shaping it into my form, giving it my life.

Not all the Tide in the world could wash away that memory, that feeling of energy. Nor could all the afternoons spent in my room, all the paddlings suffered and privileges denied, stop my frequent explorations in the back yard. Mother Nature herself was powerless to stop me; in the fall when there was less rain, I would irrigate the field with a constant stream of water, sometimes carried cup by cup from the basement. My mud creations grew more frequent and more sophisticated and once Mom resigned herself to my fascination, I had the pleasure of making gifts and presenting them to adult audiences who received them with delight—Dad would gobble up my mud cookies and pies and cakes and for a moment the sometimes distant man in the dark blue suit and tie would set down the coal grey Samsonite briefcase and enter my world of play; Mr. Campbell would actually use one of my ashtrays (the one Dad let me harden on the grill, showing me how he'd done it when he was a kid) as he sat in his back yard drinking scotch and swearing at the mosquitos and blowing smoke rings for me to catch and wear on my fingers like the magic rings of some fairy princess of mists. The transformations were always temporary—the adults had always to leave eventually and return to their world of work—nonetheless, at some point, mud became for me a medium for shaping an audience in the same way I had originally shaped the mud itself. And of course language had the same power, the power to transport people into another world—I could perhaps sense that in the language of the books that carried me off into the worlds of Stuart Little or Charlotte or Christopher Robin, though I was not adept at using it until much later.

It was this sense that guided me to my first success with language years later in my sophomore year of highschool in Mr. Wright's Fundamentals of Writing class. We were told to describe a picture of an old man that was in our text—just one paragraph. The picture was a stirring one, one that captured the loneliness of age in the wrinkles of the face and the white wisps of angel's hair that fluttered about the fragile head. I struggled with that one paragraph, trying to get the words to obey my feelings the way the mud once had. I had long ago given up mud, but I still knew that feeling of intense connection with shapeless matter that marked those earlier creations. And I just didn't feel that connection here. At midnight I gave up and resigned myself to bed and to an embarrassing scene with Mr. Wright in the morning. But at twelve-fifteen the light was back on—words were oozing up in my head and mentally I squeezed them through my fingers—a smooth, dark, rich, warm flow of words. I could feel the energy of the language in the same way I had felt the energy of the mud that first day in my bedroom. And as I returned to bed, I felt the same anxious hopefulness I had had as I waited for Dad's car to round the corner or for Mr. Campbell to finish dinner and pour his scotch.

Mr. Wright was a very big man with a very big vocabulary, who impressed on me the "largeness" of our language—its variety, richness, power, and depth. When he read to us, he would sit on the very edge of his desk, almost leaning, with his feet planted on the floor and his hands dancing magically to the rhythm of the words as he spoke them, his voice resounding through the room and sometimes spilling out into the hall, echoing loudly. He had a deep, smooth, dark voice, the kind that wells up from just below the diaphragm and reverberates in the throat and resonates in the hearing. He was an impressive figure in the classroom.

The next day while we worked on our next writing, he flipped through the papers we'd handed in, and his "Well, I'll be" startled us all. As we looked up, he grinned broadly, announcing that we had a writer in our midst, and began to read us a paper—my paper. I listened to the words, welling up in the great bellows of his stomach, and saw them dancing rhythmically from his hands. And I watched people's faces, their eyes darting about the room at first looking for the blush and the averted eyes that would mark the unknown author, but finally, caught in the rich flow of words and the dance of language, they fixed their eyes on the large dark man before them. When his sound stopped, no sound rushed in to fill up the space, and I sat mutely myself in the void of that moment, anxious yet proud, feeling the success that the silence communicated, my words holding them composed in a moment of silence and sorrow for the man who faded slowly into oblivion. Language, charged with the same energy of creation, proved as powerful a medium as the mud before it, as rich, as deep, as dark, as lovely. We have a long tradition, culturally, of invoking the heavens when we write, of looking to the skies, not the earth, for inspiration, of associating language with gods, muses, even Welty's moon. Such a tradition is misleading. It suggests that writing begins outside ourselves, beyond the realm of earthly thought, earthly experience, earthly power. Certainly such an idea misses Welty's point altogether. Her moon is not other-worldly; it is very much of this world. It is sight, sound, touch, and taste. It is a grape, a *thing*, and her experience of that thing. Mud may not be as auspicious a beginning as is communion with the moon. Still, I think I found the same essential connection in the muddy cornfield of my Pennsylvania home as Welty found in the moonlit skies of the West Virginia back country, the fusion between language and senses, between language and feeling, that quickens the mind and brings it to life, that charges language with the power of felt knowledge, and energizes both—language and knowledge—with the child-like spontaneity that refreshes. There is something primal, something essential about mud. And it is no wonder to me that we find both our religious and our scientific wonderers speculating on mud theories of creation—the Biblical "dust to dust" and the evolutionary "Man was mud and mud was man" from scientist-writer Loren Eisley. Today, as I take Mr. Wright's place in front of the teacher's desk, as I try to get students to feel what I may have sensed before I understood, it is this mud theory of creativity that I hope to pass on—the idea that playing in words is a lot like playing in mud, feeling the primal exhilaration of creativity as I break new ground, as I run my fingers through the fecund soil of my mind where I take root, where I am literally growing. Our language roots lie buried in the mud. It is there we must find them.

Probably the first thing you'll notice while watching the development of this essay is that although there are four categories of criteria—content, organization, style, and mechanics—Baer doesn't comment on all four after every phase of the process. This is just as it should be, since being concerned with the whole set of criteria at every turn is inappropriate. She has a good deal to say about content early on, about what is potentially interesting in her prewriting cluster and vignette, about how she will expand and develop this beginning of an idea. Note that she concentrates on what she's done well, not what she dislikes. There'll be plenty of time later to apply the negative side of criticism; early in the process negative thinking discourages the writer, reduces the will to continue. In fact, what people call "writer's block" usually results from the reluctance to commit anything but the best writing to paper. (At the outset, ignore what is done badly and look for what is done well to guide you in moving forward.) She considers organization too, speculating on possible patterns of arrangement, but since most of the material hasn't been generated yet, there isn't much she can say for sure at this point. Since she has written a paragraph, she can begin to consider style, and once again she looks for what works, so that she can build on it.

After her sketch, a kind of free-form outline or flow chart, she begins to be more critical, questioning the content, telling herself now what it lacks, what will have to be added as she fleshes out the skeleton of the outline in a draft. She has more to say about organization now, being able to see more parts of the emerging essay. She identifies both strengths and weaknesses here, and at this point she can still be bold in contemplating changes. Rearrangement is cheap before the writer moves from outline to draft; after that, the writing begins to congeal, and takes more energy to alter. There is little to say about style at this point, but she reminds herself that there was much that she liked in that vignette paragraph, and she wants to be thinking about that as she goes into the draft.

Upon beginning the draft, she runs into trouble, and the critic steps in and says "don't waste any more time with this; throw it out and get a better start." The style, mainly, disappoints the writer here, but there is one suggestion for improving content.

When a draft is finally produced, Baer is just getting started. Even though she has already invested a good deal of time and work in the draft, she's not afraid to question it, and she's still ready to build on what works well. This, perhaps, is the most tangible benefit of positive application of the criteria: if you use them to lead you toward your best efforts rather than to condemn your weakest ones, a draft is a wealth of potential to be developed rather than a flawed product to be patched up. It is the conviction that good writing will get even better that gives the writer the courage to make extensive changes between the two drafts shown here. Nor is she satisfied entirely with the final draft—she hadn't finished typing it before she was looking at ways to improve it even more. The writing process never really ends.

If you followed her notes carefully through the process, you might be wondering what happened to the mechanics category in the early stages. Two things, actually. The obvious one is that as an English teacher and a practiced writer, Baer knows mechanics well enough to not have to worry much about them (one of the benefits of working hard at anything—it gets easier after a while). But that's not the most important thing to be aware of. If you go back to the vignette paragraph at the beginning, you'll find mechanical errors—a missing comma in the first sentence, missing quotation marks around what are clearly quotes, what appears to be an unintentional repetition in ". . . in the classroom as I teach writing as I teach language . . ." What?! Mistakes, in the writing of an English teacher?! Yep. And she doesn't say a word about mechanics after the vignette, even though the drafts of the essay show that somewhere along the line she found and corrected the errors. She knows that of the four criteria enumerated here, mechanics especially shouldn't concern her until the end of the process. Early on it's a hindrance, a block, a hang up. Fussing over correctness in the early stages of the writing process is like wearing your tie to bed the night before a job interview: it reveals a basic misunderstanding of the purpose of proper surface appearances. By the time the writing is actually presented, the writer has dressed it up, but early on she has more important things on her mind.

The final thing I'll point out about this example is that in her discussion of her efforts, Baer has two voices; she sounds like two different people. When she says, for instance, "Try to get the same energy that you have in the last paragraph into the anecdotes," the voice is that of a teacher or editor, a critic, telling the writer to make a change. But when she says "I still need more details to create the initial feeling I had when playing in the mud . . .," she sounds like a student in conference with a teacher or perhaps in a peer editing group, explaining, partly to herself and partly to someone else, how she might improve the essay. She is not only, as Anne Frank said of herself, her own "best and sharpest critic," but her own best and sharpest student as well.

The Writer As Jekyll and Hyde

This schizophrenic nature is an essential quality of writers. The real question is not what the teacher wants, but what you, the writer, want to accomplish in any given writing situation. You want to move through the writing process toward your best possible effort at any given time, and if you are to do that, you can't wait for the teacher (or the editor, or the publisher, or the team leader) to apply evaluative criteria to your writing. You have to be both writer and editor, to have your own notion of what works and use it as a guide throughout the process, helping you make the better choice at every fork in the road.

To that end the next four chapters set forth the four criteria I've mentioned here in greater detail. As you read them remember that, misused, detailed evaluative criteria can interfere with the writing process and jeopardize its success. If you have the criteria too completely in mind early in the process, they can act as a psychological block, disrupting the creative functions of the brain that are so important in the early phases of writing. If you think the criteria are a formula that must be followed by rote, you reduce the process to a mechanical exercise that does not help you work out your own views and express your own responses. If you ignore the criteria until the process is nearly done, writing a complete draft and then setting it up next to the criteria to see if you've coincidentally produced a good essay (or if you place that unpleasant task in the hands of a teacher or editor), you turn the revision phase of the process into an awesomely difficult task, and perhaps destroy your own confidence in your ability to write.

But if you use objective criteria as Cindy Baer has in her essay, as a guide to have at hand and consult as needed throughout the process, the results are much more favorable. This complex process called writing involves choices to be made during every phase—different aspects of the given topic to choose from, different statements to be made about the topic, different supporting ideas to choose among, alternate patterns of arrangement to try, different words available for any single concept, and different sentence structures available to express any given thought. If you know what "good" is from the outset, if you keep specific criteria near to hand as you go along, the criteria can become the basis for making reasoned decisions among the many available alternatives, so that when you have finally wended your way through the process and have arrived at a complete draft, most of the choices will have been wisely made, most of what you have written will be good enough to be worth the final effort of polishing and presenting to your audience. Perhaps more important, having a more specific idea of where you are going as you go along can give you the confidence, essential in good writing, to proceed boldly.

EXERCISES

1. Find two short pieces of published writing that you like, two pieces that are very different in form, such as a newspaper column and a movie review, or a poem and an advertisement. Using the four criteria mentioned in this chapter—content, organization, style, and mechanics—list *similarities* you find between the two pieces. Then, in two or three

paragraphs, answer the following questions. What general conclusions can you draw about your own ideas about good writing? How do they correspond with my analysis of the three pieces of writing at the beginning of this chapter?

2. Find two short pieces of writing of the same sort, two poems or two sports reports, for instance. Pick a genre that you like to read. This time choose one piece that you like and one that you don't like. Using the criteria, analyze the two pieces. What specific aspects of the writing account for your likes and dislikes? Has your opinion of the pieces changed any after you've analyzed them in detail? Write a paragraph explaining your evaluation of each passage.

3. Take a piece of your own writing that is finished, preferably one that you haven't looked at recently. An essay from a previous class would be ideal, or if you prefer to use something written for the class you are in, your earliest effort would be best. Using the criteria as an evaluative tool, as a teacher would in grading the writing, evaluate the piece. Put aside any fondness you have for the piece (and for yourself) and be harshly critical. If you want to, go ahead and give a letter grade on each of the four criteria. Then write a detailed paragraph in which you discuss what you would do if you had the essay to write over from scratch.

4. As Cindy Baer has, write your own essay about your beginnings as a writer. It may be that you don't have your own thoughts about the writing process worked out as thoroughly as she has done. If you don't, write about your anxieties as a beginning writer, your problems, your questions. Develop the essay in stages, as Baer does. Your steps may differ from hers; different writers go through the process in different ways. If you don't have your own approach to the process, you might want to emulate her method and see how it works for you. However you move through the process, pause at the end of each phase and comment in two or three short paragraphs on your work according to the four criteria. Remember, you need not comment on all categories at any given stage, and you shouldn't be concerned with mechanics until the very last. Try to keep your comments positive, aimed at improvement and building on what works well, but don't be reluctant to reject what isn't working.

Chapter Three

Content

Picture this scene: It is Monday morning, and students are chatting quietly with one another, unzipping book bags, unfolding binders on their desks. The instructor is strolling back and forth in front of the class, handing back graded essays. A student in the front row waits with some anticipation, anxious to see how well she has done. She is an average student in most ways, sincere, wanting to do well, interested in writing but not very confident in her ability.

The instructor calls her name and hands back her essay, and she flips through it, reading the comments in the margins before she looks for the grade on the back. The comments are generally favorable—"good sentence here," "thesis is clearly stated," "I like this simile." There are hardly any of the editing marks that indicate mechanical flaws. So she turns the paper over. And on the back is the comment "C—Weak in content."

The student avoids the instructor's eyes and hopes that her face isn't as flushed as it feels, and during the rest of the period she is distracted, glancing through her essay again from time to time. When class is over, she waits until the other students have left, and, trying to keep the anger and frustration out of her voice, she confronts the instructor with the obvious question: "Well, what is it that you *want*?"

Perhaps the scene is familiar to you. I know it is to me, for as a beginning instructor, I caused many similar ones with that cryptic comment "weak in content." As most English instructors do, I believed that content is the most important part of writing, but like too many instructors, I didn't have specific ways to tell my students what it was that I wanted. When I finally realized this and began to devise specific criteria for judging content, I began to teach better, and coincidentally the idea for this book was begun.

But even before I could talk about content specifically, I had one thing right about it: It *is* your most important consideration as a writer. "Content" is actually a metaphor comparing any given piece of writing to a container such as a bottle or a jewelry box. This container is created with the three other aspects of writing discussed in this book—organization, style, and mechanics. All of these involve the placement of language symbols on paper—letters and punctuation, words, sentences, and paragraphs. All combine to become the container; the *contents* of the container are your thoughts or ideas.

The metaphor is useful because it suggests that this structure created with language symbols, like any other kind of container, is not necessarily full. Language can form structures that don't express any ideas, or that express very few, or that express ideas that are not particularly interesting or valuable. The container, in other words, can be empty or half full or full of something no one wants.

And as with any other container, the content justifies the container's existence. The most delicate wine bottle is only as valuable as the vintage it holds; the most finely crafted jewelry box has no value empty that compares to its worth if it is full of diamonds and pearls. Similarly, an essay, no matter how well organized, how cleverly styled, how mechanically perfect, is no better than the ideas it contains.

It would of course be impossible to label and categorize every aspect of good content or to reduce it to a system of easily followed rules. Content, after all, is human thought, in all its complexity and diversity, from Milton's poetic vision of humanity's fall to Einstein's mathematical descriptions of the forces that control the physical universe. It is possible, though, to look at writing that has been called good by many well-read people, and to observe human nature and human response, and from these observations draw some conclusions about what makes one idea more worth presenting than the next. And with a specific notion of what *some* good content is, as you write you can move toward ideas that will pique your readers' interest and stimulate their ability to think, and away from mediocrity of thought and potential boredom. You can recognize a good idea when you are on the track of one, and put your effort into improving it rather than playing anxiety-ridden guessing games about what your instructor wants.

This notion of what good content is, of the four categories of criteria discussed in this text, is the only one that you should have in mind early in the writing process. You don't create the container and then look for something to put in it; you make the wine and then choose a bottle that complements its color and suggests its taste. As you've seen in Chapter One, the writing process begins with finding ideas, and for any given topic you will probably have more ideas than you will be able to write about—some good, some mundane, some flawed. With clear criteria for content firmly in mind at the beginning of the process, you can select the better ideas to experiment with rather than wasting a lot of effort finding out that the flawed ones are flawed.

Sticking to the Assignment

In writing, it is both a blessing and a curse that the very act of trying to compose your thoughts gives rise to further thoughts. This thought-generating quality is good because it makes writing an enriching experience both for writers and readers. It causes problems, too, though, in writing a response to a specific assignment, because all the thoughts that writing generates, all the remembered details it calls up, all the connections it uncovers, and all the ideas it brings forth are not necessarily pertinent to the writing task at hand.

This is true, of course, in almost any kind of writing. In a letter to a lover who is angry with you, and whose favor you are trying to regain, you probably wouldn't mention all you lover's faults, even though they might come to mind as you write. During a business trip to Miami, even though the palms swaying gracefully along the beach and the sun-bronzed bodies arrayed on the white sand might strike you as beautiful and exotic, you probably wouldn't include a detailed description of them in a report to the president of your firm. In another instance a well-wrought description of Miami might be received as very good writing, but given the situation it would be inappropriate, off the point, and annoying to the reader.

It is just as important in writing essays for a composition class to remember what the writing situation is, and to do what you are being asked to do. The aphorism "close only counts in horseshoes" applies very well here. Most composition instructors choose assignments that will give practice in particular writing skills. If you deviate too far from the assignment, you might produce an essay that has many virtues, that would be received as good writing in another situation, but that doesn't apply the skills the instructor wants you to practice at that particular point in the course.

Thus the first step in responding to an essay assignment is to know what you're being asked to do: to carefully read the assignment, ask questions about it if need be, and be sure you understand all parts of it. The following essay assignment, which I use sometimes for in-class essays, needs careful analysis:

TOPIC:
Many of the commonest assumptions, it seems to me, are arbitrary ones: that the new is better than the old, the untried superior to the tried, the complex more advantageous than the simple, the fast quicker than the slow, the big greater than the small, and the world as remodeled by Man the architect functionally sounder and more agreeable than it was before he changed everything to suit his vogues and his conniptions.

E. B. White

INSTRUCTIONS:
Write a well-organized, two–three page essay in which you illustrate White's statement by showing a common assumption to be arbitrary, using specific examples from your own observation and experience as support. If you must, deal with one of the assumptions that White mentions.

After quickly reading through this to get a general idea of what is going on, the first step in understanding it fully is to go back and read the instructions carefully and analytically. You'll find that they tell both what to do and to some extent how to do it. Your response, first of all, is to be an essay—not a series of short answers, not a paragraph, not a short story or a poem. "Well-organized" is really redundant, since an essay should be well organized as a matter of course, and a careful reader will perceive the redundancy as a kind of emphasis. In fact, I usually throw that phrase into an essay topic for in-class writing because I know that writers under pressure to think in limited time often forget to be concerned about organization. Next, the essay you write is to be two to three pages long—handwritten pages, of course, since this was an in-class essay. The same instructions on an out-of-class assignment would leave you wondering whether to produce typed or hand-written pages, and of course it would be up to you to ask for clarification.

Besides specifying an essay response, the assignment also stipulates how the essay is to develop. You are to illustrate White's statement—not disagree with it, even though it would be possible to do so and that might be your first inclination—and not simply restate or explain it. Further, the illustrations are to come from your own observations and experience, which means that if this were an out-of-class assignment, you wouldn't be expected to do library work. Finally, you know that you may use one of the assumptions that White mentions, but note that the tone of my comment "If you must," strongly implies that I would prefer for you to come up with your own example of a common assumption.

By knowing the constraints of the writing situation and by writing within them, you avoid the possibility of wasting the effort of your writing. It is possible for several good ideas to arise out of your thinking about any given topic, and certainly the better ones should be saved to produce writing for an appropriate occasion. But it is only common sense to produce and turn in for any given writing assignment a piece of writing that sticks as closely as possible to what you've been asked to do.

Saying Something (or, Not Saying Nothing)

To return to the container/content metaphor, if you don't do what the assignment asks, your container may be full, but not of the right contents— beer in a wine bottle, so to speak. But just trying to stick to the assignment does not ensure that the wine bottle will contain wine. It is possible—you have to work at it, but it's still possible—to create a completely empty container. This "content" I am talking about, the wine to fill the bottle, consists of accurate information put together to form ideas, and it is possible to take the signs that make up language—letters, words, punctuation marks—and put them on paper in such a way as to follow the rules of language without conveying information or ideas. A clever example of this is Lewis Carroll's poem "Jabberwocky."

'Twas brillig, and the slithy toves
  Did gyre and gimble in the wabe;
All mimsy were the borogroves,
  And the mome raths outgrabe.

"Beware the Jabberwock, my son!
  The jaws that bite, the claws that catch!
Beware the Jubjub bird, and shun
  The frumious Bandersnatch!"

He took his vorpal sword in hand;
  Long time the manxome foe he sought—
So rested he by the Tumtum tree,
  And stood awhile in thought.

And, as in uffish thought he stood,
  The Jabberwock, with eyes of flame,
Came whiffling through the tulgey wood,
  And burbled as it came!

One, two! One, two! And through and through
  The vorpal blade went snicker-snack!
He left it dead, and with its head
  He went galumphing back.

"And hast thou slain the Jabberwock?
  Come to my arms, my beamish boy
O frabjous day! Callooh! Callay!"
  He chortled in his joy.

'Twas brillig, and the slithy toves
  Did gyre and gimble in the wabe;
All mimsy were the borogroves,
  And the mome raths outgrabe.

Of course the poem does communicate, for language has many dimensions, and even this curious English can amuse us, please us with its rhythm, even stir us with the subtle effects of its sounds and connotations. But in the most literal sense the poem says nothing because, aside from describing things and concepts that don't exist, many of the words don't themselves exist—"vorpal" has no dictionary meaning, and no matter how strong your feeling that you know what it means, you can never be sure that you know what Carroll meant by it unless Carroll himself translates it into "real" language for you. The poem is a very pretty container indeed, but at least in the literal sense quite empty. And of course this is part of what Carroll has done—shown the more subtle powers of words by divorcing them from their most obvious literal function.

But most writers who create empty containers don't have motives as noble as Carroll's. Usually the empty container is a result of either carelessness or desperation over having something to hand in. Here are four kinds of empty containers to avoid creating:

CLICHÉD THINKING

One way to say nothing is to say something that has been said so often that it has become a cliché. Contemporary society has such wide-spread and elaborate media that clichés pop up like banana slugs in a backyard garden, just as numerous and just as slimey. Just as soon as someone has an original insight into the popular culture and gets it into print, it becomes a fad or a trend, and pretty soon it's been written about, talked about on the tube, portrayed in movies, mimicked by thousands, until no genuine manifestion of it exists any longer. A case in point—Yuppies. Young Urban Professionals, they marched along behind Preppies, Peaceniks, Hippies, and Beatniks in a long parade of overdone stereotypes for which the mass media has called cadence. At the height of the media's fascination with Yuppies, you couldn't open a newspaper or magazine without finding another article about these exciting people: Seems they carried Gucci briefcases, owned VCRs, drove BMWs, and liked Brie cheese. The reading public had heard it all two dozen times; hearing about it again was like listening to a mediocre joke you've heard a dozen times and having to pretend it's funny—or listening to a parrot "talk"—sounds with no meaning, empty words. A few good writers managed to find novel twists on the fad (Yuppies don't exist; every era has had its yuppies), but for the most part Yuppie articles became warmed-up leftovers, and the fad mercifully faded.

BELABORING THE OBVIOUS

Another way to say nothing is to say something most people already know. When you write, you assume that your readers are alert and thoughtful, able to look around the world and see what anyone with eyes can see, hear what anyone with ears can hear. So don't insult their intelligence by telling them what they are bound to know. Every now and then I'll get an essay that tells me that olympic athletes have to have the desire to win, or that a college education can be an advantage in looking for a job. My favorite is the thesis statement "Life is the hardest thing you'll ever do." Quite true, of course, but I figured it out myself some years ago, and I wonder if the student who wrote it gave any thought at all to what her readers might already know.

HIGH PLANE DRIFTERS

As I'll point out later, generalizations are an important part of writing, but it is possible, by staying entirely on a plane of high generality, to say nothing at all. Politicians have raised this to an art form. A highly placed public figure might say something like:

> After an era of indecision, the country is once again on a firm course. The national will and the will of the people are now one again; the private interest and the public interest are no longer mistakenly seen as separate entities. We are ready to confront our problems with bold solutions, face the world with bold policies, pursue our collective goals with bold determination. We are on the road to recovery.

Like Carroll's poem, it sounds pretty, but what in the world does it *say*? Nothing, of course. What specific problems? What solutions? In which direction lies recovery, whatever that is? It doesn't say. For politicians this is a useful if somewhat dishonest way to sound as if they have good news when they don't. Student writers who float off into the upper atmosphere of generality usually do so because they haven't thought about the topic enough or because they haven't thought about how much detail their readers will need to understand the writers' ideas. I had a student once who had been a national champion in a sport, and he wrote an essay about how to become a national champion. But he didn't say what sport. He dropped the class before I could hand the essay back, and I never got the chance to ask him.

DON'T BE WRONG

You'd think that I'm belaboring the obvious myself to point out that conveying wrong information is a way of saying nothing at all. But I get an essay now and then in which a writer will talk about what went on in "the olden days" without having any specific knowledge of history, or will talk about what happens in Russia without any idea at all of life inside the Soviet Union. I recently read an essay that alluded frequently to the war in Cuba, never mind that there wasn't one at the moment. The soundest advice I can give you is "never write about something you don't know anything about." If the assignment backs you into a cul-de-sac with an unfamiliar topic, then find something out through research or observation, or negotiate with the teacher. Saying something wrong is the worst way of saying nothing.

So yes, it is possible to create an empty jug, and doing so is almost always the result of effort directed at producing something to hand in—*just* something to fulfill the most rudimentary terms of the assignment—rather than at the communication of thought. This "something to hand in" is instantly recognizable for what it is, just as an empty bottle cannot long be mistaken for a full one, and the simple way to avoid such writing is to follow the advice in Chapter One and work hard at the early phases of the writing process—gather sound, accurate information through research, observation, or reminiscence and ponder that information carefully before you write.

Saying Something Worth Saying

Gathering and carefully selecting information assure the presence of content. Sticking as closely as possible to the assignment assures the appropriateness of the content. But none of these necessarily assures the *quality* of the content. Quality can be measured almost entirely in terms of reader interest, and it is possible to do everything the assignment asks, and to convey specific, accurate information, without writing an interesting essay.

But what is "interesting"? A lot of things interest people that have nothing to do with essays—the vertigo sensation of a fast ski run down a steep, icy slope; a double scoop of mocha almond fudge in a sugar wafer cone; candle light and soft music and fine wine. But an essay can't appeal to the taste buds in the same way that ice cream can. Nor is all interesting writing interesting in the way that I mean here. There is writing that stimulates interest in ways that the essay cannot and should not: A gothic romance can appeal to maudlin sentiments, and a detective story can satisfy the urge for mystery and excitement. But essays are not light fiction.

The essay has to engage your readers' interest and keep it engaged within the limits of the form, within the constraints of your attempt to work out your feelings about a topic in a few short pages. It is no easy task. Your first impulse might be to depend on the topic to supply the interest—to write about that invigorating ski run down Headwall at Squaw Valley with the wind in your teeth and the ice under your skis. But you're gambling that your audience shares your interests, and they may not. Or perhaps you'll depend on the audience by picking a topic you know is of interest to them. This is a good strategy, and it increases your chances of success, but it's still not a sure thing. Just because your readers like to eat mocha almond fudge ice cream doesn't mean that they want to read about it, and even if they do, by writing about that particular topic, you limit the potential for interest to a single group of people. This is often the case when a beginning writer chooses a topic such as fraternity beer bashes that might fascinate a few immediate acquaintances and writes a sophomoric account of drunken revelry that seems dull and pointless to the instructor.

To be *sure* that the content is interesting, and further, to be sure that it is interesting to a mature, thoughtful, general audience, you need something more than titillation or purely subjective response. You need a main idea that is worth your readers' effort, and such ideas usually are the result of the way the topic is handled rather than what the topic is.

It is usually possible to tell whether an essay is worth reading (or worth writing) by looking at the thesis. If that one, sentence-sized, compressed version of your main idea evokes a surge of excitement, if it intrigues or puzzles or even annoys your readers into widening their eyes and leaning forward and saying to themselves "Now what is this all about?", it will probably expand into an essay that will keep them engaged and alert. If it doesn't, if the immediate response is "So what?", the response to the essay probably will be too. If you are aware of this in the early prewriting phases, when you're still trying to decide what to write about, you can save yourself a lot of effort wasted trying to make a boring idea interesting and concentrate on your most stimulating ideas.

I can't devise a formula for stimulating thesis statements for you, but many years of reading what people call good writing has convinced me that one factor does recur frequently in provocative ideas. That factor is tension or conflict.

In *A Rumor of War* Phillip Caputo says of the fighting in Vietnam:

> The rights or wrongs of the war aside, there was a magnetism about combat. You seemed to live more intensely under fire. Every sense was sharper, the mind worked clearer and faster. Perhaps it was the tension of opposites that made it so, an attraction balanced by revulsion, hope that warred with dread. You found yourself on a precarious emotional edge, experiencing a headiness that no drink or drug could match.

This excitement born of tension is not exclusively a characteristic of combat: Television and movies pit the bad guys against the good guys, athletic competition is conflict for conflict's sake, and even in courtship there are elements of "the tension of opposites." In the arts, too, conflict is an essential factor. Without conflict, novels are failures and plays aren't even plays. Tension or conflict is an important component of all writing, essays included. Ken Macrorie says:

> Strong writers, effective and interesting writers, bring together oppositions of one kind or another—long and short sentences, fast and slow rhythms. And what they choose to present from life is frequently the negative and the positive, one thing and its opposite, two ideas that antagonize each other. The result is tension. And the surprise that comes from new combinations. And news.

THE TENSION OF CONFLICTING OPINIONS

The sort of tension most commonly seen in nonfiction writing is the tension created by conflicting opinions—the tension of argument. Daily human interaction creates issues—questions about what is right and wrong, about what should be done in a given situation, about what people deserve and how they should be treated. Opinions differ on issues, and people take sides and then write to explain their opinions, to justify the stands they take, and to persuade those who don't share their opinions to change their minds. Candidate A should not be re-elected. Capital punishment should be abolished. Gun control infringes on our constitutional rights. Some issues arise, provoke debate briefly, and are forgotten, and some are as perpetual as the endless give and take where waves meet seashore. But the writing such issues generate has an increased potential for interest because it is part of a conflict, a kind of contest to see whose opinion will prevail and whose ideas will be most widely accepted. So controversy provides the opportunity for conflict of opinion; but you need not look only to public issues for an argumentative edge. It is possible to have an opinion, and for opinions to differ, about ordinary aspects of the human condition regarding which formal decisions are never made nor laws passed. Consider:

> A work of art has no importance whatsoever to society. It is only important to the individual.
>
> *Vladimir Nabokov*

This is not the kind of issue over which legislatures will debate or newspaper editors battle or judges rule, but it is a statement with which many people would disagree. Since it is not fully understandable as it is, since it needs explanation, it could easily expand into an essay, and that essay would be interesting because it would contain the tension of conflicting opinions. Here is another opinion that could be the thesis for an argumentative essay:

> What all men are really after is some form, or perhaps only some formula, of peace.
>
> *Joseph Conrad*

This seems particularly apt to provoke controversy since there is so much evidence to refute it in the wars of history and the various wars going on at this moment and the mock wars we so love to watch on the athletic field and television screen. But so much—if the case is argued well—the better. Like a figure skater who is awarded for an advanced degree of difficulty in her performance, a writer who successfully argues a dubious point provokes more interest than one who attempts to prove the obvious.

For this reason, some of the most interesting argumentative statements, rather than confronting the opinion of some small, specific group, take on the whole world by challenging a commonly held notion. Again, consider:

> Politeness ruins conversations.
>
> *Ralph Waldo Emerson*

I would have said just the opposite—that politeness is an essential quality of conversations and that *impoliteness* ruins them. So I raise an eyebrow at Emerson's assertion and sit forward a little and say "Now wait a minute." And this is precisely why an essay explaining this statement (I suspect it would be mostly an essay that defined Emerson's notion of "conversation") would be interesting. The remark snatches the comfortable seat of conventional wisdom from under me, dumps me abruptly on my assumptions, and forces me to seek my own support for what I believe—in short, it makes me think. More gauntlets flung in the face of popular opinion:

> The destiny of mankind is not decided by material computation.
>
> *Winston Churchill*

> For over a quarter of a century, I've lived in this society and been influenced by its high regard for the individual. I'm sure you have, and I'm sure our children will too. During most of this time I've thought that being an individual was a

good thing, and that promoting individuality was one of the things that made this country great. Now, after working for nearly half a decade in Silicon Valley, I'm not so sure that individuality is the boon to our society that I had always believed it to be.

Wayne George

If a nation expects to be ignorant and free, in a state of civilization, it expects what never was and never will be.

Thomas Jefferson

The entire object of true education is to make people not merely *do* the right things, but *enjoy* the right things.

John Ruskin

The reward of friendship is itself. The man who hopes for anything else does not understand what true friendship is.

Saint Aelred of Rievaulx

Serious sport has nothing to do with fair play. It is bound up with hatred, jealousy, boastfulness, disregard of all rules, and sadistic pleasure in witnessing violence: in other words, it is war minus the shooting.

George Orwell

These examples come from different times, and since popular attitudes change through the years, each statement would be more controversial in some ages than in others. With pro sports becoming ever more violent and mercenary, Orwell's statement would meet less resistance now than it did when he made it. Churchill's statement about material computation, on the other hand, is very contrary to today's talk of GNPs and economic indicators, so dated though it is, it still challenges a commonly held notion. But within its own context, each of these statements challenges the conventional wisdom and creates a tension that generates interest: Any one could be the thesis of a provocative essay.

THE TENSION BETWEEN THE NEW AND THE OLD

This tactic of challenging the conventional wisdom suggests another kind of tension that can generate interest—the tension between new ideas and old ones. Life is a constant search for novelty, for something new to alleviate the boredom of the same activities, the same sights, the same ideas day in and day out. An idea that challenges everyday beliefs is a new thing as well as a contentious thing, so it relieves the boredom and stimulates interest.

And there are other ways to create novelty in ideas. The most obvious is to find a fresh insight into a commonly discussed topic. The more concerned people in general are about a topic, the more quickly most of the obvious statements that can be made about it get made, and once they've been made, they very soon have been repeated often enough to be old stuff. This leaves it up to people capable of getting further into the topic, capable of finding the unexplored corners of it to bring to light new facets of it and keep interest alive. This applies particularly to the kind of contemporary issues about which argumentative writing is usually done, but it applies as well to timeless issues that have been discussed over and over again. Consider:

> The basic test of freedom is perhaps less in what we are free to do than what we are free not to do.
>
> *Eric Hoffer*

People have discussed freedom since before recorded history, and will discuss it however long the future continues until history ends; and as long as they discuss, they will ask what people are allowed to do, and whether they are allowed to do enough to truly be called free. But Hoffer has taken a different slant, has found a fresh aspect of the topic to discuss: What are people free *not* to do? So here is something that is worth writing about because it appeals to the desire for a change of scenery.

Of course you might already be wondering whether Hoffer's statement is all that new—whether someone might not already have had this idea of his. And by extension you might wonder whether there is such a thing as a fresh insight: "There is nothing new under the sun," says *Ecclesiastes*, and the more well read you become, the more inclined you will be to believe it. But perhaps another example will help me explain what I mean by "fresh."

> Originality does not consist in saying what no one has ever said before, but in saying exactly what you think yourself.
>
> *James Stephens*

Stephens's statement is itself a fresh insight, since the most literal definition of "originality" *is* "something new under the sun" (which of course is what intimidates you when you sit down to write). But according to Stephens's definition, everyone is capable of originality, and simply by being observant, thoughtful, and honest, you can create ideas rather than parrot those most commonly expressed; you can write, if not something new under the sun, then something fresh and invigorating for your jaded readers. Here are some more examples of statements that break new ground in ways variously amusing, intriguing, and provocative:

> What is patriotism but the love of good things we ate in our childhood?
>
> *Lin Yutang*

> The medium is the message.
>
> *Marshall MacLuhan*

> Most sorts of diversion in men, children, and other animals, are an imitation of fighting.
>
> *Jonathan Swift*

Merchants have no country. The mere spot they stand on does not constitute so strong an attachment as that from which they draw their gains.

Thomas Jefferson

Another way to create tension between the new and the old is to place the known in a novel context, to look at the topic as it is not usually viewed. Consider:

A house is a machine for living.

Le Corbusier

This is provocative to me because it is not the way I normally think of houses: I see them as places, not things, as surroundings, not objects. By giving me a new way to look at them, the statement allows me to understand their significance and function better. More examples:

Love and business and family and religion and art and patriotism are nothing but shadows of words when a man's starving.

O. Henry

If we judge love by its results, it resembles hatred more than friendship.

François De La Rouchefoucauld

Sometimes a new way of looking at the topic can be literally that—a new point of view, or a new set of eyes with which to see:

The boys throw stones at the frogs in sport, but the frogs die not in sport but in earnest.

Bion

I would normally see this slaying of frogs through human eyes—if not the eyes of callous boys who call it sport, then at least from a human perspective, disapproving of a small cruelty. But this statement suggests the frogs' point of view and makes me wonder if the cruelty is really minor. Imagine an essay developing this thought in vivid detail all from the frogs' point of view: the peaceful lily pads that are your home crushed and sunk beneath jagged stones larger than you, the sight of relatives mashed flat, the pain of a crushed limb, the enormous, oddly shaped creatures with their malicious cries, bent on your destruction. Much good writing stems from adopting an alternative point of view, and both writers and readers can learn from this kind of intellectual exercise.

It is worth noting too that at one extreme this tactic of novel contexts creates figurative language—specifically simile and metaphor (you'll find further discussion of figurative language in Chapter Five). We can place the known in a novel context by comparing it with something or by calling it something it is not, as this example from one of the essays at the end of the chapter shows:

A real friendship is like a good book. It is something that you begin with interest, set aside when disturbed by the needs of the present, pick up and throw down with disgust. But the book is never thrown away; it is placed on a shelf and dusted, to be browsed through another day. The lessons of yesterday are intact in this book and all the tomorrows are still waiting to be read.

Wendy Ichimaru Hanabusa

Hanabusa starts here with a simile—an imaginative comparison using connecting words such as "like" or "as"—and expands the simile into an analogy, or extended comparison, that allows her to work out several provocative observations about friendship. The tactic of comparing breaks the readers' minds out of the old track and gives them a fresh look at a shopworn topic. Here are some more similes:

Virtue is like a rich stone—best plain set.

Francis Bacon

What the mass media offer is not popular art, but entertainment which is intended to be consumed like food, forgotten, and replaced by a new dish.

W. H. Auden

A more extreme kind of comparison is metaphor—the naming of one thing as another. The following remark by Francis Bacon suggests Auden's food simile, but Bacon goes a step further and states his point metaphorically:

Some books are to be tasted, others to be swallowed, and some few to be chewed and digested.

It is largely the power of figurative language that makes poetry and fiction art, and the same power can make an essay interesting.

INTERNAL TENSION

So far I've talked about ways to bring conflict and tension *to* the topic; it is also possible to find and exploit tension inherent *within* the topic. People tend generally to oversimplify the world, to see things in absolute terms, to think of objects, people, and even ideas as self-contained and at ease within themselves. People point at a man and say "That man is a conservative: He believes in the free market and the sanctity of life." And they are right, yet the same man will argue for import tariffs and send his sons to war. This tendency of objects in the universe to contradict themselves, to possess seemingly unreconcilable qualities simultaneously, is called paradox.

A paradox is a self-contained contradiction, something that seems as if it couldn't be true, but still is true, and paradoxes can be the basis for interesting writing. Consider:

To talk much about oneself may also be a means of concealing oneself.

Friedrich Nietzche

I am intrigued by this; it is a puzzle; how can it be true and contradict itself? I automatically want the solution to the problem. An essay expanding this idea would explain how two seemingly contradictory actions can be one and the same action. Here are some more paradoxical statements that could become interesting essays:

> After a certain age, the more one becomes oneself, the more obvious one's family traits become.
>
> *Marcel Proust*

> And if a rider does fall, he stands a very good chance of getting "T-boned," or struck, by other riders traveling at blistering speeds. Not fun! The funny thing about motocross, though, is that these nuts, these riders, actually get off on it!
>
> *Michael Virgillo*

> The maturity of man—that means, to have reaquired the unconciousness that one had as a child at play.
>
> *Friedrich Nietzche*

> Fond as we are of our loved ones, there comes at times during their absence an unexplainable peace.
>
> *Anne Shaw*

> Painting is easy when you don't know how, but very difficult when you do.
>
> *Edgar Degas*

> Man is so made that he can only find relaxation from one kind of labor in taking up another.
>
> *Anatole France*

> Nothing in Education is so astonishing as the amount of ignorance it accumulates in the form of inert facts.
>
> *Henry Adams*

Similar to the paradox is the polarity found in a topic or object normally considered a unified whole. Humans are unique on the face of the earth, thinkers, tool-makers, a thing apart from all other forms of life. But people are animals too—predators, killers, responding to murderous animal urges as well as to the higher impulses of the intellect. Within this one creature called human are two opposite extremes—a polarity—and the creature is more interesting because of it. And ideas that juxtapose polarities are interesting too. From another essay at the end of the chapter:

> Why is the first year of marriage so hard? Do you get married, quit loving each other, and learn to adjust to life together without love? I couldn't believe that because I loved my husband more, that day at the lagoon, than ever; I knew he loved me more than ever too. There was all this wonderful, tender love inside of us, yet every time we opened our mouths we sounded like ducks that had just

had a tender tidbit stolen from them. If we hadn't stopped loving each other, what had changed our relationship so much?

Pamela Liebenberg

Unlike the paradox, wherein opposites coexist simultaneously, the polarity here is between alternate states—the alternating presence of love and fueding in her marriage. The writer identifies the polarity and sets out in her essay to explore its implications, answering in the process some questions that apply to marriages in general. More examples of statements based on polarities:

My life is spent in perpetual alternation between two rhythms, the rhythm of attracting people for fear I might be lonely, and the rhythm of trying to get rid of them because I know that I am bored.

C. E. M. Joad

Man is the only animal that laughs and weeps: for he is the only animal struck by the difference between what things are and what they might have been.

William Hazlitt

Men by their constitutions are naturally divided into two parties: 1. Those who fear and distrust the people, and wish to draw all powers from them into the hands of the higher classes. 2. Those who identify themselves with the people, have confidence in them as the most safe, although not the most wise depository of human interests.

Thomas Jefferson

The young American, to me, is restless and also charming. He can be very rude, and cute. He can be a good guy, and also a very bad guy at the same time.

Tuan Tran

Like the airplane, the computer, and the nuclear warhead, the camera is a product of a technology that is catapulting us into the twenty-first century. It has become a basic tool in our communication with the world. Its images are a natural part of our evolution, just as the cave drawings of bison and antelope were natural images to our ancient brothers and sisters. And whether its shutter opens and shuts on the lethal billowing form of a mushroom cloud, or on the squinting, squirming face of a newborn child, is entirely up to us.

Kathleen Lynch

TENSION BETWEEN THE PART AND THE WHOLE

The final kind of tension I will mention here is perhaps the most frequently found in good writing, hence the most important kind—tension arising from a conflict inherent in the human condition, a conflict between the apparent meaninglessness of the separate and individual phenomena and the feeling that there must be form and meaning in the world after all. Our ancestors walked out of the cave and looked up at the stars and wondered what the significance of it all was, and we've never stopped wondering, and never will. One of the most important functions of writing is the search for a higher meaning, and the most interesting essay is one that finds significance in the ordinary event or situation. Often this significance lies in the relationship between the specific and the general.

In her essay presented in Chapter One, "On Fear of Spiders," Nancy Heifferon starts out with something specific—her own reactions to spiders. But she does not stay at the specific level for long; she quickly expands her thought to make a generalization about her own character:

> Every time I catch, out of the corner of my eye, the sharp black scurrying on white walls, I want to run screaming from the room. And it is not, as my husband thinks, entirely a laughing matter. My silly fear of spiders keeps me from being a fully-developed and independent human being.

Later in her essay, she raises the idea to an even higher plane of generality:

> In fact, most of us, given the slimmest chance, will rely on others to take care of our unpleasant tasks. But when we do, we grant others a power over us, a power they may easily use against us. They know our weaknesses, they know their strengths. Women who flippantly claim they want men to open doors and to stand in busses for them, who find Phyllis Schafly an eloquent spokesperson, whether they recognize it or not, give up something for the privileges, something like respect. Probably the most important sacrifice any of us make when we depend on others to do unpleasant things for us is the opportunity to surmount a difficulty and to learn about ourselves, in other words to grow. Feminists, too, when we rail at men for oppressing us, must temper our bitterness with some understanding that we have often ceded control over our lives in exchange for the dirty work that men will do for us.

Thus in the course of her essay, Heifferon has taken her own experience and answered the quintessential human question: What is the meaning of this? Here are some more statements that find the general significance in the specific instance:

> In our play we reveal what kind of people we are.
>
> *Ovid*

> The more I think of it, the more it appears to me that dress is the foundation of society.
>
> *Thomas Carlyle*

> The battle of Waterloo was won on the playing fields of Eton.
>
> *Duke of Wellington*

> The walking-stick serves the purpose of an advertisement that the bearer's hands are employed otherwise than in useful effort, and and it therefore has utility as an instrument of leisure.
>
> *Thorstein Veblen*

At its extreme, this trick of linking the specific and the general involves symbol making, one of the most powerful devices of artistic writing. A symbol is a specific object that comes to represent something much larger and more important—more generally significant—such as an idea or an era or an aspect of the human condition. One of the most compelling symbols in American literature appears in the following passage from *The Great Gatsby*:

> The silhouette of a moving cat wavered across the moonlight, and turning my head to watch it, I saw that I was not alone—fifty feet away a figure had emerged from the shadow of my neighbor's mansion and was standing with his hands in his pockets regarding the silver pepper of the stars. Something in his leisurely movements and the secure position of his feet upon the lawn suggested that it was Mr. Gatsby himself, come out to determine what share was his of our local heavens.
>
> I decided to call to him. Miss Baker had mentioned him at dinner, and that would do for an introduction. But I didn't call to him, for he gave a sudden intimation that he was content to be alone—he stretched out his arms toward the dark water in a curious way, and far as I was from him, I could have sworn he was trembling. Involuntarily, I glanced seaward—and distinguished nothing except a single green light, minute and far away, that might have been the end of a dock. When I looked once more for Gatsby he had vanished, and I was alone again in the unquiet darkness.

That single specific object—a green light on a dock—represents Daisy, the woman Gatsby idealizes, his romantic quest for her, and by extension the human capacity to dream. And even the most mundane object has the potential to send the mind spinning off into more abstract orbits, as E. B. White shows in his response to the sight of a simple goose feather:

> Here in New England, each season carries a hundred foreshadowings of the season that is to follow—which is one of the things I love about it. Winter is rough and long, but spring lies all round about. Yesterday, a small white keel feather escaped from my goose and lodged in the bank boughs near the kitchen porch, where I spied it as I came home in the cold twilight. The minute I saw the feather, I was projected into May, knowing that a barn swallow would be along to claim the prize and use it to decorate the front edge of its nest. Immediately, the December air seemed full of wings of swallows and the warmth of barns. Swallows, I have noticed, never use any feather but a white one in their nest-building, and they always leave a lot of it showing, which makes me believe that they are interested not in the feather's insulating power but in its reflecting power, so that when they skim into the dark barn from the bright outdoors they will have a beacon to steer by.

For White—indeed, for anyone with a keen eye for specific detail and a keen instinct for significance—no object is insignificant, and *everything* is interesting because of its place in the overall design of life.

The types of tension discussed here aren't the only kinds of tension, and tension isn't the only way to generate interest, but quite a lot of good writing has the characteristics of conflict mentioned above, and being aware of them can help you recognize good ideas when you have them. Look once again, in Figure 3-1, at the beginning of the sample essay presented in Chapter Two.

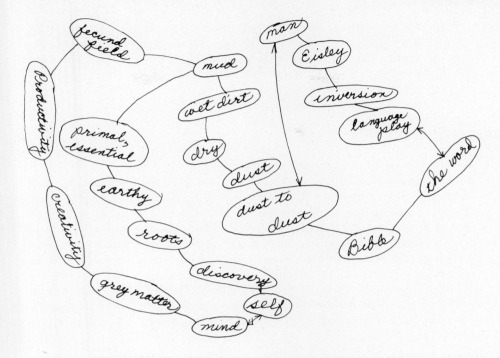

There is something primal something essential about mud. It's probably not a mistake that both our religious & our scientific wonderers have come up with mud theories of creativity — dust to dust from the Bible and man was mud and mud was man from scientist/writer Loren Eisley—incidentally one of my favorite examples of linguistic play in the classroom as I teach writing as I teach language, as I try to get students to see what I may have sensed before I understood — that playing in words is a lot like playing in mud, feeling the primal exhilaration of creativity as I break new ground, as I run my fingers through the fecund soil of my mind where I am literally growing.

Figure 3-1. An Intriguing Statement Arising from Prewriting Activities.

From the fragmentary thoughts that come out in the cluster, the writer composes the vignette, and within the vignette she finds tension—the intriguing simile "playing with words is a lot like playing in mud." Be alert for similar tension in your own initial thoughts about a writing topic.

Saying It Sensibly

By being aware of the general principles outlined above, you can come up with interesting ideas for your essays, but the most interesting ideas sour without logic. In judging content, the rule is simple: Sound logic is good; unsound logic is bad. Or to put it even more directly—your ideas have to be sensible. Generally, there are three ways to ensure that they will be: Base your ideas on sound assumptions, qualify your ideas to avoid overgeneralization, and make sure you have adequate evidence to prove your ideas are valid.

Many ideas are based on other, implied ideas; an idea based on an invalid assumption is an invalid idea. Consider the following thesis statement dealing with the invasion by the United States of the small Caribbean island of Grenada:

> The President's intervention in Grenada was necessary to protect our country from communist expansion.

What the statement *says* is straightforward: The invasion was necessary. But it also *assumes* the truth of two very large and controversial beliefs: that communism is a single, homogeneous force, and that its expansion is a direct threat to the United States. Both assumptions deal with complex issues, both the subject of heated debate among people knowledgeable about world affairs. But complexity aside, the truth of the thesis statement depends entirely upon the truth of the underlying assumptions; if communism is *not* a monolithic force, or its expansion poses no direct threat to the United States, then the writer's assertion—that the invasion was necessary—cannot be true. When you experiment with possible theses in the early stages of writing, remain aware of the underlying assumptions you make, and question them as critically as you question the conclusions you draw from them—one false assumption can invalidate an entire logical structure.

Be cautious also to qualify your statements so that they say *specifically* what you want them to say. In discussing interesting content I noted the value of generalization, but you may remember that earlier I said being *overly* general was a way of saying nothing. In a thesis statement, overgeneralization is a logical flaw, and a common one at that. It stems from the human wish to simplify a complex world. Often argumentative writing is marred by overgeneralization, and many controversial issues are debated by polarized camps that refuse to see the complexities of issues and to qualify their statements. The following thesis about gun laws is an example:

Gun laws are detrimental to the common good.

This is more an expression of an emotion than good sense; it tells what side the writer is on, but in terms of content it is illogical, encompassing as it does *all* gun laws and *all* that is to the common good. In reconsidering this as a possible thesis, even the writer would have to admit that laws forbidding the use of a firearm to commit a felony or banning the firing of guns in populous areas enhance rather than detract from the public good.

But the statement could be made more sensible by being made more specific. The original statement could become "A handgun ban in this city would be a useless burden on the taxpayers," and then more specific still "A handgun ban in this city would be a waste of money and legislative effort because it would be unenforceable." This last statement is most sensible because it is limited enough to apply accurately to those aspects of the general issue it encompasses.

Finally, the most important aspect of logic is evidence or proof—having sound reasons to believe what you believe and say what you say. The most commonly used type of logic is called "induction," and it involves the simple process of observing many specific instances and drawing a conclusion based upon these observations. People use induction to draw conclusions in all sorts of ordinary situations. Say, for instance, that you eat at the Friendly Family Diner, a franchise eatery near your home, and find the food there to be greasy. On another occasion, you dine at a restaurant of the same chain across town, and their food proves to be greasy too. On a trip to Houston, you eat at yet another FFD, only to be slimed again, and on the way home, stopping at another one, you get still more greasy food. You conclude, with sound reasons but not necessarily with unerring accuracy, that the food at *all* Friendly Family Diners is greasy. The scientific method works this way, experiments providing the specific evidence for conclusions, and writing too is very often an inductive activity. Good writers observe specific examples to see what they want to say and what it is sensible to say, and then present those examples to their readers as illustration or proof of what they say. As a rule of thumb, if you can't find *several* examples to illustrate a statement, you should doubt yourself; that statement might not make sense. If you *can* find several examples, then it's a good idea to present them to your readers so that *they* know that your ideas make sense. If you can prove it with examples, it is logical, and good writing must be logical.

Saying It Completely

The last thing that needs to be said about content relates to length. Student writers are often perplexed by length—by how long an essay is "supposed" to be and by how to make it that long. This causes teachers to assign length limits—three pages or five hundred words or whatever—and students sometimes do artificial things in response, like chopping an essay off before it makes its point (got three pages; that's it) or padding it with wordiness and repetition to stretch it out. Both result in bad writing.

The alternative is to think in terms of development of ideas rather than the length of the essay. By development I mean how much you say about your main idea. Considerations of audience usually govern the necessary degree of development. An essay expands through illustration, explanation, and proof; that is to say, your purposes are to enable your readers to envision your topic, to understand your statements about it, and to believe those statements. If you have accomplished all these purposes, the essay is adequately developed—long enough.

Whether the development is adequate for the audience is most easily judged in the later phases of writing, after you've actually written a draft. But since predicting approximate length is important in judging whether a tentative thesis is a good one, and since in budgeting your time you need to know how large the task at hand is, it helps to get an idea of how much you have to say before you write. This can be accomplished by thinking in terms of *horizontal* and *vertical* development. Consider the prewriting sketch in Figure 3-2, which I produced in writing an essay for one of my own class assignments. I had asked the class to find the general significance in a slang term or euphemism, and I chose an expression in vogue on our campus at the time, "get real."

The horizontal axis, measured on the second level of the sketch just below the word "reality" at the top, represents the number of supporting points I used to expand my thesis—each became a paragraph, making a seven-paragraph essay. The vertical axis, measured according to how far down the sketch is developed, represents the degree of detail I went into. Formed into a more conventional outline later in the process, the sketch appears again in Figure 3-3. In this kind of outline, horizontal development is measured by the number of Roman numeral headings, and vertical by how much is between them.

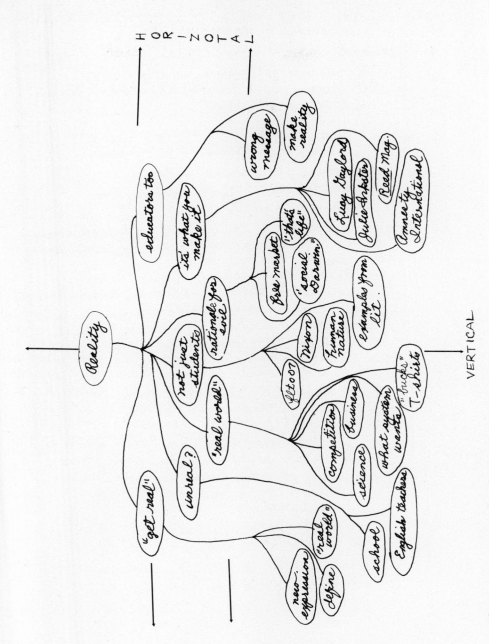

Figure 3-2. Horizontal and Vertical Development.

THESIS: We should control reality rather than conforming to it.

I - Students have a new expression: "get real".
   A. It means get serious, or stop BSing.
   B. It reveals their anxiety about what they call "the real world".

II - They mean a variety of things by "real," but generally they contrast it to "unreal".
   A. By "unreal" they mean school.
   B. Students think English teachers are particularly "unreal".

III - The "real world" is the world of work and money.
   A. Science, business, and especially computers are part of the real world.
   B. The real world is competitive.
   C. In contrast to the 60s radicals, these students want to be whatever the system wants most.
   D. Every now and then you see a T-shirt that says "Because we need the bucks."

IV - This preoccupation with reality is not just a student attitude.
   A. After flight 007 was shot down, hawkish politicians talked about the reality of getting tough with the Soviets.
   B. Nixon, that expert on reality, just wrote a book on the realities of war and peace.
   C. Dreamers of other times lamented real-worldism.
      1. Wordsworth
      2. Yeats
      3. Cervantes

Both methods of recording prewriting information make it possible to predict length and development. Properly developed paragraphs, or items on the horizontal axis, or Roman numeral headings, vary in length but on

V – The tendency to scoff at dreamers and equate reality with the _status quo_ has often made a convenient rationale for greed and brutality.
  A. "Self-interest drives the free market," we say as we stuff our pockets.
  B. "That's life," we say as we push our weaker neighbors around.
  C. "Social Darwinism" is a rationale for animal behavior.

VI – But not all students here are "getting real"– for some reality is what they make it.
  A. Lucy Gaylord the artist recently had a successful show downtown.
  B. Julie Inkster the golfer is on the pro tour now.
  C. The poets who publish in _Reed_ magazine and the activists who collect signatures for Amnesty International know that the world of the spirit is as real as the world of the flesh.

VII – Educators recently have been talking about reality too.
  A. We've focused on business, science, technology, and the race with the Japanese.
  B. The implied message is that learning not associated with high-salaried jobs is not real.
  C. The message we should convey instead is that these students, like all people before them, can create reality rather than conforming to it.

Figure 3-3. Horizontal and Vertical Development in Outline Form.

the average are about a half page, typed and double spaced. Five of them, plus a brief introduction and conclusion, make approximately three pages, or 750 words. So if you've been given a length limit, you can tell by looking at the horizontal axis whether the information you've gathered to develop your idea exceeds or falls short of that limit. Gauging length helps determine whether your idea is appropriate for the assignment.

More important, you can tell whether the essay will be adequately developed to accomplish your main purposes. If the vertical axis is inadequately expanded, the essay will not be detailed enough to enable the readers to envision and understand. If the horizontal axis is sparse, the readers might not understand or believe your idea. In other words, you won't have proven your point. A broad horizontal axis, with several main supporting points for the main idea, and a deep vertical axis—three levels or more—ensure early on in the writing process that you have enough material to work with to make your point.

"Content," then, boils down to a few controllable aspects of writing—having something to say, making sure it is worth saying, saying it sensibly, and saying it completely. Knowing this and keeping it in mind throughout the process can make your writing informative and interesting.

Examples of Student Writing

The chapter you've just read, as any attempt to describe content must be, is an oversimplification. The characteristics of content mentioned occur in a variety of combinations and in a variety of forms, slightly different wherever you encounter or apply them. The following essays show how student writers before you have produced good content in class writing assignments. Careful attention to their writing can give you a better idea of how the principles discussed above actually apply.

The Lessons of Yesterday
Wendy Ichimaru Hanabusa

In one way the following essay is a very ordinary kind of writing—just a person talking about a friend she has known since childhood. It contains the kind of subject matter that is accessible to everyone—everyday human experience. But it is also compellingly interesting.

The writer has done not one but several of the things mentioned in this chapter. Most conspicuously, she has taken advantage of the tension of polarity by describing one friendship involving two very opposite people. She enhances this tension by extensive development, both horizontal and vertical, giving a detailed picture of her friend Charlene. And finally, at the end of her essay, she sums up her feelings about her friendship—and gives us a new way of looking at friendship in general—by using an imaginative simile.

Children don't choose their friends as adults do. They aren't too concerned with race or wealth, but measure their friends by the amount of fun they can share and the mischief they can get into together. My first real friend was a girl who lived down the street, and no two such opposite girls were ever so close. Her name was Charlene, also known as Charlie, Chuck, Tuna, and Char, the only child of a double divorcée and a bartender turned restauranteur. She had step-sisters, a step-father, a step-mother, and a grandmother who had been married three times. The Caucasian trunk of her family tree had branched at her parents' level with Greek, Mexican, and Carolinian limbs as couples split to join new spouses. Her birthdays would bring quick visits and $100.00 checks without any cards, which were used to buy stereos, waterbeds, and hanging beads.

My family by contrast was frightfully dull, my parents in a lifetime marriage, my lineage consistant in race and religion, and all five brothers and sisters produced by the same two people. Birthday presents were handmade or purchased for under $10.00, and the birthdays relatively undistinguished except for an occasional cake. Our rooms were functional, bunkbeds opposite the door, dressers and desks side by side, closets without doors for easy access and to assure tidyness. Grades were monitored closely and efforts reflected in a "C" were not satisfactory, and one parent would sit with the delinquent child to review math tables or spelling lists or simply ensure that the books were read. But through all the comparisons and arguments about how Charlene's mother never made her miss a full night of television or movies with a friend, my parents were puzzled but happy that we were friends, and even then, I wondered why. I learned a large portion of my vocabulary of racial slurs from Char, and my bank of swear words had its beginning in her mother's home. I remember running home in junior high demanding birth control pills, though I wasn't sure why Charlene was so proud of them or why my mother was so upset.

It was as if I lived a part of my life vicariously through Charlene. I watched as she drew circles in the moist concrete surrounding a miniature golf course and laughed as the others placed their footprints in the wet surface. We all ran when the manager's voice yelled out over the background sound of the Bayshore freeway, our feet taking us to the local Seven-Eleven. A quick call to her mother was not fast enough, and the police arrived a moment before our rescue vehicle appeared. And at the site of the terrible deed, the manager banned our presence, the first of many places we were not to go until we matured into decent little girls. Each time we were caught, Char was the doer, I was the tag-along who was more than willing to share in the punishment or to go along with the prank, happy to share in the excitement and the thrill of being naughty if only by association.

Junior high school days faded into high school, and boys were always on our minds. Charlene was less than five feet tall and nature had shaped her silhouette in early abundance. These were the days of mini-skirts and platform shoes, Levi jeans and messy make-up, cut classes and cigarettes. She had boyfriends at our high school, at my church, at my boyfriend's school, and a few scattered in various places throughout the city, each one a prior victim of giggling girls and longing gazes. We even enrolled in wood shop classes where the odds were tremendously in our favor at 30 to 4, each project completed by a different boy in the room. They were the days of spin-the-bottle and marked liquor bottles refilled with water, secret parties and less-than-honest days. Weekend waterskiing trips with her parents and camping trips with mine were simply great new settings to meet other young men to flirt at and tease, and life and love were just games to be enjoyed for the moment because the next week would bring new players into the fun.

I really miss her now. I haven't seen Charlene since my wedding, which was not quite a year ago. Prior to that, the last time I talked with her was during her second marriage. We both had changed and too much had happened after high school, much more than I could understand. She married within a year of graduation, just months after she met and rescued her first husband from living out of the back seat of his car. He was a real low-life whose greatest ambition was to rebuild his pan-head Harley, but he was graced with an amazing amount of charm and chatter. I watched through her "Stepford" days of "whites" and "crank," the paranoid days of cocaine and the angry nights with late night cruises to see which bar he was at. One night we were unfortunate enough to find him, getting into his car, waving at a pretty girl as she started hers. He followed her out to Central Expressway, his white van in sharp contrast to the evening's darkness, traveling in an unhomebound direction. He didn't see us until a half mile on Central, and his van jerked as he tried to accelerate and shift at the same time. But, like a woman possessed, Char not only overtook him but cut him off, forced him to come to a stop, jumped out of the car and ran back to confront him. She didn't divorce him then as she didn't divorce him when she contracted venereal disease months after their wedding, nor when he consumed the profit and part of the investment of his drug deals.

I never knew how much she had changed until I visited her at her mother's new apartment and found her yellow with jaundice and weak. They were back together again, newly divorced mother and soon-to-be-divorced daughter. Charlene tried to make an unbearable situation last, somehow rationalizing that a bad marriage was better than letting family history repeat itself. The only reward for her efforts in those four long years was a painful heroin addiction and a case of an incurable rash. After her divorce we went on a whirlwind tour of Northern California, our parents believing the space could heal her wounds. We talked the hours away through the flat, hot valley of Sacramento, into the foothills of Nevada City, over the mountain to Reno, around the lake to South Shore and up to Shasta and Dunsmuir. We talked about how different our lives were during her married years. I was in college, working full-time as an accounting clerk, dating several men at the same time and trying to live life at its fullest. We talked about the people we knew, from her husband's biker friends to my engineers and accountants. The bell-bottom jean days were over a long time ago for me, and yet she was still clinging to the memories of midnight runs to Clear Lake, twenty bikers strong, with hell in the wind and drugs in her veins.

My mother never knew all the details of Charlene's life; she was just the street-wise, fast-taught friend that my mother never had. She was the girl with eyes too old for her age and the smile that covered all the pain. My mother never worried when I was with her, for she was the friend to help me when I was unsure and I was the friend who tried to help when she was too sure. My family gave her camping trips, new foods, watchful older "brothers," and stability. Her family gave me roller derby, professional wrestling, water skiing, and a sense of freedom. But most of all, Charlene taught me that you can't always help those you care about; that they must want help before it can be given; that "wrong" doesn't matter if what is "right" seems too far away to reach without losing everything that appears to be important; that a friend is someone who will speak her mind, offer a helping hand, and never say "I told you so." A real friendship is like a good book. It is something that you begin with interest, set aside when disturbed by the needs of the present, pick up and throw down with disgust. But the book is never thrown away; it is placed on a shelf and dusted, to be browsed through another day. The lessons of yesterday are intact in this book and all the tomorrows are still waiting to be read.

The Narley Stuff
Michael Vergillo

One way to exploit the tension in a paradox is to resolve the paradox. Another way is to go with it, adding to the mystery rather than solving it. The following essay was inspired by Tom Wolfe's book The Right Stuff, *and the style as well as the title is modeled after Wolfe's lively, emphatic use of language. In this essay, Michael Vergillo finds a paradox in a sport he enjoys—the participants subject themselves to physical torture and apparently enjoy it. Rather than trying to analyze the phenomenon, Michael simply portrays it, and the tension inherent in the paradox is highlighted by the tension between the details he presents (physical torture) and the tone of the essay (radical enthusiasm, Michael would call it) created by the colloquial diction, MX'er's jargon, and emphatic style.*

The sport of motorcycle moto-cross is a form of high speed, off-road racing. The races are referred to by the riders as "motos." They can be held on anything from rolling grass hills, resembling a golf course, to the roughest, rockiest, moon-like terrain. A moto might be five minutes short or thirty minutes long. Normally there are at least two motos on race day, and the top finishers from these progress to a final. Speeds can exceed seventy miles per hour, as riders bounce and skip over a giant dirt washboard, on lightning-quick, two-wheeled jack hammers. Riders sail off 45-degree drops at sixty miles per, and then take the express elevator to the bottom, five stories down! Just like "Devil's Drop" at Carlsbad Raceway in Southern California! This will often cause the feebler MX'ers to lose their lunches. And along with the thrills of playing Superman in the air, the chance of falling, or as MX'ers would say, "biting it" always exists. And if a rider does fall, he stands a very good chance of getting "T-boned," or struck, by other riders traveling at blistering speeds. Not fun! The funny thing about moto-cross, though, is that these nuts, these riders, actually get off on it! There is nothing in the world they would rather do than scream their bikes way beyond the limits of control. Or jump as far and as high as they possibly can, until they crash their brains out! So you can bet these boys wear some special riding gear.

Along with the helmet, I always wear goggles. The darn things fog up about fifty seconds before the starting gate drops. I can't see worth beans anyway, with seven tear-offs stacked on 'em. (Tear-offs are like throw away lenses, you tear one off when it gets too muddy to see through.) Then there's the upper part of an MX'er's body, which looks like that of a football player, shoulder pads and all. My shoulder pads hold my jersey out away from my body so the mud and water can slide off my helmet, down my back, and into my pants. There's no better feeling in the world! A tight, wide elastic band called a kidney belt is worn around the waist to prevent your guts from becoming a scrambled mess. The leathers, which are really nylon riding pants, are equipped with plastic hip, knee, and shin guards that do little more than shatter when a rider falls. Feet take a beating too, so the boots are heavy and padded. They resemble antique, over-the-calf ski boots, radical-looking numbers that give the rider no sense of feel with his feet. These minor discomforts are part of the fun for the hardcore MX'er. The fact that my bike is as tall as my legs are short is no big deal. A brick under my right foot is a sure fix! If something doesn't want to work, you make it work.

Because of the geographical location, moto-cross in the Pacific Northwest tends to be a bit soggy, gooey, sticky, muddy, and wet. I can remember getting out of a warm car in dry riding gear and stepping into a downpour of ice-cold Washington rain. What better way to start a day? And as I pushed my state-of-the-art, mega-buck, and highly zoot piece of racing machinery through the ocean of mud, my head filled with dreams of catching the hole shot! You see, the rider with the hole shot is the first one to the first turn, and he has the choice of the fastest line through the course. The rain was no big deal. I had plenty of other things to worry about: "Think I'll start in second cog, slide the clutch, and let the torque pull me out of the hole." Making a bike move in knee deep oatmeal is some serious work!

But by the time the one minute warning sign comes out, the MX'ers are ready to do some "go for broke" racing. When the gate falls, the most righteous MX'er loses all sense of reality. "Shower the rider behind you with rocks and dirt or you'll be eating rocks and dirt!" "Kill or be killed!" An all around good time. The starting gate is a kick in the pants, with plenty of room for thirty riders abreast. But the first turn, well, it will normally accommodate no more than eight riders. Now things start cooking! Picture thirty insane MX'ers, in Darth Vader suits, on high-output, two-wheeled crotch rockets, traveling at speeds which well exceed the legal national highway MAX, all heading for the same exact place at the same exact time! It just doesn't work!!! Wherever you look riders are catching lower cogs (gears) and standing on the binders as if their lives depended on it. And for good reason. The first turn is like an elimination process. And there are two good things about getting through it. One, you have a halfway decent chance of finishing the race. And two, you no longer have to worry about dying in the darn thing!

The rest of the race is pretty mellow. Almost always, there is a stretch of whoops or whoopdidoos. They're just a bunch of ripply bumps, about the size of small tidal waves. I like the camel humps or double jumps at the Seattle International Raceway. They're like two Sherman tanks parked about forty feet apart. The idea is to jump off the first one and clear, not touch, or land on, or bury yourself into, but *clear* the second one! But wait, there's more! Some joker always builds a massive berm that takes a 90-degree turn about five feet after the last hump. A berm is nothing more than a soft, banked dirt corner. But even so, it can cause some serious problems when an airborne rider has his Suzuki pegged W.F.O. as he flies through the air, and that good old berm is in his landing spot. I think you can picture the rest. Oh, and about "W.F.O.," I won't go into detail in polite company, but it's a racer's term for holding the throttle "wide open."

This is only a small part of the excitement and fun a MX'er might go through on any given race day. Some might say MX'ers don't have it all together upstairs. Or that they can't possibly be having fun. But in fact, they're having more fun than you could dream of. They might not have it *all* upstairs, but what they do have is the NARLEY STUFF!

Travar, Young American
Tuan Tran

The following essay illustrates three of the kinds of tension mentioned in this chapter. Since the writer sees the subject of the essay, an American teenager, as representative of his peer group, the essay finds the general significance in the specific instance. He also finds elements of paradox in the young man he writes about. But the essay's real charm lies in the fact that the writer, a Vietnamese immigrant, provides the American reader with a novel point of view, an outsider's perspective. Because of this distance rather than in spite of it, his insight into American young people is keen.

A long time ago, even before I came to the United States, I heard that young Americans were well-known for their restlessness, that street crimes such as drug addiction, prostitution, and robberies happened daily, and a lot of them were caused by juvenile criminals. People keep wondering what this young generation really wants. After living in the United States for three years, I'm not sure how I can put it. The young American, to me, is restless and also charming. He can be very rude, and cute. He can be a good guy, and also a very bad guy at the same time. Travar, my co-worker, is an example.

I first met Travar when I came to work as a dishwasher in a fast food restaurant. Travar was in charge of training me. I liked him from the first moment. He was quiet, confident, tall, and muscular. Although he was a high school kid, Travar behaved like an experienced, mature person. He was slow, patient when explaining things to me. He was calm, cool, and kind when I made mistakes. Once I broke a whole pile of dishes. He just said, "Easy, easy Tuan, no big hurry at all." Seeing a chance of making friends with an American guy, I tried to talk with him as much as I could, and we soon became friends. One afternoon, just one week after I started working, I was twenty minutes late. I called in, and as soon as I heard someone pick up the phone, I went like a machine gun: "I'm sorry, Bob (he is my manager), I'm late, but I'll be there very soon."

To my surprise, there was a pause at the other end, and then I heard Travar's voice. "This is Travar; you'd better hurry up, Tuan, because no one knows you're late yet. Meanwhile, I'll cover yours." I'll hardly forget that voice.

Besides being a good friend, Travar is also an anti-racist, which I like very much. Once, I told him "Some people told me that Mexican people are lazy and very combative; are they?" Travar looked straight at me and said, "Whoever told you that is racist, Tuan. I have a lot of Mexican friends, and they are good people to me." However, to my big surprise, although he is anti-racist and friendly to everybody, Travar hates his mother and his sister. He told me, "I'll never see them again, even the day I die." I later found out that he was thrown out of the house because he was trying to steal his mother's Jaguar. Right now, he is living happily with his step-mother and sisters. Another person he doesn't like very much is Bob, the manager. He always refers to Bob as an asshole, or a pain in the ass, and doesn't hesitate to show his dislike. Once, I heard him say to Bob, "I already said it to you, Bob, but you just sat there like I was talking to my dog at home!"

Travar's favorite hobby is driving fast cars. So far, he's owned about six cars: a Triumph, a Maverick, a '72 Toyota, a Datsun 510, and right now, a '69 Camaro. All of them were old, rusty, and damaged. He fixes the engines, paints the bodies, and sells the cars himself. In fact, he's a good mechanic;

he can fix almost any engine, from a car engine or a motorcycle to a boat engine. Very often, after fixing them up, he will drive to highway south 17 to race against any cars. He proudly reminded me that he had eight speeding tickets, one car explosion, two crashed helmets from motorcycle accidents, and an uncountable number of car accidents. But he still loves driving fast cars, and risks his life any way he can. "One thing I haven't done, you know, is rolling a Bug," he would tell me, "but someday I will, you know! Just for the fun of it! Get that Bug rolled over and step out, straighten it up a little bit, and drive away! That's great!"

Besides cars, Travar also loves partying. He lives in Fremont, but drives to Santa Cruz almost every day to have some fun. One of his friends has a "beach-out," that is, a house with the back facing the beach. They party and have fun all night under the moonlight. That is terrific! They play strip-poker and all kind of God-knows games until the morning. Sometimes, Travar comes to work when his eyes still sparkle with fun from one of those parties. He grabs me by the elbow and tirelessly tells what was going on the night before.

Watching me go to school everyday, somehow, Travar felt irritated about his insecure future. As I asked what he wanted to do later, he scratched his head a little bit. Finally, he solved the problem. "I would do anything, Tuan, as long as I would get a lot of money, a lot of money, Tuan." I understand what he meant. People don't have to be engineers or doctors to have a good life. He can be an auto-mechanic, making a lot of money while having fun. He doesn't want to waste his years in college, to become a guru or anything like that, and miss all the fun in life.

Whatever he is, Travar my friend, I like him. I like him because of the way he walks, the way he talks, and the way he manages his life. It's like saying to the world "Whatever I am, I am O. K., I am having fun, and I am controlling the game." I like him because of his kindness to friends, his straightforward mind, and his simple ideas about the world. They're like an old, good chair you can rest on when the world is rough around you.

The First Year
Pamela Liebenberg

One of the biggest hangups in the initial phase of the writing process is the fear of not having anything to write about. Everyone feels to some extent that his or her life is ordinary, not much worth mentioning. But good writers know the falsity of this—they know that everyone, simply by being observant and thoughtful, can have something to say.

In the following essay Pamela Liebenberg proves this in two ways. First she demonstrates the writer's most valuable ability—the ability to look at one thing and see another. In watching swans and ducks, she sees more than swans and ducks, just as Fitzgerald sees a green light on the end of a dock as more than a light. To her, an ordinary sight becomes a metaphor for something larger and more significant. And having made the connection between what she sees and what she feels and thinks, she then analyzes and speculates, working out a problem in her life (and a general human problem as well) in writing.

I was thinking about marriage while watching the swans, geese, and ducks swimming around the lagoon near my mother-in-law's condominium. The ducks were chasing each other, flapping noisily around the lagoon, quacking, bickering, and screaming at each other like children on a playground. The geese and the swans, on the other hand, were sedately swimming around the lagoon in pairs like synchronized swimmers in a delicate ballet, effortlessly moving to their own soft and sensuous song. I wondered how long the couples I was watching had been together; I wondered about their first year of marriage.

The first year of marriage has a reputation for being the most difficult. My husband and I are in our first year of marriage, and unfortunately I don't think that we are going to be able to belie that reputation. We had thought that we had eluded the difficulties of the first year by living together for two and a half years before gliding smoothly into the waters of wedded bliss. We had already survived the arguments at the grocery store and the arguments about budgeting and bills. He had quit yelling at me about my driving; I had quit yelling at him about dropping his dirty clothes next to, instead of into, the dirty clothes basket. We had even survived a couple of championship bouts that went at least fifty rounds. Our relationship came out of these arguments bruised but not broken; it was even strengthened by the struggle.

Those two and a half years had given us experience, so it was with confidence that we planned our wedding. We felt confident as we wrote our ceremony. We wrote the ceremony to be a celebration of an already working relationship rather than an ignorant promise to try. It was a perfect wedding, and the memory of it will make me smile forever. It was what I had always dreamed my wedding day could be. I was a beautiful princess and my husband a handsome prince. His voice rang with confidence and pride as he recited his vows; my voice trembled in awe of what we had been and were to be to each other. Our kiss was full of love and hope; the reception was the biggest, most wonderful ball that has ever been. So why was I sitting by a lagoon six months later thinking that our marriage reminded me more of the ducks than the swans?

Somehow I couldn't envision those two elegant swans pecking at each other and squabbling in their first year of marriage the way my husband and I had been. We couldn't seem to agree about anything; we were back to bickering about cereal, and this time our arguments had a vicious edge to them. The humor and the love that had tempered our anger before seemed to be missing. Why is the first year of marriage so hard? Do you get married, quit loving each other, and learn to adjust to life together without love? I couldn't believe that because I loved my husband more, that day at the lagoon, than ever; I knew he loved me more than ever too. There was all this wonderful, tender love inside of us, yet every time we opened our mouths we sounded like ducks that had just had a tender tidbit stolen from them. If we hadn't stopped loving each other, what had changed our relationship so much?

As I sat by that lagoon, a thought occurred to me; it wasn't the love that was gone but the goal. Before we had gotten married, we had talked together about being married. We had shared our feelings about each other, our fears about each other, our feelings and fears about marriage. We had planned the ceremony and the honeymoon together. We had searched out a place to get married together; we chose the music together; we wrote the ceremony together; we interviewed ministers together; we did everything concerning our marriage together. Our marriage was our common goal. We had getting married to look forward to and to work together toward. Once the ceremony and the honeymoon were over, we no longer had that common goal to plan for and to stimulate conversation.

Perhaps the first year of marriage is so difficult because the two people involved, having accomplished their first goal together, are at loose ends and need to set new goals for just the two of them to keep the relationship stimulated and moving forward. Without personal goals to share, there is nothing to do but pick at each other and try to stave off a sense of inadequacy by each proving how imperfect the other is. New tasks provide the opportunity for a couple to work together and share their thoughts, feelings, and ideas. My husband and I haven't found our new goal yet, but there will be plenty of goals to share—a home, children, even retirement eventually—goals enough to get the love more on the surface and less hidden. Over time, I hope, through the accomplishment of many goals, we'll begin to really know each other and swim together as effortlessly as the swans.

Two Weeks One Summer
Karin Smail

Finding the general significance is often a matter of finding connections between different scenes, experiences, or events. By finding a common denominator between two seemingly separate subjects, you often find that they are not separate at all—just different parts of something larger. In this way it is often possible to make statements about life in general by finding the connections among your separate experiences.

In the following personal-experience essay Karin Smail explores the general significance of a remembered childhood experience. The experience, a

*trip to summer camp, taught her a lesson, and she is perceptive enough to
see that it is generally applicable—that it applies to families and whole so-
cieties as well as to girls at camp.*

I stood there by the horse ring with my thoughts keeping me company,
providing a protective layer of warmth against the winter air. Conflicting
images darted like fireflies through my mind, each flashing its own urgent
message before being replaced by another just as urgent. Those two weeks
five years ago had been the most exciting and personally rewarding of my
twelve-year-old life. Belonging to a Girl Scout troop, I had been given the
opportunity to spend two glorious weeks in the great outdoors with 29
other scouts and as many horses—ours to cuddle, pamper, and generally
adore for the duration. I had to smile as I thought of how agonizing each
day of waiting for an answer had been, how much will power it had taken
to remain on my best behavior.

The latter had been a particularly exacting task, for my childhood up to
that point had not been ideal, due mainly to my attitudes regarding my
family and what the word "family" really meant. How many days had I
slyly integrated the subject of horse camp into the mealtime conversation?
Too many to count. How many nights had I spent staring at the ceiling
from my bed, willing whoever or whatever was up there to convince my
parents to agree to part with the $200 necessary to pay for the camp?
Again, simply too many to recall. To be sure, being the younger of two
girls had its difficulties, but in my eyes it was unbearable. My sister was
four years older, a considerable gap when one thought about it logically—
something I never took the time to do. Instead I chose to rebel against the
real and imagined injustices being inflicted upon me by my parents. I had
to go to bed so early, while *she* had practically all night to stay out with
her friends. My sister was the quieter of us, a winning personality trait
that was, I felt, an unwritten guarantee of her getting pretty much what
she wanted. It never dawned on me that her willingness to help with the
housework and yard chores was a major factor when my parents decided
whether or not to allow her to go out. No, in my eyes at that time, I was
the scapegoat, the perpetrator of all crimes, and the one who got punished
for everything. Sadly, much of the time my sister and I had together was
spent fighting over something or other, such as who got to use the bathroom first and whose turn it was to pick the television channel. The majority ruled against me most of the time. It was three against one, my
parents on my sister's side, and I lost out.
I can still recall angry conversations at the dinner table, voices raised
ever higher as accusations, protests, and denials were volleyed back and
forth over an emotional net. Chairs screeching painfully back from the
table, running feet down the hall to my room, the slamming of the door
reverberating its final message to the enemy back in the kitchen: "Leave
me alone!" Words spoken so often but never really meant, a plea that had

never asked to be heeded so much as it had begged to be ignored. I felt alone and unloved.

The horrible feelings I had had about being the most unwanted and picked-on sibling in the world abated during the two weeks at the Girl Scout horse camp. I was in heaven among the other campers, spending time mucking out stalls, cooking over wood fires, taking ice-cold showers under a garden hose·in a little clearing draped with canvas for privacy, and sharing a tent for four with six other girls. Not until later did I realize the changes I was going through in those two weeks, let alone think of the meaning of sharing and cooperating with my tentmates as in any way relating to my family life.

For in that setting, the "all-for-one" attitude was simply not tolerated. I was forced to think of others ahead of myself, and I was surprised to find myself enjoying helping out new-found friends. Cooperation was the key. If, when dinner was called, one of the girls hadn't straightened up her sleeping bag or washed out her muddy jeans from that afternoon's trail ride, all of her group had to wait until the tasks were completed. Then and only then could they begin to fix their meal. Having won the disgusted looks and anger of my living-quarters companions after choosing to disregard the rules the first night, I chose, albeit a bit reluctantly, to conform to the guidelines. The results, I noted with more than a little pleasure, were astonishing to my adolescent mind. I had friends, not just among my peers, but among the leaders as well. I laughed and smiled and truly enjoyed myself as never before, wishing the grand experience could go on forever.

The happiest and most fulfilling moment of my life until then occurred on the last day of camp. I was picked by the camp leaders to head the procession of scouts into the riding ring for the traditional end-of-camp horse show. As the leader, I was to canter once around the ring, jump a competition gate course, and then demonstrate all the riding gaits we had learned in our stay at the camp.

I was never prouder than on that warm autumn day sitting astride a horse named Sabre, and I'm sure, had they been there, that my parents would have shared my happiness. Unfortunately, they wouldn't arrive to pick me up until the following day. My disappointment faded, but slowly, and as I watched the other girls with their mothers and fathers, laughing and smiling and no doubt recounting every last detail of their stay, I had trouble focusing for the moisture welling up behind my eyelids. I felt pangs of guilt, because I knew that if I had been a better daughter, my parents would have done anything to be at the camp for the show. Slowly I began to understand what being a member of a family was all about.

The next morning, as I kicked up dust in the rutted dirt trail that wound its way a mile or so into the woods before meeting the little group of tents assembled in a rough semicircle, an eagerness I had never known began building up inside me. I wanted to see Mom and Dad again. I stood and cried uncontrollably as they strode around the bend and into view, and then I ran to them and flung my arms around them both, not wanting to let go. I told them how much I'd missed them and loved them. When I looked up to see my mother flashing Dad a startled look that quickly became a relieved smile, I knew that from then on things would be different.

As I turned, five years later, to leave the ring where the little children who were images of an earlier me circled on horseback, enraptured looks on their faces, I had to smile once again at the memory of those two weeks one summer when my understanding of myself and my parents greatly improved; or should I not use a word sounding so like a television pitch for laundry soap? All right then, let me say that I was enlightened after I returned home from my adventure. I looked at life in a different light, as differently as a twelve-year-old can. I tried harder to maintain equilibrium in my emotions; there were no more really bad days when I was impossible to deal with. I came to the realization that the world did *not* revolve around me and my wants, but rather that I was simply one of millions of others in a world where cooperation with and consideration for others was the only way.

Giving the ring one last, lingering look, I turned to go, wondering if any of the children within would experience the joy and personal triumph that I had so long ago. Somehow, I already knew the answer to my question.

EXERCISES

1. Using the ones presented on page 67 as models, do a free-association cluster and a vignette on each of the following terms:

   integrity   sensuous   ice   fortune   dust

   Begin by placing each term in a circle in the center of a blank page; then, jot down words and short phrases that occur to you, whether they seem to make sense or not, anywhere your hand takes them on the page. Enclose them in circles too, and keep adding circles as long as thoughts occur to you. When you've filled the page or run out of thoughts, use lines and arrows to indicate possible connections among the bits of information you've spilled out onto the page. Finally, write a vignette for each cluster, trying to use *all* the words in your cluster. If you can, make your vignette paragraph come full circle, ending up where it began. Look back at the kinds of tension mentioned in the chapter. Can you find any statements in your vignettes that display or suggest these kinds of tension? Would any of the ideas you produced be suitable for expanding into an essay?

2. From exercise one, choose the cluster/vignette you think would make the best essay (preferably one that contains interesting tension). Using the information in it, produce a sketch similar to the one on page 71. (Turn the paper sideways and start at the top edge, since this type of diagram tends to spread out laterally.) Put a condensed version of your main idea in the top bubble, and branch downward from it to supporting ideas on the second level. Below that, break the supporting ideas down into details, and then carry the process one level further, breaking the details down into smaller details. Once you've generated a full sketch, turn it into an outline as I've done on pages 72–73. Assuming that you've been asked to write an essay approximately three pages, or 750 words, long, is your outline long enough? Too long? Assuming that your audience is unfamiliar with your topic, will you have enough development to cause them to envision, understand, and believe your main idea?

3. Turn your outline from exercise two into a rough draft of an essay. How long is it? How effectively does it get your point across? Is it interesting?

4. Qualify the following statements to make them more sensible:

The abolition of pornography would not be an infringement on our freedom of speech.
Television is poison to young minds.
Illegal immigration will destroy this country.
Motorcycles should be outlawed.

5. Write three statements you know to be true, and then list as much evidence as you can to prove them. Example: The classrooms in Sweeney Hall are uninviting. (Evidence—cold fluorescent lights, no windows, cold white colors, hard tile floors, spindly metal chairs with formica writing arms, hissing noises from the airconditioning, chilly air.)

6. Write three statements that express your own opinions about some aspect of public affairs. Then analyze each statement, listing the underlying assumptions it rests on. Example: Money should be diverted from military spending into entitlement programs for the citizenry. (Underlying assumptions—that entitlement programs are more important than military might, that we are not dangerously behind militarily, that citizens pay for the military buildup, that citizens have needs that are not being met, that it is the responsibility of the government to meet those needs.)

Chapter Four

Organization

When I read, I often think of the essay or article or book I am looking into as a kind of landscape—a landscape of ideas and images and phrases and facts rather than of trees and rocks and hills and streams. I think of myself as a traveller, moving through a world made by a writer, following a path the writer has blazed, coming face to face with each new piece of scenery exactly when and where the writer has decided I should. Like all travellers, I may be at ease in my surroundings, or bored by them. I may be disturbed by each new sight I run across, or enthralled by it. If the scenery is rich enough with significance and arranged in a meaningful order, I may emerge from the landscape of the essay altered by what I have seen, enlightened by where I have been. On the other hand, if I find myself abandoned in a bramble of thorny ideas or tangled phrases, I may feel as lost and alone as any wanderer in the woods.

You've probably known that latter feeling, late at night, deep in the wilderness of a badly written psychology text or critical essay on *King Lear*. After struggling long enough through the clutter and deadfall of listless thoughts and dried up phrases, you have probably just wanted to find a way back out to open air and the light of day. The path through the woods may have been too vaguely marked, or the scenery too stark to hold your interest. Either way, it's not surprising if the escape instinct has taken over when you've found yourself wandering deeper into the darkening woods of badly-crafted prose. This is a chapter about how to keep your own readers from meeting the same fate.

Let me begin it by making one rather sweeping, but still I think valid, generalization about organizing essays: Any essay, in order to *be* an essay, needs some sort of an introduction, a middle section, and (probably) a conclusion. Each of these three parts helps in a different way to keep the readers on track as they move through the essay. None of these parts really has any set form; each takes its shape from the ideas it contains. There is no set length for any part, either, except of course that the middle is bound to be the longest section. An introduction or a conclusion may take only a short sentence or a full page, though either is most likely to fall somewhere between those extremes.

What follows are some of the options I have discovered—mostly through reading my students' essays and essays by professional writers—techniques for arranging each part of the essay. All, it seems to me, are good resources to have at hand when laying out a landscape of discovery.

The Introduction: Providing a Trailhead

Readers, like any travellers, often hesitate to enter new territory. It takes a certain amount of courage, an act of faith, to take the first step and embark on any kind of expedition into the unknown. Because of this, one of your first concerns in introducing your readers to your subject is to win their confidence so they will willingly follow you into the complexities of your topic. To do this, you will need to provide a trailhead—a starting point that will promise fair and interesting travelling ahead.

Fortunately, there are many specific devices for establishing such a starting point. I'm going to list some of them, discuss each briefly, and then show you some introductions that use them effectively. First, though, let me caution you that there can be no easy formula for writing introductions. Since the purpose of an introduction is to lead readers into a subject, and since each paper will have a different subject, there is no universally "right" way to proceed. First you have to know what you want to introduce and whom you want to introduce it to; then, you have to find a way to get the job done. That may mean one short paragraph or several longer ones. It may mean gradually leading up to your point, or suddenly and boldly challenging your readers' assumptions. In fact, so varied are the types of introductions that many writers prefer to arrange the rest of their essay first and then come back to write the introduction later, when they know more surely what they are introducing. Whether you write it first or last, though, you'll find that there are at least two things you'll almost always want your introduction to do:

Orient your readers to the topic: Let them know what they're getting into, what subject they will confront in the interior of your essay. Or at least make them wonder.

Entice them into the essay: Give them reason to want to read on and learn more about the subject. Generate enough interest in the subject, or create enough mystery about it, to overcome any initial reluctance and beckon them into the body.

All introductions, it seems to me, do these two things in one way or another. Consider, for instance, this short introduction by Donald Murray:

> When students complete a first draft, they consider the job of writing done—and their teachers too often agree. When professional writers complete a first draft, they usually feel that they are at the start of the writing process. When a draft is completed, the job of writing can begin.
>
> *Donald Murray*

Murray orients us to his topic by bluntly telling us how two groups of writers—professionals and students—typically view that topic, and so after only three sentences we know that the essay will lead us into a discussion of revising writing. At the same time, he entices us to read on by swiftly delivering us to a thesis, one that challenges a common misconception: "When a draft is completed, the job of writing can begin." Since most of us at least want to believe that the job of writing is largely over by the time we've finished a draft, the tension created by Murray's surprising thesis draws us deeper into the essay. We want to see how he is going to prove such a thing.

There are times, rare times, when it is a good idea to state your point so boldly and launch your readers so precipitously into the body of the essay; usually it is wiser to spend a little more time making them familiar with the subject at hand and luring them into a discussion of it.

Here, now, are some of the techniques that I have used and seen my students use to build effective introductions. Some help to orient readers; some help to entice them; some do both. Use any of them that seem useful, ignore any that don't, and don't hesitate to combine and adapt them to your own purposes.

PAINT A PICTURE

Let your readers see the subject before you begin to tell them about it. Try creating an image of a specific place or person or thing that pertains directly to your topic. Vivid images will seize your readers' attentions, arouse their emotions, prod their imaginations to life, make them care about what you intend to discuss. One of my favorite opening lines is George Orwell's from his essay "Marrakech":

> As the corpse went past the flies left the restaurant table in a cloud and rushed after it, but they came back a few minutes later.

It's a disturbing, even disgusting, image; but because it engages our imaginations, we read on, moving into an essay that lambastes Europeans for their attitudes toward nonwhite peoples. A good image is always an eye-opener.

Images in introductions are particularly useful when you intend to relate a story or argue a point of view in the rest of the essay. Before entering a story, readers want a sense of setting: they want to feel involved with the physical scene, with the time and place in which the story will unfold. Similarly, before entering an argument, readers expect to care about the issue. A short, vivid sketch of one child starving in East Africa can do wonders to make readers care about the more abstract issue of American foreign aid.

RECALL AN INCIDENT

This device is similar to the first, and in fact it may well involve creating images again. The emphasis here, though, is not on a person, place or thing, but on something that has happened. Retelling an event from your own experience, or from the news, or from history, can be a means of raising an issue, framing a challenge, or igniting a flash of recognition that will involve your reader personally in the topic. Stories, like images, move readers to care.

Of course, as with images, a story used by way of introduction should do more than just entertain and arouse interest. It should be manifestly connected to the subject you want to introduce; it should lead your readers clearly into an issue and deposit them on the doorstep of an idea worth considering.

FILL IN THE BACKGROUND

If you know much more about the topic than your readers are likely to know, you may need to fill them in on any information they'll need in order to follow you through your discussion. You might preface an analysis of a poem, for instance, with pertinent biographical facts about the poet, so long as those facts truly shed light on the poem in question. Or you might begin a discussion of current U.S. trade relations with a brief history of such relations. Take care, though, not to bore you readers by beginning with a long litany of dry statistics or facts. Keep in mind that you will have opportunities to pause and explain complexities along the way.

ASK PROVOCATIVE QUESTIONS

Like a chigger, an unanswered question can get under the skin and twitch and itch and drive one slightly mad. It can compel attention.

You can make good use of this nagging quality of questions in introducing an essay. An essay, almost by definition, must answer a significant question with its thesis, and one option for beginning is to drop the question directly at your readers' feet right at the outset. Then let the essay—perhaps slowly and teasingly, perhaps more directly and systematically—supply the answer. You may even want to open with a series of questions, each growing more telling, more aggravating, more demanding of an answer.

PROVIDE A VIEW AHEAD

If the going's going to be tough—if you must inevitably lead your readers into the brambles of a complex issue, abstract ideas or dense facts—you may want to begin by giving them a glimpse of the path they'll follow. It may help keep them on track later. Take them up to high ground and let them take a look ahead. This may mean listing arguments you'll make, showing several positions you'll evaluate, anticipating objections you'll answer, or enumerating steps you'll trace, to name just a few possiblities.

The view-ahead approach to constructing introductions has the advantage of reasurring your readers that you know where you intend to lead them. It has the potential disadvantage, though, of boring the living daylights out of both you and them. Remember that a sense of mystery—of small wonders yet to be discovered—is what moves most readers to enter an essay and to keep reading once they're in it. Knowing too surely where they're going can make people not want to go. Reserve this technique for those times when your readers are truly likely to get lost without a preview.

PIN A PHRASE ON IT

A pithy phrase of any kind—a quote, an epigram, a one-liner dropped at a party , a proverb remembered from childhood, an advertising jingle, a fragment of a nursery rhyme, or your own inventive twist on any of these— may provide a clever, engaging opener. Or a deadly one.

Memorable phrasing, wherever encountered, can seize attention by condensing great wit or wisdom into a short space. As the centerpiece of an introduction, such wit can delight readers and entertain them, leaving them eager to read on; such wisdom can encapsulate a main idea or prompt an increased interest in a topic.

Unfortunately, what seems memorable or clever to a writer may seem trite or strained to a reader. A quote from *Bartlett's* that seems witty and wise the first time you see it, may seem old and tired to a professor who has already read 700 essays on the American dream beginning: "A penny saved is a penny earned." To work well, quotes, epigrams, and the like have to be strikingly original for the context in which you use them and tightly linked to the subject at hand. Look for those that will seem like newly discovered treasures to your readers, like promises of more discoveries yet to come.

STATE YOUR THESIS (OR DON'T)

Finally, let me suggest, rather ambiguously, that you may or may not want to state your thesis outright in the introduction. As Donald Murray's introduction above shows, a good thesis may itself grab attention and propel readers into an essay. All of the various kinds of theses discussed in Chapter

Three, in fact, can generate the kind of tension that will arouse interest and sustain it through an essay. So revealing the thesis early is always an option worth considering.

But don't be too eager to give your thesis away simply in order to get started. Often a thesis has more impact if placed later in the paper. If your main idea is a controversial one, for example, you may want to lead your readers up to it gradually, first whittling away at their reluctance, moving them towards acceptance. If your thesis is abstract or otherwise difficult to grasp, you may want to pave the way leading up to it with explanations before expecting your readers to comprehend it. If your idea is unusually clever, you may want to bring them around a bend in your argument to confront it, suddenly, when they least expect it and will be most dazzled by it.

My advice is to think twice about using your thesis in the introduction. Do so only if bluntness and directness seem like the best approaches to your idea.

SAMPLE INTRODUCTIONS

Below are a few introductions I think work especially well. Some are by students, some by professional writers. They are only a small sampling of the possibilities, but they will give you an idea of how many ways the techniques I've just discussed can be combined. I'll keep my commentary on them brief, since I think they explain themselves well.

First, Joan Didion luring us into a story in which a woman will burn her husband to death in a Volkswagen:

> This is a story about love and death in the golden land, and begins with the country. The San Bernadino Valley lies only an hour east of Los Angeles by the San Bernadino Freeway but is in certain ways an alien place: not the coastal California of the subtropical twilights and the soft westerlies off the Pacific but a harsher California, haunted by the Mojave just beyond the mountains, devastated by the hot dry Santa Ana wind that comes down through the passes at 100 miles an hour and whines through the eucalyptus windbreaks and works on the nerves. October is the bad month for the wind, the month when breathing is difficult and the hills blaze up spontaneously. There has been no rain since April. Every voice seems a scream. It is the season of suicide and divorce and prickly dread, wherever the wind blows.
>
> *Joan Didion*

When I read that, I *hear* the Santa Ana wind screaming at me. I *feel* it clawing at my scalp. I *smell* the eucalyptus trees, dry and ready to burst into flames. Images abound throughout Didion's paragraph, and because of them I read on into the story already feeling as if I am there, in San Bernadino, waiting with "prickly dread" for "a story about love and death." The scene is set, and it is appropriately scary.

In the next introduction, David Yohn also uses images , but for a different effect:

The neighborhood has changed, but the house is the same. It stands as it has for over a hundred years, and probably will for a hundred more. In three-storied splendor, white columns reaching up through the first two floors—a very man-sionish set of twelve columns, topped by wide white gables decorated with plaster leaves and filigrees—it stands on top of one of the highest hills in this town of hills, Hannibal, Missouri. The house was built in the 1860's by a man who made millions shipping barges full of cement up the Mississippi River. From the third-floor windows, he could see several miles down the wide, tree-lined river, giving him plenty of time to ride down to meet his shipment. The road then must have been dirt, or gravel, subject to becoming dangerously slippery with the frequent summer storms, not the modern concrete of the Grace Street I'm standing on now.

David Yohn

About to take us through the door and into the house he grew up in (and into his childhood memories of it), Yohn first dips into the more distant past, adding just a touch of storytelling to his description to help us see and care about the house as he has seen it and cared about it.

This one is by Irwin Edman, who also begins by recalling the past:

I remember often during my early adolescence listening to older people making conversation. I vowed I would never willingly be a conspirator at such transparent hypocrisies. When I went out to dinner, I found myself saying, I should speak only when I felt like it, and I should say only what was on my mind. I used to listen while my elders pretended to have a fascinated interest in visitors with whom I knew they had only the most remote concern, and hear them discuss with affected animation matters that I knew bored them to pain. I remember having had it explained to me that this was the least that good manners de-manded. It was at this moment that I came to the conclusion that good manners and dubious morals had much in common.

Irwin Edman

Although almost devoid of images, the brief story serves its purpose of delivering us to an abrupt thesis at the end of the paragraph. And the thesis, since it states an apparent paradox, creates a tension that pulls us into the essay.

Last, consider this by E. M. Forster:

A few years ago I wrote a book which dealt in part with the difficulties of the English in India. Feeling that they would have had no difficulties in India them-selves, the Americans read the book freely. The more they read it the better it made them feel, and a cheque to the author was the result. I bought a wood with the cheque. It is not a large wood—it contains scarcely any trees, and it is inter-sected, blast it, by a public footpath. Still, it is the first property that I have owned, so it is right that other people should participate in my shame, and should ask themselves, in accents that will vary in horror, this very important question: What is the effect of property upon the character? Don't let's touch economics; the effect of private ownership upon the community as a whole is another question— a more important question, perhaps, but another one. Let's keep to psychology. If you own things, what's their effect on you? What's the effect on me of my wood?

E.M. Forster

About to embark on an exploration of a very abstract issue, Forster first takes care to frame it in concrete terms. His personal anecdote leads to a general question; the general question leads to a more specific one; and the specific one urges us into the essay, expecting an answer.

The Body: Finding a Direction in the Subject

If you have ever contemplated a vase shattered on a floor, or stood, as I have, clutching a sheet of instructions and nervously eyeing a not-yet-assembled tricycle, you've had an object lesson in organizing the middle section of an essay. You've seen that parts of any kind in disarray lack the significance of those same parts put next to each other in deliberate arrangements.

This, of course, is obvious, but it's worth pondering for a moment in relation to the way language works. Language is really little more than an agreed-on system for organizing parts. One pattern of language symbols— say the letters "crbieeg"—although composed of perfectly familiar parts, English letters, means nothing at all. Rearrange the same parts according to a plan, though, and you get "iceberg," which means something quite definite. Instantly, significance is born, simply out of the new relationship of the parts. And the same thing could as easily be done with scrambled and unscrambled versions of whole sentences, or paragraphs, or essays.

I bring this up now because readers move into the body of an essay expecting to find significance there, expecting something found to make the traveling worthwhile. Whether they eventually emerge from the essay satisfied or disillusioned depends partly on the quality of the separate ideas and facts and images and speculations they find there. But it also depends, to a much larger extent than most novice writers realize, on how those separate parts are arranged.

What I'd like to do in this section is to suggest some ways in which you can effectively assemble your various ideas into patterns of larger significance. Professional writers and students have used the techniques I'm about to discuss for years, centuries I suppose, to move their readers from idea to idea. But all that means is that they've proven useful to many writers writing about many topics, and I think you'll find that if you look upon them as resources rather than as binding regulations for correctness, they'll help you to arrange your own landscape of ideas and blaze a clear trail through it.

Before I launch into them, though, let me issue one caveat:

- Always let your content determine how your paragraph or essay will be arranged; don't on any account choose a pattern of arrangement first and then cast about for ideas that might fit into it.

When it comes time to organize a paper, begin by examining your pre-writing notes, your outline, your rough draft—whatever jottings you might have assembled before writing a full draft. Sort through the jumble of ideas on your desk or the entries on your computer screen. Look for the order within these notes, the structure implied by them. Then, choose a pattern of presentation that will help you to unfold the best of your ideas clearly. Usually, you'll find that one of the patterns I'm about to suggest, or some combination of them will work best. But if not, don't hesitate to invent new ones to suit your own material.

Now for the patterns themselves. I'll offer a little advice about how you might use each in your essays and then illustrate each with a student or professional example. I've included only paragraph-length samples here, but keep in mind that any of these patterns might as easily be used either to arrange just a few sentences within a paragraph or to structure a whole essay.

FROM FIRST TO LAST

Arranging is probably easiest when your subject concerns events. Events, after all, tend to follow one another in clear, simple sequences, and retelling them, telling stories, is a natural human inclination, something we're all fairly well practiced in. Still, there are a few particulars I try to keep in mind when I find myself stringing together a tale, whether of fact or fiction. Let me pass them along in the form of tips for you to consider the next time you find yourself narrating a story.

- Pace the events you unfold carefully, moving the readers from event to event at just the right clip. Include those details that help to develop your main idea or sustain your readers' interest; leave out any that don't. Many a tale has become tedious for being too long in the telling.

- If flashing forward or backward in time serves your purpose better than a straightforward, first-to-last progression, then by all means flash; but don't jump around in time so much that you might leave your readers wandering in confused circles as they try to follow a twisted story line.

- If there is a central event, a climactic incident in which your main point is revealed, try to lead the readers up to it gradually but surely. Don't give away any surprises too early. If you can, create a sense of mystery about how things are going to turn out in the end.

- Use transitional markers like "next," "then," and "after a while" when you must—when the readers honestly might get lost without them. Resist the temptation to overuse them, though. If the events are well paced, one will lead to the next without much explanation on your part.

Consider the simple elegance of John Updike's paragraph below. He's describing the last time that the great Ted Williams played ball at Fenway Park. Notice, in particular, how Updike paces the events he's describing, moving us gradually, but not too gradually, toward the climactic moment of that fall afternoon:

> Fisher, after his unsettling wait, was low with the first pitch. He put the second one over, and Williams swung mightily and missed. The crowd grunted, seeing that classic swing, so long and smooth and quick, exposed. Fisher threw the third time, Williams swung again, and there it was. The ball climbed on a diagonal line into the vast volume of air over center field. From my angle, behind third base, the ball seemed less an object in flight than the tip of a towering, motionless construct, like the Eiffel Tower or the Tappan Zee Bridge. It was in the books while it was still in the sky. Brandt ran back to the deepest corner of the outfield grass, the ball descended beyond his reach and struck in the crotch where the bullpen met the wall, bounced chunkily, and vanished.
>
> *John Updike*

FROM STEP TO STEP

Another very simple pattern of organization, often called the process pattern, works well for a surprising array of topics. The pattern itself simply involves leading your readers from the first step in a sequence to the last step. You'll find it useful in two different kinds of writing situations:

1. When you want to instruct someone how to perform a task; or

2. When you want to analyze how something occurs in a progression of steps.

In the first instance you might want to explain to someone how to assemble a birdhouse; in the second, how the finches that inhabit it court, mate, and raise their young. Or in the first you might propose a method for running a winning political campaign; in the second, how John Kennedy defeated Richard Nixon for the Presidency in 1960. In this last case, the organization might resemble the "from first to last" pattern I discussed above. But here there would be an important distinction: Moving from step to step, you would be deliberately breaking the progress of the Kennedy campaign down into separate *stages* in order to explain how it worked. The emphasis now would be on dividing the events into groups in order to explain how the victory was accomplished.

Again some suggestions:

- Make at least a scratch outline before you write, divided into the major phases you will discuss. This will give you a broad overview of the process and keep you from skipping any steps or getting them in the wrong order. Then go back and fill in the smaller steps that occur in each phase.

- If the process you are going to trace is especially complicated, you may want to share your overview of the main divisions with your readers early in the paper, so that they, too, will not get lost among the smaller steps.

- Avoid, on the one hand, the temptation to get too detailed, breaking the process down into too many small steps. (No one building a bird-house, for instance, needs instructions in how to hold a hammer.) On the other hand, don't remain too general in tracing the steps: What's obvious to you may not be obvious to your readers. (They may, in fact, need to be told to nail the bird house together before painting it.) Let your common sense and an honest assessment of your readers' needs be your guide here.

- Keep the steps in rigid sequence from first to last. But don't be afraid to pause and sum up earlier steps or offer helpful explanations along the way.

Even the simplest, most familiar things sometimes take on a new interest when a good writer breaks them down into a process and holds each step up for examination. Here's E. B. White examining how a racoon climbs down from a tree:

A coon comes down a tree headfirst for most of the way. When she gets within about six feet of the ground, she reverses herself, allowing her hind end to swing slowly downward. She then finishes the descent tailfirst; when, at last, she comes to earth, it is a hind foot that touches down. It touches down as cautiously as though this were the first contact ever made by a mammal with the flat world. The coon doesn't just let go of the tree and drop to the ground, as a monkey or a boy might. She steps off onto my lawn as though in slow motion—first one hind paw, then the other hind paw, then a second's delay when she stands erect, her two front paws still in place as though the tree were her partner in the dance. Finally, she goes down on all fours and strides slowly off, her slender front paws reaching ahead of her to the limit, like the hands of an experienced swimmer.

E. B. White

FROM HERE TO THERE

Suppose you wanted to describe something, anything—your grandmother's face, a vista from your uncle's front porch, the layout of a new computer's keyboard. In each situation, you would first need to select the most essential details of the person, place, or thing in question. Then you would also need to arrange the selected details. But where to begin with this arranging, and how to proceed? A detail here and a detail there?

If you simply throw descriptive details before your readers as those details occur to you, the readers are likely to move through a confusing landscape. They will catch glimpses of what you want to describe, fragmentary and disjointed images, but they'll never form a whole impression of the thing itself. Much better, it seems to me, to reveal the essential details in a spatial order—that is, as they would appear to your readers if they stood before the thing and moved their eyes across it.

You could, for instance, describe the computer's keyboard by moving your reader from left to right, or top to bottom. Looking out with you from your uncle's porch, your readers might first encounter the nearby details, your aunt's horse grazing in a dry, dusty pasture below the porch; then more distant images, the green brush-choked hillside falling away into a canyon; and finally, far beyond the canyon, the Pacific ocean, grey and still in the afternoon. Or you might begin describing your grandmother's face only in general terms, but gradually focusing in on details that seem significant—her brittle nose and thin, fragile mouth, perhaps. In each case, your readers, because they moved in a particular direction through space with you, would be able to see not only the separate parts, but also the relationship among those parts that forged them into a whole.

I have only two tips here:

- Arrange the details so that your readers' eyes move in a direction that is appropriate for the particular thing you are describing. Moving rigidly from right to left across a computer's keyboard makes sense. Moving as rigidly across your grandmother's face will seem mechanical, lifeless, cold.

- In fact, beware of rigidity of any kind. It's easy to seem too mechanical with a spatial arrangement. Unless your main concern is precision— as, admittedly, it might be in techical writing—you will probably want to let your readers' eyes leap about a bit while still maintaining a general movement in some particular direction.

Edward Abbey, in the example I've chosen, looks out over a vista. Notice that as he turns, you turn, looking with him farther off into the distance with each new direction:

The view is open and perfect in all directions except to the west where the ground rises and the skyline is only a few hundred yards away. Looking toward the mountains I can see the dark gorge of the Colorado River five or six miles away, carved through the sandstone mesa, though nothing of the river itself down inside the gorge. Southward, on the far side of the river, lies the Moab valley between thousand-foot walls of rock, with the town of Moab somewhere on the valley floor, too small to be seen from here. Beyond the Moab valley is more canyon and table land stretching away to the Blue Mountains fifty miles south. On the north and northwest I see the Roan Cliffs and the Book Cliffs, the two-level face of the Uinta Plateau. Along the foot of those cliffs, maybe thirty miles off, invisible from where I stand, runs U.S. 6-50, a major east-west artery of commerce, traffic, and rubbish, and the main line of the Denver-Rio Grande Railroad. To the east, under the spreading sunrise, are more mesas, more canyons, league on league of red cliff and arid tablelands, extending through purple haze over the bulging curve of the planet to the ranges of Colorado—a sea of desert.

Edward Abbey

FROM SIDE TO SIDE

Like many college teachers, I often find myself asking my students to hold two things up next to each other for comparison's sake in a single piece of writing—two poems, two opinions, two remembered experiences. When I do this, I sometimes recall an anthropology professor who once assigned me to do a term paper contrasting Mayan and Aztec religious beliefs. By requiring me to write about both religions simultaneously, she was able to stretch the resources of my mind and find out what I knew about both cultures. More importantly, though, she could see what I knew of the intricate relationship between the two. I hated that assignment, but I learned more from doing it than I had thought possible.

Comparing and contrasting are more than just academic calisthenics, though. They are basic ways of thinking and making meaning. You can distinguish between an eagle and a parakeet now only because at some point in your infancy you learned a process for systematically sorting out similarities and differences—in this case, details of size, color, shape, behavior, and sound—and evaluating their significance. You still use this same process in your everyday thinking and, more often than you may be aware, in your everyday writing. Try to advance an argument about combatting terrorism and you will probably wind up comparing alternative solutions. Try to explain the advantages of one new computer system and you will likely have to contrast it with others.

Organizing this kind of writing, whether in a single paragraph or a whole paper, comes naturally. One danger, though, is that your readers might get lost as they try to follow you back and forth between the two things you want them to consider. My suggestions have mostly to do with keeping them on a zigzagging trail:

- In the early stages of the writing process, draw up a list of the particular *points of comparison* you will make between the two things you are discussing. Evaluating two computers—the Apple Macintosh and the IBM PC, for instance—you might want to address such points as cost, compatibility, memory, availibility of software, ease of use, and so on.

- Plan to use only those points of comparison that are genuinely helpful in making your main point. If you are trying to assert that one computer is more practical than the other, the amount of memory each holds is relevant. The color of their consoles probably is not.

- When it comes time to arrange the paper, you have two equally valid options. You might, on the one hand, discuss each half of the comparison fully in turn (first analyzing the Macintosh along all of your points of comparison, then turning around to do the same for the IBM PC); or you might, on the other hand, move back and forth between the two on a point-by-point basis (discussing first the memory of one computer and then that of the other).

- Deal with *each* point as it applies to *both* sides of the comparison. In other words, if you talk about the software available for one computer talk as well about what's around for the other. Don't feel, though, that you have to write discussions of equal length for both sides of a point. There simply may be more to say about IBM software than Macintosh software.

- Be ready to supply plenty of transitional phrases—sign posts such as "on the other hand," "similarly," "but," "alternatively,"—to blaze a clear path between the two main subjects.

In this next sample, Carol Panek focuses on a single, specific point of comparison to draw a contrast between the main characters of two short stories and to make an assertion about them:

I see a definite dissimilarity in the awareness of each character. Trexler constantly looks at his situation and evaluates the possibilities in minute detail; therefore, his decisions influence what will happen. His pattern is of quickly, deeply felt experiences. For example, in the doctor's office he *feels* the doctor's eyes on him, he *shoves* his chair back, he *presses* his advantages, he *identifies* himself with other people. All the verbs E. B. White uses to describe him are as strong as Chekhov's to describe Ryabovich are weak. Experiences in Ryabovich's life affront him unexpectedly: he is invited to tea (a social obligation), emotions take possession of him, he is unable to restrain his uneasiness, someone makes him happy, something has come into his life. Everything that happens is beyond his control. In particular, that Trexler "feels time passing," while for Ryabovich "the days flow by," illustrates the inequality of their awareness. The patterns continue through the stories, and reflect the degree of control each man gains over his life.

Carol Panek

FROM GROUP TO GROUP

Another option is to break your subject down into parts, assemble those parts into groups held together by some logical principle, and then lead your readers from one group to the next. This, in fact, is what my co-author and I have done in this book, breaking the general subject of what makes for good writing down into parts and then grouping those parts under four main headings: content, organization, style, and mechanics. Since anything that is made up of parts can be divided and regrouped, the strategy works for many topics, for anything from airlines to appetizers, from poems to politicians. And what makes it even more useful is that most subjects that can be categorized in one way can be recategorized in a variety of other ways to suit different purposes in different kinds of writing.

Since I've suggested it, let me take what little I know of the topic of airlines as an example. Writing informally to a friend about my own experiences, I might group the airlines I've travelled on simply, along lines such as these: "The Reliably Reliable," "The Generally Reliable," "The Erratically Reliable," and "The Irredeemably Unreliable." Writing a somewhat more formal kind of paper about the routes of major airlines, I might divide the same subject like this: "Local Carriers," "Regional Carriers," "Transcontinental Carriers," and "Overseas Carriers." Or in a still more formal kind of report, I might want to group the airlines according to any number of statistical categories. Miles flown annually, passengers carried per month, gross revenues—any of these, or many others, might provide the best system for dividing the topic in a given writing situation.

More tips:

- Search for the principle of divison that will best help you reveal your main idea; don't rest easy with the first that comes to mind. Dividing airlines by miles traveled per year might not do as much to reveal which ones offer the greatest safety to passengers as would dividing them by the number of accidents or near misses per year.

- Take care that when you slice up the pie you make all the cuts with the same knife. You'll notice that in my first airline example above all the groupings have to do with reliability. Reliability is the knife with which I have cut up the topic. If one of my categories had been, say, "The Best Restaurants in the Sky," it would have resulted from a concern other than reliability and thus violated the principle by which I set out to divide the subject. It would not have fit in with the rest.

- If you create a new grouping system, and label the groups with names that might be unfamiliar to your readers, try to illustrate and define each label with a few representative examples. My first method of grouping airlines, for instance, using labels such as "The Irredeemably Unreliable" calls for specific examples to illustrate those terms and make them meaningful.

- Once you've chosen your groupings, consider the order in which you would like to have your readers come across them. If one category helps to explain another, the helpful one should come before the other. If one is particularly convincing, you might want it to come last, where it will have the most impact.

The example is by Lewis Thomas. One of the reasons I like it is that he takes us quickly and quietly from one to the other of his four groupings without calling unneccessary attention to what he is doing. Wisely, he allows his content to outshine his organizational scheme:

> Not all social animals are social with the same degree of commitment. In some species, the members are so tied to each other and interdependent as to seem the loosely conjoined cells of a tissue. The social insects are like this; they move, and live all their lives, in a mass; a beehive is a spherical animal. In other species, less compulsively social, the members make their homes together, pool resources, travel in packs or schools, and share the food, but any single one can survive solitary, detached from the rest. Others are social only in the sense of being more or less congenial, meeting from time to time in committees, using social gatherings as *ad hoc* occasions for feeding and breeding. Some animals simply nod at each other in passing, never reaching even a first-name relationship.
>
> *Lewis Thomas*

FROM CAUSE TO EFFECT

Recall, if you can, the first words you spoke this morning. Something prompted you to say them—a longing, a comment, a dream, a slamming door—they had a cause, or causes. Consider, also, what happened when you spoke them. Someone, if only yourself, heard them, reacted to them, felt their effect, and was in some, probably small, way altered by them. Everything you do or see or touch or say has causes and effects. The world is an intricate machine of interrelated actions and reactions, and because of this all writers inevitably spend a great deal of time explaining and reconstructing cause and effect relationships for their readers.

Discussions of causes and effects are often confusing, simply because almost anything worth writing about has a myriad of complex causes and effects. The best general advice I can give to help you simplify your own discussions is, again, to design a straightforward organizational plan early in the writing process. To help with planning, the first two of my tips here will concern patterns that you might use to guide your readers over this tricky terrain.

- If you want to discuss the various causes or effects of a single phenomenon, consider sorting them out along the lines I suggested above in "From Group to Group." You might arrange the effects of your decision to quit smoking, for instance, under such headings as "physiological," "psychological," "familial," "economic," and "social."

- Other times, you will find that your best bet is to string together a chain of causes leading up to one final effect or a chain of effects stretching away from a single cause. The outbreak of World War One, for example, came as a result of a long and elaborate chain of events. I think all of the advice I offered for writing "From Step to Step" would apply in such situations.

- Whenever you assert that one thing is the cause of another, be particularly careful to make sure that you are correct. When one event follows another, our tendancy is often to assume that the first caused the second. But it ain't necessarily so. The lizard who had been sunning himself all spring on a rock near my front porch suddenly disappeared last week, about the same time that my cat lost her appetite and refused dinner one night. Assuming murder, I cursed the cat and pushed her off my lap whenever she tried to nest there. The day before yesterday, the lizard reappeared on the rock. The cat now rests comfortably again on the lap of a man who tries to apologize to cold, green eyes.

- Because cause and effect relationships are often so complex, be liberal in your use of connecting words and transitional phrases, especially where shifting back and forth between causes and effects. Markers such as "consequently," "as a result," "therefore," and "because" will help keep the path clear for your readers.

In the paragraph below, Kathleen Lynch explores the effects of her family's decision to stop watching television. For the most part, she simply lists effects here, but notice that one of the effects (an increase in leisure time for reading the newspaper) becomes a cause of another effect (an increased consideration of the paper's contents). She links together action and reaction, forging a chain that her readers can easily follow:

The most immediate and apparent difference was the sense that we had so much more *time*. I know that the twenty-four hour day lasts exactly twenty-four hours, no matter what one does with one's life. But I certainly *felt* that my daily allotment of time had expanded. I have always been a "reader," but now I found myself reading much more, and much more intently than before. I was also beginning to read material I usually "didn't have time for." I rediscovered books that had waited on our shelves for years, treasures we picked up at yardsales and flea markets (in hope of reading them on that proverbial rainy day). I also read the newspaper more thoroughly. Before, I had skimmed the front section while sipping my coffee and worked the crossword puzzle in the "Living" section with the second cup. That ritual hasn't changed—it's still "all I have time for" in the morning. But the space in the evening that was filled by local and national newscasts (and the hundred or so commercials peppered throughout them) is now "free" time again. That is when I read the rest of the paper: local news, California news, political commentary, "Science and Medicine," and even the "Garden" section on Thursdays. I like getting news information through the written word.

It allows for more consideration of and reflection on the reported events. On a TV newscast, one item is followed rapidly by another, or by a commercial, and there is little "air space" for contemplating any of it.

Kathleen Lynch

FROM OBSERVATIONS TO CONCLUSION

Unsupported opinions don't count for much in college writing, or any-where else. What do count are opinions accompanied by the hard evidence that has lead the writer to embrace them in the first place. Coming across assertions without evidence in student writing, college instructors typically grumble something about "con artists," make a few caustic comments in the margin, and start looking forward to the next paper.

So how does one arrange the evidence that supports an opinion? Actually, there are two basic strategies. The first I'll briefly explain here; the second I'll save for the last in this series of patterns.

In my own writing, I often lead up to a controversial point by first taking my readers through the observations I have made in order to arrive at the opinion; then, I deliver them to the idea itself. That way they can see exactly what I have based my conclusion on—whether it is collection of facts or a chain of reasoning—before I ask them to accept it themselves. Usually they are more willing to accept my idea when I finally get to it if they have already seen the evidence. The strategy requires a little advance planning and enough self-discipline to keep me from blurting out my main point too soon, but it works well enough to make the effort worthwhile.

Just a couple of tips here:

- Whether your evidence takes the form of separate, individual facts or a train of connected thoughts, try to build toward your most convincing support. You don't want the trail to lead your readers off into weaker and weaker evidence just before delivering them to your main assertion.

- You may need to use a lot of connectors again here—transitions such as "further," "additionally," "what's more," "next," and "finally"—to assure your reader that this accumulation of evidence is, in fact leading to some end. Otherwise it may simply seem a catalog of random facts.

In this example, Carl Sagan leads us toward his conclusion that chunks of asteroids are bound to land on earth from time to time. To convince us, he holds off on stating his claim until he has first filled us in on a few basic facts of astrophysics:

Many asteroids have orbits that are highly eliptical or stretched out, not at all like the almost perfectly circular orbits of Earth or Venus. Some asteroids have their far points from the Sun beyond the orbit of Saturn; some have their near points to the Sun close to the orbit of Mercury; some, like 1685 Toro, live out

their days between the orbits of Earth and Venus. Since there are so many asteroids on very elliptical orbits, collisions are inevitable over the lifetime of the
solar system. Most collisions will be of the overtaking variety, one asteroid nudg-
ing up to another, making a soft splintering crash. Since the asteroids are so
small, their gravity is low and the collision fragments will be splayed out into
space into slightly different orbits from those of the parent asteroids. It can be
calculated that such collisions will produce, on occasion, fragments that by accident intercept the Earth, fall through its atmosphere, survive the ablation of
entry, and land at the feet of a quite properly astonished itinerant tribesman.

Carl Sagan

FROM STATEMENT TO SUPPORT

The last pattern I'll discuss is simply the reverse of the previous one. Here
you make a general assertion first and then follow it with specifics—facts
or reasons or events or examples—that back it up. This is the pattern you've
probably had the most practice with.

The advantage of moving from a general statement to specific support is
that your readers enter the body of your material knowing what you are
getting at. Because they know your intentions, they can evaluate the evidence as they encounter it, weighing the truth of your main assertion against
the support you bring to it. If the writing works well, they accumulate
evidence as they move along and eventually emerge convinced of the idea
they encountered at the beginning.

Here are two last suggestions:

• The overall movement in this pattern is what's most important—the
  chance for the readers to gradually collect evidence. Don't feel com-
  pelled to start with a topic sentence and move in lockstep fashion to
  the first piece of evidence. You may well want, for instance, to introduce
  the main idea with a sentence or two or restate the main idea again at
  the end of the passage.

• As in the previous pattern, it may be wise to arrange your evidence so
  that your readers encounter increasingly convincing details as they
  progress. This is especially true if the main idea is one that they are
  likely to balk at.

The short, somewhat cryptic sentence that opens the paragraph below
urges us on because it seems to contradict itself, a paradox. We need support before we can make much of a sentence like this; we need some
explanation and we need proof. The support comes in the form of a single
example, concerning the ways of a certain man. The details of his behavior
are unfolded gradually, and it is only gradually that we come to understand
the first, general, idea through those particular details.

Eccentricity ritualizes behavior. It's a shortcut through unmanageable emotions
and strict social conventions. I knew a sheepherder named Fred who, at seventy-

eight, still had a handsome face, which he kept smooth by plastering it each day with bag balm and Vaseline. He was curious, well-read, and had a fact-keeping mind to go along with his penchant for hoarding. His reliquary of gunnysacks, fence wire, wood, canned food, unopened Christmas presents, and magazines matched his odd collages of meals: sardines with maple syrup; vegetable soup garnished with Fig Newtons. His wagon was so overloaded that he had to sleep sitting up because there was no room on the bed. Despite his love of up-to-date information, Fred died from gangrene when an old-timer's remedy of fresh sheep manure, applied as a poultice to a bad cut, failed to save him.

Gretel Ehrlich

A Path through the Thicket: Ducks and Blazes

The organizational patterns I've suggested here are only a sampling of the possibilities. To be honest, I had intended to discuss others—"From Question to Answer," "From False to True," "From Problem to Solution." But I think by now you get the idea: there are as many new patterns as new subjects, and the best writers are those who find ways to combine old strategies or forge fresh ones.

Finding a pattern for laying out the principal landmarks, though, is not the whole job in arranging the middle of an essay. The other important challenge is to make sure that the path from one point to the next, from landmark to landmark, is clear and unambiguous. Readers can get lost easily in even a well-laid-out forest of words, and to keep them on track you'll often need to provide sign posts.

In my Boy Scout days, we learned to leave piles of rocks, called "ducks" wherever the trail we were hiking was unclear, to point the way for others who might come later. When we were in woods, we left blazes on trees instead, chopping off a patch of bark to expose a bare, white spot, a signal that this was, indeed, the trail. That was scouting lore, and there is a writing lore that teaches similar skills. What follows concerns some of the ducks and blazes of good writing.

TRANSITIONAL TAGS

Earlier, I several times urged you to consider using short transitional phrases like "on the other hand," "similarly," and "furthermore" to help connect your ideas. In general, it's a good idea to provide an explicit transition wherever there seems to be a noticeable gap between two ideas; but you should also be aware that phrases like these are a rather conspicuous and self-conscious way to point out your direction. Too many obvious transitions will tend to clutter your sentences and may distract your readers from the ideas you want them to pay attention to. After all, if your content is well enough arranged in the first place, the connections among the parts should already be fairly obvious.

Assuming, though, that you've put your ideas in the clearest possible order and still find that you need a transition, perhaps the best thing to do is to keep the connecting device as inconspicuous as possible. With this in mind I have two suggestions:

- When you select a transitional phrase, look for wording that fits in with the surrounding language in terms of its formality and its tone. Try to find wording that does not call out, "I am a transition!"

- Take great care to use a word or phrase that expresses the *precise* relationship you intend between the two ideas. A carelessly chosen transition may call undue attention to itself or, worse, alter your meaning in unintended ways.

Let me try to illustrate both principles with a pair of simple sentences.

Brenda kissed Martin lightly on the cheek. Martin blushed.

Actually these sentences don't really need any kind of transition between them. The connection is obvious; we know that the first event caused the second. But suppose that for some reason you wanted to underscore the cause and effect relationship here. Probably the *least* fortunate thing you could do would be to pop a great, huge, heavy formal connector between the two sentences:

Brenda kissed Martin lightly on the cheek; consequently, Martin blushed.

That "consequently" sits there like a rock, a multisyllabic barrier looming between the two statements rather than knitting them together. Surrounded by more formal and elaborate language, the word might be a good choice, but here it is simply too pretentious for the context. It calls too much attention to itself.

What *would* work here, then? Any number of simpler, less obtrusive connectors might fit more naturally into the surrounding language, making the connection clear, but doing so more quietly. Each would mean something slightly different, though. All of the possibilities I've listed below fit in with the simplicity of the sentences, and any one of them would be better than "consequently" or "therefore" or "as a result." But as you can see, only the first two really insist on the cause and effect relationship, and some of the others alter the meaning, subtly swinging the sentences in different directions:

Brenda kissed Martin lightly on the cheek, *so* Martin blushed.
Martin blushed *because* Brenda kissed him lightly on the cheek.
Brenda kissed Martin lightly on the cheek, *but* Martin blushed.
While Martin blushed, Brenda kissed him lightly on the cheek.
Brenda kissed Martin lightly on the cheek, *and* Martin blushed.
Brenda kissed Martin lightly on the cheek; *then*, Martin blushed.
Although Martin blushed, Brenda kissed him lightly on the cheek.

PARALLELISM

A more subtle kind of trail marker is parallelism, a common stylistic device you'll come across again in the next chapter. For now, let me just explain that parallelism involves arranging any equally important pieces of information in equal grammatical structures. Before you decide that "equal grammatical structures" sounds too technical for you and skip this section, read through the following paragraph by Geoffrey Moorhouse, writing about Calcutta. Look for patterns of similar phrasing:

> It is the traffic that makes it all unique. A traffic in trams grinding round corners, a traffic in approximately London busses whose radiators seem ready to burst, in gypsy-green lorries with "Ta-ta and By-by" and other slogans painted on the back, in taxis swerving all over the road with much blowing of horns, in rickshaws springing unexpectedly out of sidestreets, in bullock carts swaying ponderously along to the impediment of everyone, in sacred Brahmani cows and bulls nonchalantly strolling down the middle of the tram-tracks munching breakfast as they go. A traffic, too, in people who are hanging on to all forms of public transport, who are squatting cross-legged upon the counters of their shops, who are darting in and out of the roadways between the vehicles, who are staggering under enormous loads, who are walking briskly with briefcases, who are lying like dead things on the pavements, who are drenching themselves with muddy water in the gutters, who are arguing, laughing, gesticulating, defecating, and who are sometimes just standing still as though wondering what to do. There never were so many people in a city at seven o'clock in the morning.
>
> *Geoffrey Moorhouse*

You'll seldom see a more conspicuous example of parallel structures than all those "in" phrases and "who" clauses. Read the passage again and I'm sure you'll observe two things. One is that you don't have to know the names of the grammatical structures to recognize and use parallel series like these—though it helps. You can simply let your ear be your guide to using parallelism. The other thing you'll observe is how the parallel series here work to help carry you along through the passage: Each time you come to "in" or "who" here, you know you're still on the track, still following one train of thought; each says, "Keep going. This is more elaboration of the idea I began with."

REPETITION

Ordinarily, experienced writers try to avoid repeating the same words or phrases too often for fear of boring their readers or seeming unimaginative. Ironically, though, skilled writers do sometimes find themselves deliberately repeating phrasing in order to help guide their readers through their ideas. Repetition is either good or bad, never neutral. If it is subtle enough to remain inconspicuous, it's perhaps the best means of linking ideas. If it clutters the landscape with reduncancy, it is vile stuff.

The trick is to make sure that you only repeat *key* words and phrases, and that you drop in the repetition just often enough to assure continuity without creating monotony. Consider this passage by Theodore White. I've underscored the repetitions to make them more conspicuous:

> Fundamentally, the present prosperity of America was engineered by <u>the scholarly discipline of economics</u>, whose most eloquent spokesmen <u>succeeded</u> in persuading both the Kennedy and Johnson administrations to use their <u>wisdom</u>. Their <u>wisdom</u>, brilliantly as it has <u>succeeded</u> in the general economy, is, however, a parochial one, a study of <u>greeds and desires</u> divorced from humanity. Deep within the <u>scholarly discipline of economics</u> is a concept of man's world as <u>a universe of random particles</u>. The <u>desires and greeds</u> that move these <u>random particles</u> are unpredictable for any single individual. But when measured all together as <u>a universe of random particles</u>, they become, as a mass, thoroughly predictable and generally controllable. Economists can graph, chart and predict the influence of almost any government intervention, curb, tax law or stimulus on this <u>universe of random particles</u>. In the getting, making and distribution of material things the <u>wisdom</u> of economics has had stunning <u>success</u>.
>
> *Theodore White*

The amount of repetition here is extraordinary; you won't often want to depend so heavily on it as White does. But the example points out, I think, how gracefully one can link thought to thought without resorting to explicit transitions. Because his content is abstract and potentially confusing, White knows the burden is on him to keep his readers from getting lost, and his way of doing that is to repeat his most important ideas frequently. Sometimes the repetition is immediate—as with "wisdom" at the end of the first sentence and the beginning of the second; other times it is delayed—as with "succeed" in the first sentence and "success" in the last. Either way, the effect is to make travelling from the beginning of the paragraph to the end easier than it could otherwise have been.

PARAGRAPHING

When readers begin a new paragraph, they believe they are entering a new bit of territory in the larger landscape of the essay. They take the break between two paragraphs as a signal, an indication that here is a change of direction, that new concerns must lie just ahead. As a result, the paragraph indentation is any writer's most useful trail-marker, indispensible whenever it's time to leave one subject behind and enter another.

Unfortunately, too many student writers arrive at college believing that rigid rules govern the construction of "correct" paragraphs. I won't deny that there are well-put-together paragraphs and shoddy paragraphs, but I don't think that rules are the way to approach the subject. In fact, I'm going to approach it by tearing down a few of the most common rules:

1. *A paragraph must have a topic sentence.* Not so. In fact most of the paragraphs in this book don't have any such thing. While a clear para-

graph does usually deal with a single idea or subject, stating the idea or identifying the subject in a special sentence is often unnecessary. Save topic sentences for situations where you really need to bring your readers directly face to face with what you're getting at.

2. *A paragraph is never a single sentence.* A variation of this rule is that paragraphs must never be short in any way. But short paragraphs do have great value in at least two situations: when you want to emphasize a thought, and when you want to construct a transition between two fully developed ideas. In either case, do be aware that by being short the paragraph will call a great deal of attention to whatever it says.

3. *A paragraph must never be more that eight sentences.* A paragraph should be just as long as it needs to be to fully develop the idea you set off as its territory. It's true that readers may get lost in longer paragraphs that mash too many ideas together, and if you find yourself writing several longer paragraphs in succession you should consider whether you couldn't break them down into a few shorter ones. But if it takes most of a page to develop a single idea, keep going. Just be sure that the ideas themselves are well laid out and that you've provided other trail-markers to help the readers navigate.

Let me reiterate: Good paragraphing has more to do with common sense than with rules. When you feel that you are moving from one main subject to another, start a paragraph. When you don't, don't.

BETWEEN PARAGRAPHS

I've already suggested that each new paragraph is a new piece of territory, concerned with a new subject. That means that there is always a gap of sorts between two paragraphs, a leap to be made from one subject to the next. If in the new paragraph you are about to go off in a radically different direction, the readers ought to know what direction as early as possible. If you are going to elaborate on a topic discussed earlier, again, they ought to know what you are referring back to so they can hold your earlier ideas in mind. What I'm suggesting is that you pay particular attention to the need for transitions as you move from paragraph to paragraph.

The techniques for bridging the gap between paragraphs are the same as for any other situation where you might need a transition: explicit transitional tags, parallelism, and deliberate repetition. You might, for instance, begin each in a series of paragraphs dealing with related subjects with phrases that are conspicuously parallel in structure. Despite grammar school injunctions to the contrary, you might start a new paragraph with a simple conjunction like "But" or And," or with a more formal transition like "However" or "Furthermore." Or you might end one paragraph and begin the next with the same phrase, repeating it to establish continuity.

Let me use Theodore White as an example again. What you see here is, first, the ending of what is actually quite a long paragraph; second the whole of the next paragraph, itself a short transitional bridge; and third, the opening sentence of the third paragraph, again a much longer one in the original text:

¶..."Remember the Maine." " Remember the Lusitania." "Remember Pearl Harbor." All American wars had begun with a date, a cause, a reason.

¶In Vietnam there was no phrase to which one could pin emotion; Americans were required to fight a war without hate. The real culprit—ignorance—could never be made clear.

¶For the ignorance, every branch of American government and every institution of American learning could share the blame....

Notice how the middle paragraph manages to tie the two longer ones together, not only by what it says, but by its wording. With the word "phrase," it points back to a long series of phrases with which the earlier paragraph ends; and with the word "ignorance," it anticipates the subject of the next paragraph, pointing the readers in the direction of the new topic.

This kind of deliberate linking together of paragraphs is relatively easy to accomplish if you know in advance what you are going to write, but even if you don't, you can usually come back and revise last and first sentences so that each last sentence leads somehow into the next first. Offhand, I can't think of a better way to assure that your readers remain on track all the way through an essay.

The Conclusion: On Not Dropping People over Cliffs

You may have had the experience of reading something that ended too suddenly, that ended without an ending. It's strangely discomforting— something like running up against a door in the dark or taking a step ahead and finding only air underfoot. And it's definitely not a good way to end an essay; you don't want your trail to emerge suddenly from the woods only to deposit unwary readers on the edge of a precipice that falls away into the white nothingness of blank paper.

Your conclusion is worth paying attention to for a more positive reason as well: It is your last and best opportunity to win your readers over to your way of looking at the topic. You want your readers to leave the essay feeling as you do, sharing your point of view, believing in you. So the question is: How to seize the moment?

Earlier I said there can be no formula for writing an introduction. This is even more true of writing a conclusion. Convincing conclusions are not tacked on; they arise out of what has come before in the essay. Remember that the readers will have moved through your landscape, explored your ideas, encountered your selection of facts before arriving at the conclusion.

If you can look back to the landscape the readers have travelled through, put yourself in their place, consider what questions or doubts they might still have, and address them as fellow travellers who have shared an experience with you, you can write an effective conclusion.

Again I'm going to suggest a few specific techniques I have used or seen my students use. Many of these will be familiar to you from my discussion of introductions earlier. That's because, like introductions, conclusions are largely concerned with grabbing and holding people's attentions. Once again, don't hesitate to adapt any of these strategies to fit the circumstances of your own essays.

GLANCE BACK OVER THE TERRAIN YOU'VE COVERED

If one way to begin an essay is to take your readers up on high ground and let them take a look at where they're going, then one way to conclude might be to take them up again and let them look back over the country they've covered. By recapitulating the main points of interest you've touched on, by reviewing the content, you can refresh their memories and at the same time help them see the significance of all these separate points taken together. A review is particularly useful at the end of an unusually long or abstract discussion, or when many smaller facts have been interspersed with more important ones and you want to sort out the most important.

GENERALIZE WISELY

Whether or not you review main points, the conclusion is often your best chance to offer a general statement about your topic, a wider observation supported by the particular evidence you've offered along the way. Having already encountered the specific facts, readers will now be more likely to accept your more general ideas about the topic. Often, in fact, this is the place to state your thesis, especially if it is controversial and depends on your readers' understanding of many smaller facts or arguments. Be sure your evidence is really conclusive, though, before formulating too sweeping a statement at the end.

LOOK AHEAD, BEYOND THE ESSAY

Another reason for going up on a high place in the conclusion might be to look still farther ahead, into the unknown, future world beyond the essay. Based on what you have told and shown your readers, you might, for instance, make a prediction of future consequences, call upon your readers to take some initiative, envision (and share your vision) of a time when things might be different, offer suggestions for solving a problem you've exposed.

ASK MORE PROVOCATIVE QUESTIONS

If you want your readers to leave the essay thinking about an issue you've raised, you'll find that question-asking works here as well as in introductions. Even a single, well-framed question can prick the consciences, pull the heartstrings, or entice the imaginations of readers. Perhaps the best questions are the unanswerable ones, but anything that will cause your readers to stop, scratch their heads, and ponder your topic will serve .

PIN ANOTHER PHRASE ON IT

Quotations, too, are as good for ending as for beginning. I would just remind you of my earlier caution against popping in irrelevant quotes. To work here, a quoted phrase must seem a natural extension of the idea you have been developing all through the essay. If it sums up your point or gives emotional impact to what you have been getting at, few things are more effective.

RECALL ANOTHER INCIDENT

In an introduction, an anecdote is useful mostly for capturing attention, but in a conclusion it can do something more useful still: It can transform an abstract idea into a concrete experience, translating a dry, distant concept like apartheid or sex discrimination into immediate, personal terms—terms your readers can identify with and take to heart.

POP A SURPRISE

Sometimes it's both fun and rewarding to bring your readers around the last bend in the trail only to leave them suddenly face to face with something totally unexpected. An unforeseen ending, after all, is usually more memorable than a predictable one. The surprise might be one last startling piece of evidence to support an argument you've been building, or an unexpected end to the story you've been telling, or even your thesis itself if you've been keeping your readers wondering precisely where you would come down on an issue.

COME FULL CIRCLE

An ending device I often use in all kinds of writing is to bring my readers back to where they started from. It also seems to be one of my students' favorite strategies, perhaps because it is so natural and unobtrusive. To try it, simply look carefully back at your introduction. You may find a key phrase, or idea, or image there, something you can revive in your conclusion. If you started a story, you might want to finish it; if you asked a question, you might want to answer it; if you created an image, you might want to recreate it.

SAMPLE CONCLUSIONS

Since conclusions depend so much on what has come before, it's hard to find examples that can stand easily by themselves. But below are a few that illustrate some of the strategies I've mentioned. Notice that again the writers have often blended techniques to achieve their ends.

The first is the ending of Pamela Liebenberg's essay from the last chapter. If you read it there, you'll remember that she begins with the image of swans swimming on a pond but only as a way of moving into a discussion of the tensions in her marriage. Here's how she concludes that discussion:

> Perhaps the first year of marriage is so difficult because the two people involved, having accomplished their first goal together, are at loose ends and need to set new goals for just the two of them, to keep the relationship stimulated and moving forward. Without personal goals to share, there is nothing to do but pick at each other and try to stave off a sense of inadequacy by proving how imperfect the other is. New tasks provide the opportunity for a couple to work together and share their thoughts, feelings, and ideas. My husband and I haven't found our new goal yet, but there will be plenty of goals to share—a home, children, even retirement eventually—goals enough to get the love more on the surface and less hidden. Over time, I hope, through the accomplishment of many goals, we'll begin to really know each other and swim together as effortlessly as the swans.
>
> *Pamela Liebenberg*

Notice how she mixes methods here. First she draws a generalization out of her personal experiences: Having provided the details earlier, she can now more reasonably conclude that—like hers—many new marriages suffer if the couples don't have goals to share and strive for. Then she looks ahead, beyond the essay, to the future she envisions for herself and her husband. And finally, with her last sentence, she brings us back to the image of the swans with which she opened the essay.

The next example, by Carl Sagan, is composed almost entirely of questions. Notice how one question leads to the next:

> How would we explain the global arms race to a dispassionate extraterrestrial observer? How would we justify the most recent destabilizing developments of killer-satellites, particle beam weapons, lasers, neutron bombs, cruise missiles, and the proposed conversion of areas the size of modest countries to the enterprise of hiding each intercontinental ballistic missile among hundreds of decoys? Would we argue that ten thousand targeted nuclear warheads are likely to enhance the prospects for our survival? What account would we give of our stew-

ardship of the planet earth? We have heard the rationales offered by the super-powers. We know who speaks for the nations. But who speaks for the human species? Who speaks for Earth?

Carl Sagan

The questions are big ones, difficult ones. Because they are, we stop and wonder and think about the issue. But what really makes the conclusion so powerful, I think, is not just the stopping power of the questions them-selves, but the implied answers to the last two. Read the paragraph again, answer those last two questions for yourself, and I think you will have the thesis of Sagan's whole essay even though you may never have read it.

Finally, let me conclude, too, by recalling an introduction I showed you earlier in this chapter. It was the first introduction I discussed, and it was by Donald Murray:

When students complete a first draft, they consider the job of writing done—and their teachers too often agree. When professional writers complete a first draft, they usually feel that they are at the start of the writing process. When a draft is completed, the job of writing can begin.

Now here's Murray's conclusion, some thirty paragraphs later:

A piece of writing is never finished. It is delivered to a deadline, torn out of the typewriter on demand, sent off with a sense of accomplishment and shame and pride and frustration. If only there were a couple more days, time for just another run at it, perhaps then . . .

Donald Murray

Two things to consider here: To begin with, note how the first line of the conclusion comes back to the first line of the introduction, echoing the opener even as it contradicts it. Readers remember where they started and will recognize the place if you return them to it. Second, note the ellipsis, those three dots at the end. They are Murray's, not mine. They signify something more to come, yet there is no more here. Murray has simply run out of time. Ending his own essay with an ellipsis, he drives home his point more forcefully than he could by stating and restating, "there's never enough time to finish a piece of writing." Good conclusions are imaginative ones; they always arise out of an intense desire to finally get the point across before time runs out. As now it has for me . . .

Examples of Student Writing

Each of the following essays takes a different form. Like snowflakes, finger-prints, and human faces, no two essays follow quite the same pattern. What all good essays do have in common, though, is this: The landscape they unfold to their readers is not only rich with significance but pleasant and easy to travel through. As you explore these essays, note how their authors have drawn on a common pool of techniques, attempting to make the going easier for you.

Ghosts
David Yohn

When a description moves us, it is because the writer has selected just the right details and found just the right order in which to arrange them. Often that means a spatial order, moving the readers from here to there, from detail to detail, in order to unfold the scene. But a spatial arrangement can be deadly dull if it is too mechanical for the topic or if the writer calls too much attention to the order of the details and not enough to the message revealed by those details.

In the following essay, David Yohn shares his childhood memories, giving us a tour of the house he grew up in. He leads us from room to room, but he does so without focusing undue attention on this technique. Our attention is, instead, on his rich images, images that recreate the place in our minds. As you read the essay, notice how Yohn uses his paragraphing and subtle transitional phrases to tell us when it's time to move on to another room. Notice also how at the end he comes back to his beginning.

The neighborhood has changed, but the house is the same. It stands as it has for over a hundred years, and probably will for a hundred more. In three-storied splendor, white columns reaching up through the first two floors—a very mansionish set of twelve columns, topped by wide white gables decorated with plaster leaves and filigrees—it stands on top of one of the highest hills in this town of hills, Hannibal, Missouri. The house was built in the 1860's by a man who made millions shipping barges full of cement up the Mississippi River. From the third-floor windows, he could see several miles down the wide, tree-lined river, giving him plenty of time to ride down to meet his shipment. The road then must have been dirt, or gravel, subject to becoming dangerously slippery with the frequent summer storms, not the modern concrete of the Grace Street I'm standing on now.

The house, sitting ten feet above the street on limestone, surrounded by a black, wrought-iron fence, rises like a skyscraper, much higher than any other house nearby, smiling its white-toothed smile, a warm, lonely face. It looks at me exactly as it did the first time I saw it. I was eight years old then and full of stories about haunted houses. This house looked like a haunted fortress. Its bricks—polished, smooth, shining as teeth do after they've been brushed—appeared indestructible. The drain holes punctuating the wall surrounding the first-floor porch were placements for cannons; marksmen crouched behind each column ready to repel the invading hordes. The front door, solid oak, had a big knocker like in Frankenstein movies. To either side stood tall, stained-glass windows, the kind usually found in churches. Once I thought I saw movement behind one of the windows. I ran all the way home, thinking about the rich and powerful ogre who must live in that house.

Two years later, when my family moved in, the house changed from a thing of fear into a place of wonder, a place for exploration and discovery. My father bought the house in 1967; it had been sitting empty since 1925 when the builder, childless and with no family of any sort, died. When we moved in, it was probably the first time the house had heard the screaming of small children playing tag, or seen a ten-year-old boy, me, the oldest of my mother's six children, prowl through its hidden places.

My favorite of these hidden places was the vast third floor. It consisted of a gigantic central room forty by sixty feet, with ten foot high ceilings. The room echoed. On either side wall were four windows which, when opened, allowed cool breezes to blow across the room. I called this the ballroom, although it was never finished and bare bulbs hanging from wires down the center of the room were the only lights in it. It was never used for dancing until, in the ninth grade, I threw a party there. A narrow hall extended from the back of the room to an equally narrow stairwell leading down. On either side of the hall were a series of small rooms. Too big to be closets, too small to be very useful, these rooms held the treasures of the house. The former owner had used them as storerooms; they had not been cleaned out since.

I found many things there—a set of flags of the world from before WW I; an antique, cherry wood chest my mother refinished and used for her sewing things, lots of odds and ends I thought were junk but which Dad seemed to think were valuable; and something I thought was valuable, an old fruitcake can with $1,000 in Confederate money in it. I was rich. I dreamed of buying cars and motorcycles, boats and baseball teams. My mother, without understanding the reason for my interest, watched me pore for hours over the Sears catalogue. Several days later, when I tried to buy a soda at the corner store, I found out my money was worthless. Heartbroken, I showed it to my mother who, bubbling about how pretty the can was, dumped the money into the trash and put the tin in her china cabinet. I went to my room and cried.

The china cabinet was built into the wall in the dining room. It was massive, as was everything in the house, made of walnut and oak, handmade in the old style, without nails. Its leaded-glass windows reflected the open, walnut beams in the ceiling. On either side of the cabinet were swinging doors leading into the kitchen, presumably for the servants. Whenever we ate in the dining room, Mom, wearing her best apron, would make a grand entrance through the doors, carrying dinner. Dad, sitting at the head of our big oak table, smiling wryly, would say something like, "That'll be all, thank you," to which Mom would curtsy, say, "Very well, sir," and run out through the swinging door. We would all laugh, throwing our heads back like young birds. On these occasions, Dad lit the brass gas lamps lining the walls, their light flickering off our plastic plates and stainless forks, making the room warm and welcoming. Mom, when she came back into the room, would light a candle off one of the lamps and place it in the center of the table. We all bowed our heads to give thanks for the chicken or pork chops, whether we liked eating them or not.

Off the dining room, through heavy sliding doors, was the family room, with the house's only fireplace. The other twenty-one rooms were heated by radiators. Dad had installed a gas-burning furnace in place of the coal-burning original, which meant the radiators now got extremely hot. In winter, spitting on one would create a loud sizzle and a flash of steam. My brothers and I would have contests to see who could get the loudest sizzle. Mother thought the radiators were leaking. Above the radiator in the family room, dominating one wall, was a large stained-glass window full of red roses, green leaves, and naked pink cupids. It would have created a light show on the floor if the sun could have shown through it. But, being on the north side of the house, it was always dark. Mom used to talk about moving it, but we all knew she would never try.

Attached to the family room was the music room. This room, with its long walls and high ceilings, housed the family's record player and the old, upright piano. One wall was curved—from the outside this part of the house looked like a turret on a castle—giving the room strange acoustics. Our piano, out of tune and faded, sounded like an expensive grand piano in this room. I loved to sit and make up songs for myself. The music room also served as the kids' playroom. It always seemed to be strewn with Legos, army men, doll clothes, and blocks. Great wars were waged and kingdoms conquered in this room. Miss America was crowned here a hundred times. And, after we watched it actually happen on TV, men again walked on the moon in our music room.

At Christmas time, the music room became a wonderland. Dad would find the biggest, fattest tree in town and fill the rounded wall with it. The star at the top would brush the fifteen-foot ceiling; the branches would stretch twenty feet across the room. We decorated the room with cut-out snowflakes and construction-paper reindeer. Mom played Perry Como Christmas carols on the record player. The house rang with the laughter of children. Arguments about who'd get the biggest presents erupted into snowball fights in the yard. Sugar cookies mysteriously disappeared from racks where they were cooling. The tang of cinnamon filled the kitchen; the smell of candies oozed down the hall. Anticipation built as December seemed to grow longer until, finally, it was Christmas Eve. With Dad reading " Twas the Night Before Christmas," and with eggnog and cookies for everyone, we sat around the roaring fireplace, excitement pounding in our hearts. Then, when the eggnog was gone, we went to our beds, trying to get to sleep as quickly as possible so morning would come, trying to stay awake to hear the sleigh bells.

At five AM I woke up. I hurried to each room to wake the others. All six of us knocked on Mom and Dad's door until they answered. Dad made us wait at the top of the stairs while he went down to see if Santa had come. Whispering excitedly among ourselves, we tried to stretch over the bannister to see the tree. Finally, after what seemed like years, Dad called for us to come down. "Walk down those stairs!" Mom said as we ran down them. Turning the corner, we stopped. The tree was ablaze with lights, candy canes hanging where none had the night before. The floor was covered with packages, bright red and green, some big, some small, some so huge they were unbelievable, bearing names, our names, "Etta," "Chris," "Anne," and the rest. We entered this church slowly, eyes wide, mouths gaping. Dad, standing to one side with a freshly brewed cup of coffee in his hand, smiled broadly, saying, "Go ahead! Dig in!" The next few hours were spent in gleeful tearing, excited sharing, surprised joy.

I start up the stairs toward the house. Twelve years ago Dad sold it to a lady who said she wanted to make it into a museum—Mark Twain had slept here or something. I'd like to see what it has become. I reach for the handle of the wrought-iron gate but can not turn it. A cold breeze stirs my hair. I look up at the smiling face of the house. Nothing's changed, I think, and turn away. On the way back to my car, I cannot resist one more glance at the house. I know now it is haunted. I know now a ghost is a memory that cannot fade away.

Work and the Silicon Valley Individual
Wayne George

Experienced essayists seldom follow a single organizational pattern from start to finish. Rather, they blend the different patterns, shifting into new ones whenever doing so helps to guide the readers more effectively through a new topic.

Here Wayne George combines a number of organizational schemes to unfold his main idea. Beginning with a personal anecdote (and returning to it to conclude), he moves us at various times from causes to effects, from step to step, side to side, and from observations to a conclusion. As you read the essay, you might find it helpful to note in the margins where you think he is employing each strategy.

The other day, while grocery shopping, I noticed a mother and a young boy in the breakfast cereals section of the supermarket. They were playing an age-old game. The mother was trying to get her son to pick out a box of cereal. As she would point out a brand, the boy, who might have been three, would cross his arms, shake his head sternly, and emphatically say, "NO!" The mother, who had apparently been getting this response quite often lately, suddenly grew irate and, throwing her hands in the air, exclaimed, "Fine! You don't need to have anything for breakfast. You can starve for all I care!" Turning her back, she started pushing her cart down the aisle. The child, caught between shock and indignation, stood still for a few seconds and, when his mother did not turn back around, let out a little whimper and ran after her.

They call it the "terrible twos." It is when we first learn the concept behind the word "no." In the next few years it often becomes our favorite word. We use it just for the sake of using it, even when we don't really mean it. Early on, we realize that by saying no we are not just expressing an idea or mood or opinion, but we are establishing our identities. By diligently telling adults "NO," we attempt to take control of our lives into our own hands. We let adults know that we are individuals, not clones made over in their images. But we need not worry about our individuality. The concept is a cherished one in America, and all through our lives the idea of individuality will be reinforced.

After all, we are a country that was made by individuals. In elementary school we are introduced to the great individuals who shaped our nation. Men like Washington, Jefferson, and Franklin designed this to be a country that protects the interests of the individual. Little else will be said about the collective actions of the Continental Congress, except that these men were part of it. We will be required to do reports on the great individuals of science, like Newton, Edison, and Einstein. Very seldom will we look at the accomplishments of teams of scientists.

At home, after we are done working on our reports, we will sit down in front of the television set. On the news we'll see countless "human interest" stories about interesting or eccentric individuals. In itself, watching television will promote our individuality by promoting isolation. We don't have to interact with the television or the other people in the room, as we would if we were playing family games.

When we do feel like playing games, we are more likely to grab a roll of quarters and head on down to the video arcade. Here, we will pit ourselves against the machines or against other players, aiming for the overall high score or trying to improve our own best scores. Few machines promote player cooperation.

No, if we want to learn player cooperation, we'll have to go out for Little League or play sports in high school. If we work hard and get to be better than everybody else, we might even get a scholarship to a college or university. In college, we may or may not be noted for being a team player, but the players who show outstanding individual effort will surely be noticed. Though the championship may be won by a team, it is the player who is voted Most Valuable who gets the attention, the glamour, the contract. And it's the same in the pros. Few fans may know the names of the individual linemen on a football team, but they all know the name of the quarterback the linemen are protecting, and the running back they are blocking for; and it's the running back, not the lineman, who will get the six figure salary and the interview after the game.

Of course, not all of us will go out for sports. If we want to go to the college of our choice, we'll have to compete for the good grades. If we really want a university to notice us, we'll become a class officer or club president. These are the people that college boards say show, "outstanding individual achievement." Once in college, we'll still be competing for grades. If we have a better G.P.A. than the other student, we will have a better chance of landing that job we want.

Out in the working world, we will be expected to make it on our own. We will try to climb the pyramid, whether social, financial, political, or occupational. If we make it to the the top with no help, we will be revered by our society as "self-made" men or women. If we drop out somewhere along the way, and especially if we leave an executive position to become glassblowers or wood carvers, then we may well be showcased on "Evening Magazine," and all the children sitting at home watching television will again learn the rewards of being an interesting and unique individual.

For over a quarter of a century, I have lived in this society and been influenced by its high regard for the individual. I'm sure you have, and I'm sure our children will too. During most of that time, I've thought that being an individual was a good thing, and that promoting individuality was one of the things that made this country great. Now, after working for nearly half a decade in Silicon Valley, I'm not so sure that individuality is the boon to our society that I had always believed it to be.

I started on the production line of a company in Sunnyvale that man-ufactures rotating disk memory drives for computers. I was amazed at how much back-stabbing and political infighting went on even at this level in the company. Instead of working together to put out a good product, the operators spend most of their time trying to attain a better paying position by climbing over the backs of their fellow workers. Many are too busy pointing fingers and laying blame for problems on the workers around them—struggling to insure that their neighbors don't get the promotion they might get—to think about cooperating and building a good product.

When I began working with engineers and executives, I was disappointed to find that this lack of cooperation extended to the higher levels of the company as well. These people spend most of their time in meetings, yet they accomplish little in those meetings. Of course, they have been raised and trained to work and think as individuals. It is little wonder that they have difficulty when trying to work together as a team. The result, though, is that it can takes weeks to handle problems that might have been taken care of in a couple of days, and this can create undue pressure in any production situation.

Of course, in Silicon Valley there is always an easy way to deal with undue pressure. If it's too hot, one can always just get out of the kitchen. There is very little company loyalty in the Valley. At any time, any engineer or executive can get a job with another company, and get ten percent more pay. Many are barely with a company long enough to learn anything about the product they are making. Just about the time they learn exactly what the production problems are, they are off to a start-up company, and some new engineer must then spend the next six months learning the production process all over again. Only a few will stay long enough to actually correct any problems.

New companies are starting up all the time in the electronics industry. Many of them are started by an individual with a new idea for a product or a new production technique. I worked for such a company. The man whose name the company bears left a large corporation to start his own outfit which, under his supervision, quickly became a leader in the marketplace. Unfortunately, after a few years, he left to form another new company. Once again this company became the market leader while his original company began to falter and lose more business, and more money, each year. When companies are founded on the ability of an individual, they generally decline when that individual departs.

In America there is almost a cult belief in the importance of individuality. As a result, industries like the electronics industry in Silicon Valley suffer. A favorite pastime of people in the Valley is to compare the industry with its counterpart in Japan. The Japanese industry always comes out on top. In Japan, no individual, not even the top executive, is more important than the company. Japanese workers often stay with the same company until they retire. All employees work together to build the best product possible. Some companies in Silicon Valley are now starting to take note of this difference and are working to promote more employee cooperation. But they will have a hard time overcoming the individuality that has been engrained in their workers for a lifetime.

I wonder what the little boy I saw in the supermarket will be doing in twenty or thirty years. Perhaps, by chance, he will be working as an engineer or executive in Silicon Valley. If he is, I hope somewhere along the line he will have learned that sometimes it's important to subdue a strong sense of individuality in order to work well within a group.

The Bird Courage
Carol Panek

For the most part, comparison and contrast writing is easy to organize: You can simply discuss one topic first, touching on certain points of comparison, and then turn around to discuss the second topic, touching on the same points in the same order; or you can zig-zag between the two topics, moving from side to side. But beware of easy formulas when making comparisons: The organizational pattern itself can loom too large in the paper and obscure your ideas. Remember that the purpose of drawing a comparison is always to make a point, to reveal an idea, not simply to make a pretty pattern.

In this next essay, Carol Panek leads us on a trail that takes us back and forth between her observation of two characters from stories by E.B. White and Anton Chekhov. As you follow her discussion, I think you'll find that she keeps her organization in the background, directing your attention instead to her ideas about the two characters. Notice also that while Panek focuses on particular points which apply to both characters, she spends more time on one character, Riabovich, than on the other. Although a comparison or contrast should treat both subjects fully, no rule says that time and space must be allocated to both in precisely equal parcels.

The main difference between Officer Riabovich in "The Kiss" and Mr. Trexler in "The Second Tree from the Corner" is the degree of control each exerts over his life. Riabovich, moving through life as slowly as Chekhov moves us through the story, is almost completely unaware of what he is and what affects his life. Throughout "The Kiss," everything happens *to* Riabovich; nothing really happens by his own will. Exterior forces control his life, and he seems to accept this control with befuddled resignation. In contrast, Mr. Trexler feels and notices every detail around him; in fact, he is so over-aware that he contracts neurotic symptoms of diseases he hasn't got and transfers himself into other people's identities. Trexler makes things happen in his life, and he knows it. He lives knowing he is responsible for himself, with no one to fall back on. The deep contrast between the two personalities explains the far different self-image each character assumes. Riabovich's inability to look ahead and think for himself results in a poor self-image, while Trexler attains a better opinion of himself through his self-awareness and ability to understand his own imperfect life.

Trexler habitually looks at his situation and evaluates the possibilities in minute detail; therefore, his decisions influence what will happen. His pattern is of quickly, deeply felt experiences. For example, in the doctor's office *he feels* the doctor's eyes on him, *he shoves* his chair back, *he presses* his advantage. The verbs E. B. White uses to describe his actions are strong, transitive, active ones. On the other hand, experiences in Riabovich's life affront him unexpectedly: he is invited to tea (a social obligation), emotions take possession of him, he is unable to restrain his uneasiness, someone makes him happy, something has come into his life. Everything seems to happen *to* him; everything seems beyond his control. The patterns continue through the stories and reflect the extent to which each man is aware of the forces that control his life.

Riabovich never takes responsibility for his life and instead accepts the external control, unaware of the effect of doing so on his self-image. The most prominent external influence on Riabovich is the military itself. Military life is strict and regimented. The officers are expected to follow orders and adhere to the rules of both brigade and society. Riabovich can hide behind the obligations and orders to avoid making his own decisions and observations. Out in society, he adopts the idea that he has an "undistinguished" appearance, and after confiding the story of the wonderful kiss to his comrades, he half-heartedly agrees when Merzlyakov calls his ladylove a "lunatic," even though he thinks very differently.

When Riabovich returns to the place where he has been kissed, his pattern of letting things happen to him begins to lead him toward realizing the truth. He has sincerely expected a messenger to come and invite the officers to tea, where he will somehow meet the lady who kissed him. Later the reality of the situation occurs to him as he watches the river water running, just like his life, "he knew not where or why." Even at the end, though, he denies that he is responsible for his life; he blames fate for his aimlessness: ". . . he recalled how Fate in the shape of an unknown woman once caressed him . . . and his life seemed unnaturally thin and colorless and wretched."

Trexler feels the opposite effect. He realizes the problems and inadequacies of his life and works to understand them. For instance, he realizes that he is always "getting himself into" impossible situations, not that the situations are always finding him. He thinks deeply and clearly about the circumstances of his life. Paranoia affects his reasoning somewhat and often leads him to neurotic feelings of illness, yet he knows this too. He notices a routine developing in the psychiatrist's sessions and, in contrast to Riabovich, takes action to improve the situation by transferring himself into the doctor's seat. The change of identity, whether good or bad, leads to Trexler's realization of truth. The weakness he perceives in the doctor gives him strength.

Trexler gains confidence in himself after thinking through this sickness carefully and realizing that he really has a deep, personal, indescribable need. He realizes that this imperfection is acceptable, that healthy people have problems with personal satisfaction, and that his life isn't so different after all. When his fear has subsided, he even recognizes that courage lurks in the shadows of his fear: "the flashy tail feathers of the bird courage" that Trexler glimpses are "in the jungle of his fear," meaning that the bird is still within his grasp, not out of reach. These late understandings help Trexler's self-image because he feels proud and content in his self-discovery.

Unfortunately, Riabovich never betters his self-image because he resigns himself to fate and an ordinary, unsought future. He has attained, temporarily, a new view of himself as a father, husband, and lover, but he can't maintain that image in the larger world where he depends so much on other people for his opinions of himself.

Small Change
Kathleen Lynch

Repetition, parallelism, transitional tags, and paragraph divisions are all trail markers; all of then help point out new directions to readers. But they are also the raw material out of which bridges are made. Between any two para-

graphs, there is always something of a gap. The first paragraph finishes with a topic, the second takes up a new topic, and in between there is nothing but empty space. Readers coming to such a gap must pause, measure the chasm, and leap across to the new topic. If the gap is too wide or the readers come across it without warning, they may well fall into it. Knowing this, writers often build bridges between their paragraphs, letting the last sentence of one paragraph and the first sentence of the next serve as anchors for the span.

In this essay, Kathleen Lynch leads us from a single cause to its many effects. As we follow her trail, we start with a quote, end with a question, and move easily from paragraph to paragraph in between. To see how she carries us across the gaps between paragraphs, look especially at each of her opening sentences. In almost every case, you'll see that she has thrown a verbal bridge back across to the previous paragraph to make sure we can follow her into the new idea.

"You must change your life," says the final line of Rilke's poem about looking at the statue of David. It is a disturbing and stirring declarative sentence. It unsettles us because it challenges the status quo at a personal level. But it also inspires. Implied in the statement is the belief that we *can* change our lives. With all the small burdens and occasional rewards of daily life, we often come to feel that we are unable to affect our destinies. Life seems like something that happens *to* us, and we are borne along by its flow. But Rilke believes we can and must make choices and changes to alter the course of our existence. So do I.

The change does not have to be monumental. Even a seemingly insignificant adjustment can lead to a wealth of new experience. Just such a change took place in my house last January. The day after the Super Bowl, my husband and I lugged our weighty, solid-state color TV from the family room to the garage. And as the kitchen door closed on the television's blind eye waiting in the darkness, our lives changed.

Banishing the television may not seem very drastic. Like most people, we would certainly not have defined ourselves as TV addicts; in fact, I believe that we watched a lot less than most of our peers. It was not until we removed it from our home, though, that we realized the subtle and insidious power it possessed over us. The ways in which our life changed without TV are the measure of that power.

The most immediate and apparent difference was the sense that we had so much more *time*. I know that the twenty-four hour day lasts exactly twenty-four hours, no matter what one does with one's life. But I certainly *felt* that my daily allotment of time had expanded. I have always been a "reader," but now I found myself reading much more, and much more intently than before. I was also beginning to read material I usually "didn't have time for." I rediscovered books that had waited on our shelves for years, treasures we picked up at yardsales and flea markets (in hope of reading them on that proverbial rainy day). I also read the newspaper more thoroughly. Before, I had skimmed the front section while sipping my coffee and worked the crossword puzzle in the "Living" section with the second cup. That ritual hasn't changed—it's still "all I have time for" in the morning. But the space in the evening that was filled by local and national newscasts (and the hundred or so commercials peppered throughout them) is now "free" time again. That is when I read the rest of the paper: local news, California news, political commentary, "Science and Medicine," and even the "Garden" section on Thursdays. I like getting news information through the written word. It allows for more consideration of and reflection on the reported events. On a TV newscast, one item is followed rapidly by another, or by a commercial, and there is little "air space" for contemplating any of it.

Contemplation of another sort became more likely with the absence of our TV. I found myself going into reveries more often, considering the details of my life, the woof and warp of relationships. I began spinning plans for my future and developing new ways to address old problems. All of my thinking became more complex and more creative. These expanded ruminations have catalyzed ideas for my artwork and given me a calmer and more thoughtful manner of dealing with some of the difficulties my relatives are going through.

There are changes in our immediate family dynamics too. My husband and I have always been close and connected, but now we seem to spend a different kind of time together. Our conversations expand to fill their natural space; they are not abbreviated or interrupted by a "good show" or the eleven o'clock news. We listen to more music together, and we make love more often. There is more time to take heed of one another and to be fully attentive.

There is also more time for solitude. Sitting alone watching TV, one does not experience solitude. The images on the screen—the gorgeous colors, the beautiful people, the stirring jingles, and the flashing action—surround the viewer. They may amuse, entertain, and even inform, but they do not allow one to move into that state of attentive quietness and aloneness which deepens awareness.

My own awareness of the power television holds over us has increased greatly. Its images are often masterful, stunning, and inviting. And they have the power to manipulate us at a very deep level. I remember a particular hamburger commercial that was beautifully filmed and edited. It was so effective that when the singers asked, "Aren't you hungry. . . ?" my body said, "Yes, I am!" even though I had eaten a full meal less than an hour before. That's manipulation. It is also power. Somehow that box of metal and glass and electronic gadgets had managed to emit a force that got inside my body and mind and lied to me.

Sometimes the manipulation is more subtle. I was particularly drawn to nature shows and enjoyed seeing the great and diverse natural marvels they featured. I sat in my suburban house in front of a gadget and observed countless hours of "nature." Now I wonder about the nature I missed. How many times did I miss seeing a thumbnail slice of moon hovering over my yard? How many cricket songs and cicada clacks and mating cat howls were drowned out by the fabricated sounds of the TV? And why had I never watched the adagio dance of the mollusks as they laid their silvered trails across our walk at night? Partly, at least, because I was watching TV— getting Nature-in-a-Box, without the smells, the ambiance and nuances; without the fullness of natural sounds. Even "good" programming has the power to seduce us away from a full attentiveness to the world around us.

Attentiveness. Perhaps that's the key. I pay better attention to my life, to the people in it, and to myself, now that the TV is gone. I no longer surrender any of my attention to the great physical and psychological presence of television. As a result of this small change, my life has become fuller, richer, and more peaceful. I feel more relaxed and alert—more as if I'm using my time rather than spending it. On a recent trip to Sacramento, I told a sister that I had put the TV in the garage. She stared in amazement and gasped, "How *could* you!?" Now that I see the qualitative difference it has made in my life, my response would be, "How could I not?"

EXERCISES

1. Consider the quotations listed below. Choose one that you would like to write an essay about, treating the quotation as an idea to be proven or disproven by the essay. Then write an introductory paragraph for such an essay, using any combination or any one of the techniques discussed in this chapter under "The Introduction: Providing a Trailhead" to orient your readers to the topic and entice them to read on.

> A man of words and not of deeds
> Is like a garden full of weeds.
>
> *Mother Goose*

> Those who make peaceful revolution impossible will make violent revolution inevitable.
>
> *John F. Kennedy*

> Nice guys finish last.
>
> *Leo Durocher*

> Political language . . . is designed to make lies sound truthful and murder respectable, and to give an appearance of solidity to pure wind.
>
> *George Orwell*

> A hungry man is not a free man.
>
> *Adlai Stevenson*

The price we have to pay for money is paid in liberty.

Robert Louis Stevenson

2. Write down each of the following topics. Under each, list the methods of arrangement that you believe would be most appropriate for organizing a written discussion of that topic or some more specific version of it. Be prepared to discuss your selections in class, explaining how and why you might use each method to organize a given topic. When possible, propose new methods of arrangement not included among those listed here.

Topics:

A. Drug use among teenangers

B. Your school's health center

C. The case for or against the military draft

D. Self-esteem

E. The Statue of Liberty

Methods of Arrangement:

From First to Last
From Step to Step
From Here to There
From Side to Side
From Group to Group
From Cause to Effect
From Observations to Conclusion
From Statement to Support

3. Choose three of the topics from exercise number two. Write a fully developed paragraph on each of those three topics, or on some more specific version of each, using the method of arrangement you feel works best for the topic. After each paragraph write both the topic and the method of arrangement you have chosen.

4. Write the middle section of the essay you began in exercise one, adding it to the introduction you created there. Develop the middle by using the pattern or patterns of arrangement you find most appropriate for your topic. Feel free to revise the introduction in light of what you say in the body of the essay.

5. Write the conclusion of the essay you worked on in exercises one and three above. Use one or more of the techniques discussed in this chapter under "The Conclusion: On Not Dropping People over Cliffs" to end the essay effectively.

6. Read the following passage, carefully noting and underlining the transitional devices Carl Sagan uses to keep his readers on track. Then write a brief analysis of those transitional techniques and how they work to tie the ideas in the paragraph together.

> The global balance of terror, pioneered by the United States and the Soviet Union, holds hostage the citizens of the Earth. Each side draws limits on the permissible behavior of the other. The potential enemy is assured that if the limit is transgressed, nuclear war will follow. However, the definition of the limit changes from time to time. Each side must be quite confident that the other understands the new limits. Each side is tempted to increase its military advantage, but not in so striking a way as seriously to alarm the other. Each side continually explores the limits of the other's tolerance, as in the flights of nuclear bombers of the Arctic wastes; the Cuban missile crisis; the testing of anti-satellite weapons; the Vietnam and Afghanistan wars—a few entries from a long and dolorous list. The global balance of terror is a very delicate balance. It depends on things not going wrong, on mistakes not being made, on the reptilian passions not being seriously aroused. . . .
>
> *Carl Sagan*

Chapter Five

Style

The Mole had been working very hard all the morning, spring cleaning his little home. First with brooms, then with dusters; then on ladders and steps and chairs, with a brush and a pail of whitewash; till he had dust in his throat and eyes, and splashes of whitewash all over his black fur, and an aching back and weary arms. Spring was moving in the air above and in the earth below and around him, penetrating even his dark and lowly little house with its spirit of divine discontent and longing. It was small wonder, then, that he suddenly flung down his brush on the floor, said 'Bother!' and 'O blow!' and also 'Hang spring-cleaning!' and bolted out of the house without even waiting to put on his coat. Something up above was calling him imperiously, and he made for the steep little tunnel which answered in his case to the gravelled carriage-drive owned by animals whose residences are nearer to the sun and air. So he scraped and scratched and scrabbled and scrooged, and then he scrooged again and scrabbled and scratched and scraped, working busily with his little paws and muttering to himself, 'Up we go! Up we go!'; till at last, pop! his snout came out into the sunlight, and he found himself rolling in the warm grass of a great meadow.

So begins a book you might have read—Kenneth Grahame's *The Wind in the Willows*. It was read to me in the fourth grade by Mrs. Miller, a small, kindly woman in a pearl grey dress and bifocals who stood in front of her desk, leaning casually against it, as she read. Although I remember absolutely nothing else of the fourth grade, or of her either, for that matter, I can still see and hear her as plainly as if she were reading right now. Two years later I checked the book out of the library and read it myself, and then again two years later, surreptitiously because I was well aware that I was "too old" for it. I've read it three or four times since then, once on a camping trip in the Santa Cruz mountains, most recently on rainy Northern California afternoons in an officemate's comfortable chair beside the shelf of books he uses in his children's literature class.

When I checked the book out as an eighth grader and sneaked it home in my binder, I worried a little bit about still being interested in a "kid's" book about a mole and a rat and a frog. Now I know that it is not the content that brings me back again and again to a child's story long past my childhood, although the book does have some interesting things to say about friendship. No, it is the style that makes *The Wind in the Willows* precious to me—the rhythm of the sentences, the clarity of the images, the kind and wise voice of the narrator. If you have a favorite book you read again and again, or if you have a favorite author and every trip to the bookstore brings with it a tingle of excitement because there just might be a book by that author which you haven't read yet, I'd hazard a bet that it is the author's style that draws you to the writing. Here is an example of a style that gained its creator a large and loyal following:

> I drove down to Hollywood Boulevard and put my car in the parking space beside the building and rode up to my floor. I opened the door of the little reception room which I always left unlocked, in case I had a client and the client wanted to wait.
>
> Miss Anne Riordan looked up from a magazine and smiled at me.
>
> She was wearing a tobacco brown suit with a high-necked white sweater inside it. Her hair by daylight was pure auburn and on it she wore a hat with a crown the size of a whiskey glass and a brim you could have wrapped the week's laundry in. She wore it at an angle of approximately forty-five degrees, so that the edge of the brim just missed her shoulder. In spite of that it looked smart. Perhaps because of that.
>
> She was about twenty-eight years old. She had a rather narrow forehead of more height than is considered elegant. Her nose was small and inquisitive, her upper lip a shade too long and her mouth more than a shade too wide. Her eyes were gray-blue with flecks of gold in them. She had a nice smile. It was a nice face, a face you get to like. Pretty, but not so pretty that you would have to wear brass knuckles every time you took it out.

Even if you're not a fan of the genre, you'll recognize the voice of the hard-boiled detective. This is Raymond Chandler's Phillip Marlowe, a private eye in the smoggy metropolis of Los Angeles. I can point to specific things that create the voice of the character—the first person narration, the short, matter-of-fact sentences and sentence fragments, the detailed description that characterizes the ever-observant private "eye" and in this case the incorrigible girl watcher as well, the humorously exaggerated similes that bring in images of the seamy underside of life such as whiskey glasses, dirty laundry, and brass knuckles, the use of "you" to imply that the reader shares this shabby/glamorous life with the narrator, and yes, an unhealthy dollop of sexism and macho in that final remark about taking the face rather than the person out. This is a style that has transcended its origin and become part of the popular culture; other writers imitate it and detective programs on television often use voice-over narration that recreates this tough, cynical, ironic voice that Chandler created. Consider how different is the voice in a scholarly discussion of the character Marlowe:

In everything that can be called art there is a quality of redemption. It may be pure tragedy, if it is high tragedy, and it may be pity and irony, and it may be the raucous laughter of the strong man. But down these mean streets a man must go who is not himself mean, who is neither tarnished nor afraid. The detective in this kind of story must be such a man. He is the hero; he is everything. He must be a complete man and a common man and yet an unusual man. He must be, to use a rather weathered phrase, a man of honor—by instinct, by inevitability, without thought of it, and certainly without saying it. He must be the best man in his world and a good enough man for any world. I do not care much about his private life; he is neither a eunuch nor a satyr; I think he might seduce a duchess and I am quite sure he would not spoil a virgin; if he is a man of honor in one thing, he is that in all things.

The sentences here are longer, more inclined to be interrupted by mod-ification and qualification. The word choice is conspicuously more ab-stract—where we had concrete images in the first passage, we have ideas in the second, abstractions like "redemption," "tragedy," "honor," and "inevitability." While the voice in the first is worldly and cynical, this one is decidedly idealistic, even romantic. But who is this scholarly idealist, talking about Chandler's detective? Does it surprise you to find that this is Chandler too, in his essay "The Simple Art of Murder"? For of course Chan-dler is not Phillip Marlowe, and the style is not the writer; rather, it is the writer's creation, arising in part from what the writer is and believes, but also in part from the occasion, the topic, and the nature of the audience. Only very seldom does a writer's style become so consistent and so rep-resentative of the writer's own views that style and writer are virtually in-separable. Ernest Hemingway is a case in point:

Ahead the road came out of the forest and went along the shoulder of the ridge of hills. The hills ahead were not wooded, and there were great fields of yellow gorse. Way off we saw the steep bluffs, dark with trees and jutting with gray stone, that marked the course of the Irati River.

"We have to follow this road along the ridge, cross these hills, go through the woods on the far hills, and come down to the Irati valley," I pointed out to Bill.

"That's a hell of a hike."

"It's too far to go and fish and come back the same day, comfortably."

"Comfortably. That's a nice word. We'll have to go like hell to get there and back and have any fishing at all."

It was a long walk and the country was very fine, but we were tired when we came down the steep road that led out of the wooded hills into the valley of the Rio de la Fabrica.

The road came out from the shadow of the woods into the hot sun. Ahead was a river-valley. Beyond the river was a steep hill. There was a field of buckwheat on the hill. We saw a white house under some trees on the hillside. It was very hot and we stopped under some trees beside a dam that crossed the river.

Bill put the pack against one of the trees and we jointed up the rods, put on the reels, tied on the leaders, and got ready to fish.

"You're sure this thing has trout in it?" Bill asked.

"It's full of them."

Hemingway saw the world as a harsh place where people have trials to face and burdens to bear. Those trials must be faced and those burdens borne with dignity and stoicism, according to Hemingway, and that is best done by confronting things one at a time as they come, not pondering or lamenting too much the nature of life, and by taking solace in the simple pleasures life offers (like trout fishing and hiking). His style, one of the most recognizable among modern American writers, portrays his philosophy—simple sentences; rambling coordination that creates a simple, straightforward movement through time; prepositional phrases that depict a matter-of-fact movement through the landscape of the story; "it" and "there" sentence openers; homey details; simple adjectives, especially general ones such as "nice;" and curt, unembellished dialogue. All help to portray people who move through life one day at a time, enduring, enjoying the small pleasures, and not complaining. Knowing now a little about Hemingway's style, you should be able to identify the writer of the next passage:

Hank went into the bathroom to brush his teeth.

"The hell with it," he said. "She shouldn't have done it."

It was a good bathroom. It was small and the green enamel was peeling off the walls. But the hell with that, as Napoleon said when they told him Josephine waited without. The bathroom had a wide window through which Hank looked at the pines and larches. They dripped with a faint rain. They looked smooth and comfortable.

"The hell with it," Hank said. "She shouldn't have done it."

He opened the cabinet over the washbasin and took out his toothpaste. He looked at his teeth in the mirror. They were large yellow teeth, but sound. Hank could still bite his way for a while.

Hank unscrewed the top of the toothpaste tube, thinking of the day when he had unscrewed the lid of the coffee jar, down on the Pukayuk River, when he was trout fishing. There had been larches there too. It was a damn good river, and the trout had been damn good trout. They liked being hooked. Everything had been good except the coffee, which had been lousy. He had made it Watson's way, boiling it for two hours and a half in his knapsack. It had tasted like hell. It had tasted like the socks of the Forgotten Man.

"She shouldn't have done it," Hank said out loud. Then he was silent.

Hemingway, right? Wrong. It's Raymond Chandler again, this time trying with some success to spoof Hemingway, whom he admired.

My point in all of this is twofold. First, style is no accident, no natural talent that great writers have and you and I can never hope to attain; rather, it is a controlled thing, the result of choices made among words, sentence structures, and imagery. Second, style is not fixed, as if it were the writer's personality and therefore unchangeable; rather, the choices that result in style are guided by external factors as well as internal ones—the nature of the topic, the demands of the occasion, and the needs of the audience. In the rest of the chapter, I'll try to show the nuts and bolts of style and give you an idea of how to manipulate them to accomplish different purposes.

Diction: In the Beginning Was the Word

Word choice is more important than people generally are aware. If you compare language to math, for instance, you'll find that most people are much more inclined to think that precision is more important in math than in language. Admittedly, approximate math is sometimes permissible, and when someone asks you what you paid for your new car, you'll probably round $7,942.37 off to $8,000.00. On the other hand, you certainly wouldn't round off when you were paying for the car. In a situation where money is changing hands, precision counts, and approximation is bound to hurt someone.

There are consequences, too, of approximate use of words, costs that are paid in efficiency of communication. In spoken language, there are ways to avoid the costs: facial expressions, body language, gestures that lend some of the precision that inaccurate word choice lacks. Because there are ways to supplement the words themselves when we speak, people often speak carelessly, throwing in the occasional "you know?" or "you get my drift." And sometimes this careless habit carries over into writing, where the audience can't see expressions, hear tone of voice, or interpret gestures. In writing especially, word choice must be precise rather than approximate.

If you have ever used a thesaurus, you know that any given concept can be portrayed with several, often many, different words. What you may not know is that there is really no such thing as a synonym—that no two words are exactly alike in the effect they have on the reader. The thesaurus may list *trash, garbage, refuse, debris*, and *litter* all under the same entry, but there are subtle differences among them. *Trash* and *garbage* are more unpleasant sounding than the others. *Litter* sounds more trivial, less important. *Debris* suggests the aftermath of disaster. Whoever would suggest that these so-called synonyms can be plucked out of the thesaurus at random is an approximate user of words, a rounder off of meaning. There are several factors to consider when making fine distinctions among available words.

LEVELS OF USAGE

As there are different degrees of formality in clothing, there are different degrees of formality in word choice. Just as you wouldn't wear your ragged T-shirt to a company retirement banquet, there are words that you might use on the job, or over an after-work beer, or during the company softball game that you wouldn't use in a testimonial speech for the retiree or a written report to a manager on the job. Words can range from the offensively vulgar to the pretentiously over formal, with several different levels in between. The following sentences all say approximately the same thing, but each uses words at a different level of formality. The first version is the way it was written in one of the essays that appear in this text:

The writer's version: Charlene tried to make an unbearable situation last, somehow rationalizing that a bad marriage was better than letting family history repeat itself.

Pretentiously formal: Charlene attempted to render untenable circumstances more permanent, by some means rationalizing that a malignant nuptial tie was preferable to allowing ancestoral occurances to recur.

Formal: Charlene attempted to perpetuate an undesirable situation, somehow rationalizing that an unsuccessful marriage was preferable to allowing family history to repeat itself.

Ordinary: Charlene stayed in a bad situation, somehow convincing herself that a bad marriage was better than all the divorces in her family.

Slang: Char hung in there, conning herself that a bum rap was better than the route the old lady and old man had taken.

The writer's sentence is a mixture of the formal and the ordinary, a sound choice for the writing situation, which was an essay for an out-of-class assignment. I think you can see that of the variations I've presented here, hers is by far the best. *Roget's College Thesaurus* was very useful in helping me mangle it.

ABSTRACT VS. CONCRETE

Abstract words stand for ideas. Concrete words stand for objects, events, and people. Concrete words describe the phenomena people find ready made in the world around them, while abstract words describe the constructs of the human mind, the inventions of the intellect that didn't exist until people conceived of them. Honor, truth, beauty, and love are abstractions; tapioca pudding and lamp posts and .38 revolvers and feather pillows are concretions.

Both of these classes of words have their place in writing, but to exercise the options they provide effectively, you need to understand the relationship between them. Abstract words are fine words to use, even necessary words if your content is to be sophisticated and significant. Inventions of the intellect such as truth and beauty are excellent topics to explore, and much of the good writing throughout history has been in exploration of the abstract. But abstract words alone create a hazard: not all readers will interpret any given abstract word the same way. What is beauty to one reader might not be to another. By using abstract diction, you leave your writing open to interpretation, and therefore exercise less control over what you communicate.

Concrete words, on the other hand, put specific images in the readers' minds. The more concrete the word, the more specific the image. If you write abstractly of "the beauty of San Francisco," some readers will assume you mean the architecture, some the setting, some the cable cars, and so on. If you write concretely of "well-kept Victorian houses roosting on hills overlooking the sparkling bay," everyone gets the same message. Consider the following examples:

Abstraction: The beauty of nature (This is an abstraction that students, especially urban students, are often tempted to write about.)

Concrete manifestations: silence
clear blue lake water
bold Stellar jays, filching scraps from the
camp site
twilight thickening under the towering
redwoods

It would seem, then, that the concrete is generally more desirable than the abstract, but to avoid abstraction would be to limit your available options, so the best thing to do is to use both the concrete and the abstract where each is most appropriate. Abstract words are best for establishing topics, for telling the readers *what you are going to write about*. Concrete words are appropriate for illustrating the abstractions, for *showing your topic to the readers*. Here are some examples from the essays in this text of students using concrete diction to illustrate abstract ideas:

Abstractions: Infidelity, misplaced loyalty

Concrete manifestation:

One night we were unfortunate enough to find him, getting into his car, waving at a pretty girl as she started hers. He followed her out to Central Expressway, his white van in sharp contrast to the evening's darkness, traveling in an unhome-bound direction. He didn't see us until a half mile on Central, and his van jerked as he tried to accelerate and shift at the same time. But, like a woman possessed, Char not only overtook him but cut him off, forced him to come to a stop, jumped out of the car and ran back to confront him. She didn't divorce him then as she didn't divorce him when she contracted venereal disease months after their wedding, nor when he consumed the profit and part of the investment of his drug deals.

Wendy Ichimaru Hanabusa

Abstract statement:

The picture I hung in my kitchen is enigmatic.

Concrete explanation:

Without captions, one could imagine several possible interpretations of the picture. It could be a tired traveler resting in the shade as he journeys through the countryside. Or it could be one of the lost souls of Downtown San Jose, still sleeping off a drunk while more enterprising citizens set up tents in the background for the annual crafts fair.

Kathleen Lynch

GENERAL VS. SPECIFIC

General words refer to whole classes of objects; specific words refer to individual members of those classes. *Furniture* is a general word, denoting as it does a variety of different objects ranging from tables to sofas to cabinets. *Desk* and *piano stool* are specific words, denoting objects that belong to the general group indicated by *furniture*. As do abstract and concrete words, both the general and the specific have their place in effective word choice. The key to using each effectively lies in being aware of the difference between these two kinds of words and in knowing when each is appropriate.

First note that there are degrees of generality and specificity. Figure 5-1 illustrates different levels between the extremes of general and specific.

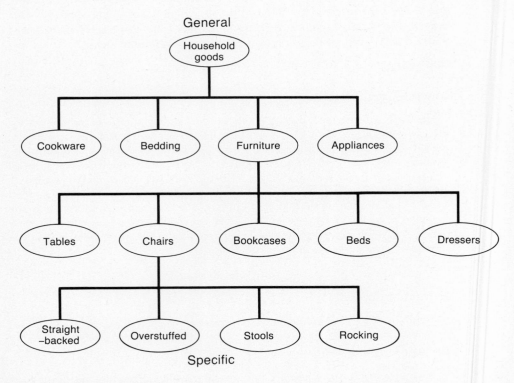

Figure 5-1. Levels of Generality.

What rung of this ladder of generality you climb to in choosing a word depends entirely upon on the thought you want to get across. Like abstract words, general words are appropriate for announcing topics, for making broad statements, for telling your readers what you intend to illustrate. Specific words are appropriate for illustrating your generalizations, for providing your readers with *detail* and *imagery*, for being sure that the readers fully understand. Thus these two types of diction work well together as a team, the general terms alerting the reader for the specifics that will follow or summing the specifics up, the specific terms far outnumbering the general and making them understandable. Here are some examples from an essay by Leif Lindseth that appears at the end of this chapter:

General term:

It is a place that collects *trash*.

Specific terms to illustrate:

From the Interstate come the usual beer cans, paper wrappers, cigarette butts, pieces of tires, broken trim, and the larger objects that have blown out of trucks, such as boxes and mattresses.

General term:

Everywhere, the old pieces of wood have been dabbed with *color*.

Specific terms to illustrate:

There is a man whose legs have been painted with blue and red stripes, wearing a yellow bucket for a hat, signaling to the planes that fly over with red flags in his hands. Another man with a four foot red and white striped nose has a yellow peace sign painted on his chest.

This carefully considered mixture of general and specific terms makes the writing easy to follow and easy to understand. Writing that stays at too high a level of generality, presenting a majority of general terms with few specific terms to illustrate them, is vague and hard to read.

JARGON vs. PLAIN TALK

Jargon refers to the special language invented by any group to meet its own particular needs. Professional groups such as doctors and plumbers are most inclined to need and invent jargon, with hobby groups such as sky divers and downhill skiers running a close second. When a doctor tells the head nurse that he has a Code Blue in the ICU, you or I might not know what he is talking about, but the nurse does, and because he and the doctor share a specialized language, they are better able to do their jobs efficiently. When a sky diver says that she blasted out at eleven thousand, went O/C, dropped into a tight frog to get stable, did a quick style series, pulled, and sat down in the peas, it might sound to the uninitiated as if she is speaking a foreign language, but the curious terms are necessary to describe phenomena and techniques that don't exist outside the world of free fall and colored silk.

Jargon exists because there is a need for it, but it can be and often is misused. Its main purpose is to expedite communication among members of a specialized group. It can also be used to convey the texture of an interesting activity, as the sky diving jargon above does. But as a writer you have to keep one thing in mind: Your readers might not understand. This depends, of course, on the audience. Members of the group that uses the jargon understand it completely, and when you are writing *within* such a group, you can use jargon frequently without thinking very much about it. But if your readers aren't members of the group, you must be aware that the jargon may be unfamiliar to them. In this case, either avoid the jargon, replacing jargon terms with their plain talk equivalents, define the jargon as you go along, or use it in such a context that the readers can't fail to deduce its meaning. Our sky diver might have addressed an audience unfamiliar with the sport thus:

> I left the plane at an altitude of eleven thousand feet, went out of control for a moment, went into a tight frog position to get stable, did some somersaults and turns to practice my style, opened my 'chute, and landed in the pea gravel around the target.

Now you know that a tight frog is a position, and if you think about it, you can probably picture it. You know what a sky diver means when she says "style," and you know that the target is surrounded by pea gravel. The sentence hasn't lost the texture of the sport, but it is easier to understand.

And now one final caution about jargon: It can be used for some unadmirable ends. Pretentious people use it to sound as if they know more than they do. Unknowledgeable people use it to conceal their lack of knowledge. Selfish people who would prefer not to share their in-group knowledge use it to exclude outsiders, much the way that children at play will invent secret codes and passwords to keep other children out of the clubhouse. If you'll just remember that writing is a process of communicating and sharing, not an act of self-conscious posturing or deceit, you can be aware of the drawbacks of jargon and use it appropriately.

CONNOTATIONS AND ASSOCIATIONS

I mention connotations and associations last because I think they are most important. Earlier in this chapter I compared language to math symbols to point out that we use it too approximately sometimes. In one way, the comparison was a bad one, for math, complex as it is, is a one-dimensional language. Its one dimension is literal, or denotative. Any given math symbol means what it means, and that's that. Not so with words. Words have dimensions beyond the literal, and it is in those dimensions that their real power often lies.

A word's *denotation* is its literal, dictionary meaning. "Cash" literally means money, specifically money ready to hand, such as bills and coins, as opposed to checks or money orders. But when you use the word, you call up reactions that go beyond the literal meaning.

Connotation refers to the readers' emotional responses to the word. Words can have favorable or unfavorable connotations; they can provoke positive or negative responses. "Cash" has a favorable connotation for most people, since money, especially money ready to hand, is usually a pleasant thing to have.

Association refers to the ideas, objects, and experiences a reader might automatically relate a word to. "Cash" is rich in associations: it suggests buying power, immediate gratification, the absence of debt, wheeling and dealing, loot and robberies—any number of things that other terms for money, like "funds" for instance, would not. Other associations arise from other ways the word is used: As a verb it means to turn a check into cash; in slang, "cash in" means to make a lot of money; in gambling, it means to quit; figuratively, it can even mean to die.

All of this gives words substantial power beyond their literal meaning, and the writer who is aware of this power can use it to guide the readers' responses and enrich their experience of reading. This excerpt from Wendy Hanabusa's essay at the end of this chapter shows how she has selected words carefully for their pleasant connotations and associations:

> Indeed, Angel Island is a beautiful sight, a peaceful playground surrounded by blue, nestled between the Peninsula and the East Bay. Serenity abounds as two young boys send delicate threads into the unsuspecting blue-green shallows; couples amble down manicured paths, drinking in the sun and making the breeze laugh with their passing. A quaint building, lush green carpet at its feet, plays host to feasting families at the white wooden tables before it. Smiling rangers greet the new arrivals, their island charge clean and composed. But it is the blackened road that we choose to follow...

"Serenity," "delicate," "lush," "amble," "laugh"—all strike pleasant chords in the readers' emotions. Only "blackened" at the end has any negative connotation or unfavorable association. And here is the scene to which that blackened road leads—an abandoned detention area where Chinese immigrants were imprisoned upon their arrival in this country:

> The yellowing wood forms barren rooms, save the displays that unlock their story, a tale of promise and lost hope, of broken men and pressing dreams. Corroding poles, in stark formation, gaze mindlessly at the walls; their arms, now mercifully gone, once held hundreds of men in their close confines. The mute, musky tomb once bulged with life, its barred windows offering glimpses of the sea. And from behind the bars' cruel grin, the Chinese saw the water they had just crossed to escape China's desperation and to enter a brave, new world.

At the end of the blackened road the reader finds words like "barren," "lost," "broken," "tomb," "barred," and "cruel." The mood changes; the feelings change; the writer is recreating her own experience and controlling the experience of reading by controlling connotations and associations.

Sentence Structure: Let Me Count the Ways

Word choice is an important factor in style, but it's not all there is to it—not by a long shot. The stylistic wealth of the English language lies not so much in its word horde as in the formula that has evolved for putting words together. Look at the following words:

and	dispassion	it	or	the
before	eye	its	passion	we
camera	for	on	put	without
closes	glass	opens	scene	

Of course, even as I've displayed them here in an alphabetical list, these words are not without power to create images, suggest concepts, even affect your emotions in subtle ways. *Camera* creates a concrete image. *And* signals the concept of combining. *Passion* and *opens* provoke favorable responses while *dispassion* and *closes* provoke negative ones. But the individual effects of the words aside, as a group, they don't tell you much. What does *passion* have to do with *camera*? *And* connects two somethings, but which two? Arranged as I've put them here, the words are really a mess. But let's apply that formula I mentioned, and see what happens.

> For the camera, without passion or dispassion, opens and closes its glass eye on the scene we put before it.

> *Kathleen Lynch*

The name of the formula is "sentence," and sentences turn images, concepts, and connotations of individual words into ideas. The sentence above is an idea from an essay that appears at the end of this chapter.

Sentences are another primary tool of style—perhaps the the most important of all. How you shape your sentences can affect how your writing sounds, whether it is pleasing or not, how the readers respond to it. The sentence is a powerful tool, and its power can be expressed in one word—variety.

If you've ever looked at a sentence you've written, known it didn't say what you wanted to say, and despaired because you didn't know what to do about it, you probably need to step back and look at the enormous variety that the syntax, or word order, of English makes possible. Nothing *has to be* the way you wrote it the first time . . . or the second, or the third, or the fourth. Consider Lynch's sentence above. It's a pretty good sentence the way it is—rhythmic, emphatic, clear. But she didn't have to write it as it is. She had myriad options:

She could have used several short, choppy sentences:

> The camera is without dispassion or passion. It opens and closes its glass eye. We put the scene before it.

or:

> The camera has no passion. It has no dispassion. It opens its glass eye. It closes it. We put the scene before it.

Or she could have combined the shorter sentences in a variety of ways:

> The camera has neither passion nor dispassion; therefore, It opens its glass eye and closes it. But we put the scene before it.

or:

> The camera has neither passion nor dispassion, and it opens and closes its glass eye, and we put the scene before it.

or:

> The camera has neither passion nor dispassion: it opens and closes its glass eye—we put the scene before it.

Rearranging the order of elements was also a possibility:

> As we put the scene before the camera, which has neither passion nor dispassion, it opens and closes its glass eye.

or:

> The camera opens and closes its glass eye as we put the scene before it; it has neither passion nor dispassion.

How about changing the grammatical forms of the elements?:

> The camera, having neither passion nor dispassion, opens and closes its glass eye as the scene is put before it.

Or condensing by leaving some of them out:

> The camera's glass eye, without passion, opens on the scene before it.

Or repeating one of them:

> The camera is without passion; the camera is without dispassion; the camera opens and closes its glass eye on the scene we put before it.

Just fiddling around here, I've come up with ten versions of Lynch's sentence, any one of which she might have used if she hadn't liked her first attempt, and I haven't even begun to show the extent of the possibilities. If you're adept at math, perhaps you can get a ballpark notion of the number of variables and the number of ways they can be combined, and conclude that there are literally thousands of ways that this sentence can be written. I myself never realized this potential for variety until one of my writing teachers in college told me that an eighteenth-century rhetorician named Erasmus used to have his students write one sentence a hundred different ways. It seemed improbable to me that one sentence would have a hundred variations, so I took a sentence from Hemingway, a rather uncomplicated sentence as many of his are, and sat down to try Erasmus's exercise. By the time I had six hundred, and realized that one grammatical transform could be performed on all six hundred, doubling the number, I decided that I had better things to do with my time than finding out how many variations were possible. But never after that did I feel that I had to settle for one of my own sentences if I wasn't entirely happy with it.

This immense variety the syntax of the language provides is in and of itself valuable—variety for variety's sake. But it becomes a truly useful tool of style only if you are aware of the the specific effects of varying sentences. These effects are subtle, and almost as varied as syntax itself, but I can illustrate some of the more obvious ones for you, and they can become your criteria for choosing among the myriad options. Sentence variation gives you control over *pace*, *rhythm*, *emphasis*, and *clarity* in your writing.

PACE

I use the term *pace* to refer to the rate at which the readers move through your sentences. Different factors affect this rate, and not all of them are under your control. The readers' ability to read is the most obvious controlling factor, and there's nothing you can do to change that. In some cases you won't even have any way of gauging it, although often foreknowledge of the general age of your audience gives you a hint as to how quickly or slowly they will read. Diction can also affect pace, since difficult words, or abstract words, or words the readers are unfamiliar with will slow them down. This you can control, and you should try to by using the simplest words that will get the job done and by defining new and difficult terms clearly early on as David Leonard does in his description of surgical lasers at the end of this chapter.

But perhaps the most significant factor controlling pace, one over which the syntactical flexibility of English gives you a good deal of command, is punctuation. Basically, punctuation marks represent pauses, and different punctuation marks represent different degrees of pauses. English punctuation marks can be divided into three rough groupings:

light pause
,
near stop
; : —
full stop
( ) ! ? .

Of course you can't just throw the punctuation in for no other reason than to affect the readers' pace (want the readers to stop here, better put a question mark in the middle of the sentence). But the syntactical flexibility of English allows you to exercise a fine degree of control over what punctuation marks you use, and where, while still following the rules. For instance, dependent clauses can legally occupy three different positions in the sentence, and each is punctuated differently:

The camera opens and closes its glass eye *when we put the scene before it*.
When we put the scene before it, the camera opens and closes its glass eye.
The camera, *when we put the scene before it*, opens and closes its glass eye.

The first version has no pauses at all, the second has one light pause, and the third has two. Fast, medium, and slow, just like an electric blender. Or consider the various options for combining sentences:

> The camera opens and closes its glass eye *when* we put the scene before it.
> The camera opens and closes its glass eye, *and* we put the scene before it.
> The camera opens and closes its glass eye; we put the scene before it.
> The camera opens and closes its glass eye. We put the scene before it.

No pause, light pause, near stop, stop—take your pick. Flexible English syntax gives you almost complete control over pace *within the rules for correctness*. Of course it helps to know those rules, and the next chapter, Mechanics, will give you some help in understanding them.

But how to decide *when* to vary the pace? When is fast appropriate? When is it best to slow the readers down? There is no pat answer to these questions. One principle to follow is to slow the readers down when the content is either difficult or particularly important, making sure that they proceed at a safe pace and don't overlook or misunderstand anything. Then you can speed the pace up at the easy parts for the readers' convenience. And it's a good idea to vary the pace just for variety's sake if the content is of a pretty consistent level of accessibility and importance.

But perhaps the best advice I can give you is *make the form match the content*. If what you are writing about trips along at a breathless pace, use sentences that do the same. If the subject matter is ponderous and elephant-like slow, make the sentences lumber along. From Wendy Hanabusa's essay at the end of this chapter:

> Obediently we follow the trail, absorbing nature's gifts in a slow, simple pace, until another path startles our spirits and beckons our souls. It is a steep, uncaring road that takes us back to the sea. Crumbling foundations lie by its side behind futile warnings although only a quick glance and a passing thought are granted to the cold cement steps and ruins, the day much too wonderful to dwell on their meaning, the grade too steep for ponder.

The first sentence is slow, like the pace it describes, and the last plunges along almost unchecked down the slope.

Every situation is different, and there are as many reasons for varying pace as there are ideas to write about, but pace should be under your control, not at the mercy of chance.

RHYTHM

Language has rhythm just as music and dancing do. There are two kinds of language rhythm—the rhythm of words and the rhythm of sentences. If you've studied poetry, you know that rhythm can be controlled by regular variation of stressed and unstressed syllables, and that poets often convolute the word order of their sentences for this kind of rhythm. Poetic rhythm has little application in writing prose, but there is a larger kind of rhythm—the rhythm of sentences—that can be controlled, through syntactical variation, without making the sentences poetically convoluted.

Like pace, the rhythm of sentences is controlled by punctuation. The pauses signalled by punctuation marks break sentences into units of different lengths; the relationship among the lengths of those segments creates a kind of rhythm. Consider Figure 5-2. Of the bars displayed in it, some

Figure 5-2. Rhythm.

can be said to represent rhythm and some not. The first shows no rhythm, or even any potential for rhythm because it is not divided into parts. Imagine it as a sound and it would be something like a factory whistle, a single, unwavering, unbroken note. Since the second is broken into parts, it shows the potential for rhythm, and further, since the parts are relatively equal in size, it can be said to represent rhythm. As a sound, it would be something like a telephone busy signal—monotonous, but rhythmic. The third bar is broken into parts, but it does not display rhythm; rather, it shows the opposite. The parts, being of different sizes and showing no predictable pattern, create cacaphony rather than harmony. Imagine an orchestra tuning its instruments before a performance for bar number three. The fourth bar, although its parts are not equal in size, shows rhythm because there is a regular and predictable progression from short to long. This rhythm is the most complex of the four, something like a pianist playing notes in a scale.

Punctuation marks break sentences down into units like the segments of these bars, and the more regular the units, the more rhythmic the sentences. Read the following sentences, more of Wendy Hanabusa's, aloud, and you can hear the rhythm:

> The yellowing wood forms barren rooms, save the displays that unlock their story, a tale of promise and lost hope, of broken men and pressing dreams. Corroding poles, in stark formation, gaze mindlessly at the walls; their arms, now mercifully gone, once held hundreds of men in their close confines.

Lined up so that each element between the punctuation marks has its own line, they show the regularity in size that enhances the rhythm:

> The yellowing wood forms barren rooms,
> save the displays that unlock their story,

a tale of promise and lost hope,
of broken men and pressing dreams.

Corroding poles,
in stark formation,
gaze mindlessly at the walls;
their arms,
now mercifully gone,
once held hundreds of men in their close confines.

The first sentence contains paired elements of relatively equal size; the,
second has two three-part series, each gradually increasing in length. The
measured cadence creates the rhythm you hear when you read the sentences aloud.

The easiest way to achieve this kind of rhythm is through the use of
parallelism. Parallelism is the placing of similar grammatical structures in
rows or series. Wendy's first sentence here has two prepositional phrases
at the end of it:

. . . of promise and lost hope,
of broken men and pressing dreams.

This, then, is a two-part parallel series of prepositional phrases. Within each
is another parallel series—two objects for each preposition:

. . . of

promise
hope

. . . of

men
dreams

This placing of similar structures together can create strong rhythms that
are completely under your control, for you decide how many items are in
a parallel series, and by including or omitting modifying words and phrases
within the parallel items, exactly how similar in length they will be. The
following paragraph by Charles Dickens shows how the rhythms of sentences can be controlled through parallelism:

It was Sunday evening in London, gloomy, close, and stale. Maddening church
bells of all degrees of dissonance, sharp and flat, cracked and clear, fast and slow,
made the brick-and-mortor echoes hideous. Melancholy streets, in the penitential
garb of soot, steeped the souls of the people who were condemned to look at
them out of windows in dire despondency. In every thoroughfare, up almost
every alley, and down almost every turning, some doleful bell was throbbing,
jerking, tolling, as if the Plague were in the city and the dead-carts were going
round. Everything was bolted and barred that could possibly furnish relief to an
overworked people. No pictures, no unfamiliar animals, no rare plants or flowers,
no natural or artificial wonders of the ancient world—all taboo with that enlightened strictness, that the ugly South Sea gods in the British Museum might have
supposed themselves at home again. Nothing to see but streets, streets, streets.

Nothing to breathe but streets, streets, streets. Nothing to change the brooding mind, or to raise it up. Nothing for the spent toiler to do, but to compare the monotony of his seventh day with the monotony of his six days, think of what a weary life he led, and make the best of it—or the worst, according to the probabilities.

And here are some more parallel structures from the essays included in this book:

We talked the hours away through the flat, hot valley of Sacramento, into the foothills of Nevada City, over the mountain to Reno, around the lake to South Shore and up to Shasta and Dunsmuir.

Wendy Hanabusa

Most of us wouldn't even notice this piece of land; we see San Francisco across the bay, or we see the bay itself as we drive by; or, maybe we see Angel Island or Alcatraz, the bridges that span the bay, or the boats and ships that sail upon it.

Leif Lindseth

Surgical lasers are medical instruments which use radiant energy to vaporize, coagulate, or photoradiate tissue.

David Leonard

We see our sons in a news tabloid beaming at the camera, revealing forever the momentary elation of conquest, the severed ears of Vietnamese sons dangling from their bayonet tips, pinned to their shirts, and held aloft like small flags.

Kathleen Lynch

Parallelism is an enormously natural and accessible technique to have so much power, and it is hard to overuse it. I recommend applying it at every opportunity, and then editing if you think you've overdone it.

Before I go on to discuss emphasis, I want to mention one more way to enhance the rhythm of your sentences, a way that combines both the rhythm of words and the larger rhythm of sentence elements—the literal repetition of words or groups of words for stylistic effect. Careless, unintended repetition can result in the weakest kind of style, but controlled, intentional repetition at the beginnings or ends of structures can create the most powerful kind of rhythm. Here are some examples:

Burse Dills is a man, a big, big man, 285 pounds worth.

Paul Anderson

And indeed they waited. Day by day, week to week, month after month for the final verdict, freedom or extradition, prosperity or poverty.

Wendy Ichimaru Hanabusa

They looked upon themselves as men who lived by higher standards of behavior than civilians, as men who were the bearers and protectors of the most important values of American life, who maintained a sense of discipline while civilians abandoned themselves to hedonism, who maintained a sense of honor while civilians lived by opportunism and greed.

Tom Wolfe

And what freeway would be complete without billboards? There are three of them here; one is rather standard—a piece of plywood painted with a rainbow— while the other two have plywood cut-outs tacked up on their open frameworks. One shows the sun in several positions in its trip across the sky, while the other shows a bird flying just below the sun.

Leif Lindseth

The mouth seemed formed less to speak than to quiver, less to quiver than to kiss. Some might have added, less to kiss than to curl.

Thomas Hardy

Ask not what your country can do for you; ask what you can do for your country.

John F. Kennedy

So rhythm can be controlled through syntactical variation. But what will your criteria be? How will you know when to write rhythmically and when not? That's a hard question to answer with a generalization, but I can advise you to avoid extremes. A complete absence of rhythm is harsh and unpleasant to the readers, while an overabundance of it can set up a singsong cadence that might lull them to sleep. As with most aspects of style, variety for variety's sake isn't a bad idea. A better general rule is the same one I suggested for pace—make the form match the content. If the material you are writing about is harmonious, pleasing, and regular, use rhythmic sentences to describe it. If it is chaotic, unpleasant, or random, use unrhythmic sentences. Build a container that suits the contents.

EMPHASIS

By *emphasis* I mean what you call most attention to within a sentence. Not every part of any given sentence gets the same amount of emphasis; some positions are more and some less emphatic. Figure 5-3 illustrates the variation of emphasis within the sentence. Generally speaking, things on the

Figure 5-3. Zones of Emphasis.

ends stand out, and are more noticeable. So the first and last positions get the most emphasis. The last position has the most potential for emphasis because the readers remember best what they encountered last. This is true of structures other than sentences, too. In a movie you wouldn't expect to see a car chase, a gun fight, and the conclusion of a romance in the first scene, and just a lot of talk after that. The dramatic parts come last, in the

climactic position. Of course, if the ends get the emphasis, the middle is
left as a deadly swamp of lost emphasis, and what you put in the middle
gets less attention.

But the diagram is an oversimplification. Most sentences are broken down
into smaller units by internal punctuation, and when they are, this theory
of zones of emphasis applies to the separate units as well as to the whole
sentence as in Figure 5-4. In a sentence broken into parts by punctuation,

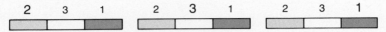

Figure 5-4. Smaller Zones of Emphasis.

there are zones of minor emphasis as well as zones of major emphasis; the
very first and last elements still achieve the major emphasis, and the mid-
dlemost part of the sentence still achieves the least. In Figure 5-5 the emphasis graph is applied to a real sentence from Leif Lindseth's essay. It

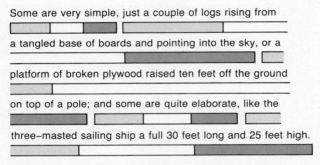

Figure 5-5. Zones of Emphasis in a Real Sentence.

serves to illustrate that Leif has done a pretty good job of causing important
concepts to fall into the zones of heaviest emphasis—"simple," "pointing
into the sky," "on top of a pole," "elaborate." I would quibble with him over
putting "25 feet high" rather than "three-masted sailing ship" in the most
emphatic last position. Once you are aware of this potential that certain
positions in the sentence have for enhancing emphasis, you can use the
syntactical flexibility of English to control emphasis. Thus this sentence
from Wendy Hanabusa's essay, which has the word "onward" in the emphatic last position, did not have to:

> The hillside crevices whisper with mystery though the blackened earth leads us
> silently onward.

> The hillside crevices whisper with mystery though the blackened earth leads us
> onward silently.

Though the blackened earth leads us silently onward, the hillside crevices whisper with mystery.

Though the blackened earth leads us silently onward, mystery whispers from the hillside crevices.

Though the blackened earth leads us silently onward, mystery whispers from the crevices in the hillside.

The hillside crevices whisper with mystery although we are lead onward by the blackened earth.

Each variation places a different word in the emphatic last position, so although they all say literally the same thing, each has a slightly different effect.

Another way to enhance emphasis is through repetition. Stylistic repetition not only enhances rhythm, but emphasizes the word or words repeated. This is a principle of emphasis that applies to more communication activities than writing. Lecturers repeat important points for emphasis, as do ads and warning signs. Speech makers are particularly inclined to use repetition for emphasis, and when Winston Churchill told his people during World War II, "We shall fight on the beaches, we shall fight on the landing ground, we shall fight in the fields and the streets, we shall fight in the hills; we shall never surrender," he wasn't giving deployment instructions—he was using the syntax of the language to give him a chance to repeat some important words. In the following sentence, Leif Lindseth makes subtle but effective use of repetition for emphasis:

Somebody, for whatever reason, found himself with some extra time and took a walk along the mudflats. *He saw* the piles of trash and driftwood, and *he saw* his audience whizzing by on the interstate and started to build.

This unknown person's ability to see what other people overlook is the important thing about him, and Lindseth emphasizes it by repeating "he saw." How much can you use repetition without overdoing it? Let's turn again to Dickens for an idea:

Fog everywhere. Fog up the river, where it flows among green aits and meadows; fog down the river, where it rolls defiled among the tiers of shipping and the waterside pollutions of a great (and dirty) city. Fog on the Essex marshes, fog on the Kentish heights. Fog creeping into the cabooses of collier-brigs, fog lying out on the yards, and hovering in the rigging of great ships; fog drooping on the gunwales of barges and small boats. Fog in the eyes and throats of ancient Greenwich pensioners, wheezing by the firesides of their wards; fog in the stem and bowl of the afternoon pipe of the wrathful skipper, down in his close cabin; fog cruelly pinching the toes and fingers of his shivering little 'prentice boy on deck. Chance people on the bridges peeping over the parapets into a nether sky of fog, with fog all around them, as if they were up in a balloon, and hanging in the misty clouds.

There's no trick to figuring out how to manipulate emphasis. You're the writer, so you know what is most important in your sentences. Put the most important elements in the most emphatic positions, use stylistic repetition for the most important parts of all, and avoid losing essential things in the unemphatic, swampy middle sections.

CLARITY

Even though clarity should be your first consideration, I mention it last because it is possible, once you become aware of all the possibilities of sentence variation, to get carried away with them. As you seek to control your pace, your rhythm, and your emphasis, don't forget that your primary purpose is to communicate clearly. The syntactical flexibility of English gives you a lot of options, but not all those options are equally clear. Look at the different possible placements of a single phrase in one of Leif Lindseth's sentences:

> A lion *with tears streaming from its eyes* points to a curious pile of wood . . .
> *With tears streaming from its eyes*, a lion points to a curious pile of wood . . .
> A lion points *with tears streaming from its eyes* to a curious pile of wood . . .
> A lion points to a curious pile of wood *with tears streaming from its eyes* . . .

Leif chose (wisely) the first version of the sentence. As the phrase "with tears streaming from its eyes" moves ever further from the word it gives information about, it becomes progressively less apparent just what it does modify. By the time we get to the last version, the pile of wood instead of the lion seems to have tears streaming from its eyes. The moral: place modifying phrases at a distance from what they modify *only if you are sure the readers can tell what they modify*. Here's another sentence to consider:

> Students on the downtown campus complain of traffic, parking problems, frequent incidents of rape and mugging, and dust from construction projects.

Anything seem wrong to you? The sentence is grammatically correct. It's meaning is clear too; no possibility of misunderstanding this one. And yet there is something about it that doesn't ring true. That something is the order of the items in the series. My orderly mind wants to see those four items put in less-than-random order: from most serious to least serious will do, or *vice versa*, but to have the most serious item—rape and mugging—buried in the middle of the series violates my sense of hierarchy. The syntax is sending conflicting messages. The placement says that dust is most important, while the content says that rape and mugging are. As you vary your sentences, try to avoid even minor misunderstandings like this.

But this is a negative approach to syntax and clarity. Besides avoiding unclear structures, try to use syntactical variety to *increase* the readers' understanding whenever possible. These are sentences from David Leonard's technical report at the end of the chapter. I've rearranged them somewhat:

Using a laser to vaporize tissue is specifically called laser surgery. In this application, a very fine, dense beam of radiant energy is converted to intense heat at the target tissue. The vaporization of intracellular liquid, identical to water boiling, is the response.

The sentences are fairly clear, but they can be better. Here is the way Leonard actually wrote them:

Using a laser to vaporize tissue is specifically called laser surgery. In this application, a very fine, dense beam of radiant energy is converted to intense heat at the target tissue. The response is identical to water boiling; intracellular liquid vaporizes.

With "The response ... " at the beginning of the third sentence, the transition between the sentences is much smoother, the whole concept much clearer. By beginning the third sentence with a word that shows its relationship to the second, Leonard has kept his readers from falling into the gap after the period of the second sentence. It's a courteous thing to do for the readers, this making of transitions, and it increases the chance that your ideas will get across intact. Here's Leonard again, keeping his readers on the track through a complex explanation:

Usually within one-hundredth of a MICROSECOND an excited electron will regain a lower energy level. Since the atom has less energy after the transition than before, energy must have been released. The released energy is exactly equal to the energy gained during excitation. The energy is given off as a PHOTON, a minute particle of light. This process is called spontaneous emmission.

This is only a sampling of the ways in which clarity can be guarded and enhanced by careful consideration of sentence arrangement. As you write, the best thing to do is to try to stay aware of your readers, seeing your sentences through their eyes and hearing them through their ears, so that you can spot potential confusion and rearrange your sentences to avoid it.

Pace, rhythm, emphasis, and clarity—all can be controlled by sentence variation, and there is ample variety available to make your degree of control a fine one. But by now you've probably begun to wonder where this kind of sentence work fits into the writing process. Is it done in the revision stage? Should you do it as you write, pausing after each sentence to consider and revise? Is it possible to do it unconsciously, hitting the most fortunate variation on the first crack? I can't give you a pat answer. For me, it is all of the above. Sometimes I stop in the middle of a sentence and rearrange it. Right now I'm composing this chapter on a word processor, and with the ability it gives me to alter my typing as I go along, I'm more inclined to revise as I go than if I were typing on a typewriter or composing long-hand. I also go back over a finished draft, often several times, reconsidering and rearranging sentences, and usually I can do a better job then because I have the whole piece in front of me and can tell better how all the sentences relate to one another. And yes, most of the time, my first choice is sound, and needs no revision. Thank heavens for that; it would take quite a long time to revise *every* sentence in the manuscript for this book. Perhaps it will encourage you to know that the more practiced I become as a writer, the more often my first impulse in writing a sentence is a good one. I theorize that every *conscious* revision I make, every sentence I struggle with to make less awkward and more effective, trains my ear and sharpens my instinct to allow me to write more effortlessly the next time.

I hope this theory will apply to you as well, that you'll become more adept in phrasing sentences with each essay until you can write effective sentences with ease and confidence. But until then stay aware of the immense potential for variety inherent in every sentence you write, and never settle for less than the best variation for the occasion.

Images: Avoiding the White Wall Syndrome

In front of my classes, I often find myself talking about the *ideas* that words and sentences convey, the logic, the abstractions. When I do I have to remind myself that language also creates *images*—vivid, detailed images if the language is adeptly used. It is quite natural that this should be so, since people think as often in images as they do in the abstract, perhaps more often, really. Think of a friend you had in elementary school, and images of that friend come into your mind, images from the playground, from the classroom, from the school cafeteria, real, remembered images of how your friend looked and acted. Remember a vacation at a cabin by a lake, and scenes from it blossom, the view out the window of the car on the way there, your first view of the cabin and the lake, the scenery gradually transforming from strangeness to delight to familiarity until your last regretful view out the back window of the car as you had to leave. If you try to tell someone about the place, perhaps to recommend it, you will probably try to use words and sentences to recreate the images projected on the movie screen of your mind.

There is a tendency among people in general, among the publishers of certain kinds of books such as science texts, and even among some writing teachers, to see the ability that the mind has to create images, and the corresponding ability that language has to create images, as a kind of luxury or embellishment, appropriate perhaps in poetry or "creative" writing, but more out of place in more "practical" or "formal" writing situations. In an attempt to seem serious and businesslike, writers and editors sometimes pare away the vivid descriptions, the comparisons, and the figurative language that come naturally to mind during the writing process, leaving only the logic and the abstractions. The resultant writing engages only part of the brain, leaving that portion where imagery occurs vacant as the screen at a drive-in theater at mid-morning, a blank white wall.

This, I think, is a terrible mistake, especially if the audience for the writing is contemporary and American. Contemporary America is a culture of images more than thoughts. Our recreations are movies and television. Advertisers work primarily with imagery. Hardly an American alive goes to a new or interesting place without a camera to record and reproduce images of the place for memory and sharing. There is hardly an activity in our lives that leaves the imaging portion of the brain unengaged, and if reading does this, it is unnatural and unpleasant.

The manufacturers of the computer on which I am composing this chapter apparently agree with me on this issue, because they engage the imaging portion of my brain at every turn, either with actual images or with suggested ones. The machine is an Apple Macintosh, famous for its "user friendliness." Most of that friendliness comes from presenting complicated computer functions to people like me, who know little about computers, as simple, familiar images. If I want to eliminate something I've typed, I throw it in a little trash can that is pictured down in the corner of the screen. The screen itself is called a "desk top." I look at the projects I'm working on through "windows." The little control device that lies beside the keyboard is a "mouse." User friendliness consists simply of teaching me the unknown through images of the known.

The chief competitor of Apple, a very serious and businesslike bunch, apparently hold themselves above this sort of thing; their monitor deals in words, not images, and even their company logo is reduced to an acronym rather than words that might call up some pale images. Both products were sitting side by side in the store, and I bought the Apple. Imagery helps me learn, and I recommend that in any kind of writing you take pains to keep the imaging portion of your readers' minds engaged, sparing them that blank white wall where the images ought to be.

DETAILED DESCRIPTION

As you write and think, images naturally come into your mind. In fact, it's hard to keep this from happening. Sit and try to imagine that blank white wall, excluding any other images from your mind. I'll bet you can't do it for more than a couple of seconds at a time. When you write, images of your topic come to mind, and sometimes it is easy to forget that the readers can't see into your head, that just the presence of the images in your mind doesn't guarantee that they will appear in what you write. As a result you might find yourself *mentioning* images rather than *describing* them. Consider the following sentence:

> Even those who lost loved ones in the war were unaware of what was going on.

The topic of this sentence is a potentially moving one, but what images does it call up? If a friend or relative of yours was killed in Vietnam, then you will call up your own images, but to the reader who hasn't directly shared the experience, the wall is blank, or at best covered with dim, vague images of battle scenes from old movies or from funerals of people who died other than in the war. But this isn't really the way this sentence was written. It comes from Kathleen Lynch's essay at the end of this chapter, and this is how she really wrote it:

> Even those whose brothers and sons came home to Travis Air Force Base in black zippered sacks were unsure of what was going on.

Here is the reality of the idea. You can see the young men, the relatives, the body bags right down to the zippers. Kathleen has obeyed the oldest and wisest rule for writers—show, don't tell. In the same essay, she mentions a picture that is familiar to most people who lived during the early part of the Vietnam war era, but she does not assume that the readers will be able to remember it; she describes it:

> In 1963, it gave us an image of Reverend Quang Duc's death. And though most of us who saw the photograph will not recall his name, we will never forget the vivid image of the man sitting on the asphalt of the main street in his home town. His robes were soaked with gasoline and he prayed, then lit the match he held and burst into flame. In the picture one can see the shock of pain on his face, the flames eating the cloth on his torso and the flesh on his right cheek. You can see the parked cars behind him, the onlookers and the soldiers. Though I was only nineteen when I saw that picture, it worked on me in a profound and terrifying way.

Kathleen included a Xerox of the photograph with her essay when she handed it in. I debated including it in this chapter, but decided that to do so would be redundant, given the effectiveness of her description.

But I've been talking exclusively about *visual* images here, and I don't want to give the impression that all imagery is visual. Imagery is perceived through the senses, and there are, after all, five of them. The best writing can suggest images recorded by all parts of the sensory apparatus. Again, from Lynch's essay:

> I was usually preparing dinner when the television screen flashed the faces of countless humans who had eaten less food in a month than the amount I was readying for our table. It became easy to disregard these faces, simply by not looking, or by turning off the set. But already, I knew they were there. In the morning the faces were back. Through the fragrant mist of fresh coffee and the buttery burst of steam from my croissant, I saw them staring at me from the newspaper page.

The pictures she is discussing here are of starving people in Ethiopia. The two telling descriptive details, the details that so vividly illustrate the difference betweeen American plenty and Ethiopian hardship, appeal to the senses of touch, smell, and taste—the steam from the coffee and croissant.

You'll be more inclined to provide your readers with this kind of detailed description if you remember one thing: The images cast on the screen of your mind by your mental projector are only visible to you, and if you want the readers to see them too, you have to use detailed description to project them onto the potentially imageless page in front of them.

COMPARISON

Detailed description has one drawback: It takes up a lot of space. If the writing situation demands brevity, sometimes you can't afford the luxury of painting pictures with words. But there is a simpler, more compact way to engage the readers' imaging capacity—comparison. By comparing what the readers don't know and can't picture to some familiar object, you can help them construct images of what they've never seen. You do this in your everyday language without thinking about it, telling someone a place is a couple of city blocks away even if you are not in the city, or calling a car "fire-engine" red, or saying a fish you caught was as long as your leg. It's a quick, easy way to call up images.

It can also be more effective than detailed description sometimes. Imagine that you are reading a manual for maintenance on your car, intending to change the oil, which you've never done before. Imagine that it describes the oil filter as "a cylinder, roughly elliptical at one end, 13 cm. in height and 8.5 cm. in diameter, with a threaded cylindrical protrusion 2.9 cm. in diameter extending from its flatter end." That's an accurate description, and if you think about it long enough, you'll probably locate the oil filter. But how readily does a picture of the device come to mind? If you're very familiar with metric measurements, perhaps you can picture the size. If you remember your highschool geometry, "cylinder" brings a quick image to mind. If you're a mechanic or a machinist, "threaded" creates a picture. But if the manual is written for laymen, or even if it isn't, why not say something like "shaped like a soda can with a little pipe coming out of one end"? The familiar image of a soda can comes instantly to mind, everyone knows what a pipe looks like, and, in fact, that's pretty much what an oil filter looks like. The comparison doesn't sound very "professional," but it works, and that's what counts. In his book *The Klamath Knot*, David Raines Wallace uses a comparison with an easily visualized scene to explain a complicated geological process:

> Plate tectonics, though, gives even a geological simpleton like me a way of interpreting the Klamath knot. Geological maps of the region look to me like a jammed conveyor belt. I once worked in an apple cannery where I noticed that the cans of apple juice got stacked up in just such arc-shaped belts when the conveyor belt was stuck (an interesting observation that was cut short when the foreman saw cans tumbling to the floor). The arcs of Klamath rocks, sedimentary rocks formed on the Pacific coast, may have been jammed against the western edge of North America by forces similar to those that splattered apple juice on the cannery floor.

The humorous comparison makes the process not only more envisionable, but less threatening as well.

Here are some more examples, from David Leonard's discussion of surgical lasers at the end of this chapter, of comparisons used to help the readers envision complicated technical devices and processes:

Using a laser to vaporize tissue is specifically called laser surgery. In this application, a very fine, dense beam of radiant energy is converted to intense heat at the target tissue. The response is identical to water boiling; intracellular liquid vaporizes.

Before liquids can vaporize, protein rearrangements cause clotting. The same process occurs on a larger scale when an egg is cooked.

In this case, the surgical laser is like a scalpel except the blade is made of light instead of steel.

We teachers admonish one another to teach the unknown in terms of the known; it's good advice for writers, too. Comparison with familiar, easily envisioned objects can assuage the readers' anxiety over new material with friendly images that make understanding easier.

FIGURATIVE LANGUAGE

Detailed description creates images of people, objects, places, and events discussed in your writing. Comparison brings in images of objects outside your subject but similar to it so that readers can picture the subject itself. The most powerful tool for creating images brings in images outside the subject and related to it in various ways, but it brings them in *for the power that these additional images themselves possess*. This tool is called *figurative language*.

"Figurative" simply means something that is not literally true. When you call your car a lemon or a beast, you are using figurative language. Specifically, you're using *metaphor*, a figure of speech that makes an imaginative comparison. A similar figure is the *simile*, which is a more straightforward yet still imaginative comparison using "like" or "as." (He took off like a scared rabbit.) Another is *personification*, which compares inanimate objects to people by discussing them as if they were people. (This little car has a lot of guts.) There are many more kinds of figurative language, but all of it contains this element of imaginative comparison, and all of it creates imagery.

But the images created by figurative language do two things that the imagery of literal comparison doesn't do: They affect the emotions, and they make connections at a higher level of abstraction than literal comparisons do. Consider the following personification from Wendy Hanabusa's essay describing an old incarceration barracks:

Corroding poles, in stark formation, gaze mindlessly at the walls; their arms, now mercifully gone, once held hundreds of men in their close confines . . . And, from behind the bar's cruel grin, the Chinese saw the water they had just crossed to escape China's desperation and to enter a brave, new world.

The bars are given human abilities and qualities here, standing in formation like soldiers, able to gaze, mindless, grinning cruelly. The personification gives us a double set of images—the literal image of rusting metal and the imaginative vision of the bars as people. If the figure of speech only did this, the writing would be much richer for it, but it does more. It makes us think about the people who made the bars and put men behind them, and beyond them the universal human impulses that have caused people to inflict injustice upon one another throughout the history of the species. Figurative language communicates on more levels than literal language; it is language raised to its highest power. Here's a simple metaphor from Kathleen Lynch's essay:

> Photography itself is really an infant, as technological innovations go.

Think of infants, their innocence, their limited abilities, and think of how they develop, grow, become more capable and powerful. The metaphor encourages us to think not only of what photography can now do, which is the topic of Lynch's essay, but to speculate on what it will grow into, for good or ill. Here Wendy Hanabusa gives us a glimpse into the oppressed spirit of the the Chinese incarcerated on Angel Island by describing their graffiti in figurative language:

> Confined in the poles' cold arms, with no space to move freely, their fingers traced the verses of promise upward on the walls. Line by line, each man added to the saga, perhaps to lend a breath of life to the monotony, surely to express frustration and fear. The poems circle the rooms, edging up the doors' frames and across window sills, searching for cracks that will bring them closer to the sun.
>   The poems, like Chinese spiders, scatter as the layers of paint peel only to release more of their somber siblings. The sorrow and desperation of their confusing incarceration crawl from the depths and meet the fresh sea air, their creators long since gone. The salted breeze picks up the tiny, spindly legs and breathes life once more into the spiders' beings, lifting them onto its back to gently land on our very souls and tug on the sinews of our hearts.

There is more to contemplate in this short passage than in many six-page essays I've read that stay on the literal level of language. Poems turned to spiders, the irrepressible human spirit, eventual escape from confinement to go on out into the new world and proliferate—the image is complex, and rich.

Your first response might be, "Oh, it's nice, but the kind of writing I'll probably have to do won't be so poetic." It is true that the everyday writing tasks that most people face, memos and reports and letters, usually don't reach the level of figurativeness that this passage displays, but I think you'll be selling yourself short if you foreswear entirely the power of figurative language. It can persuade people. It can motivate them. It can even inspire them to be more than they are. And all of these things have their place in the real, practical world. Often a well-chosen figure can get the job done where literal language can't.

Impulses at the Source of Style

So far in this chapter I've talked about the component parts of style, about the nuts and bolts that put it together. I haven't said much about what influences writers to make the choices they do, about what accounts for the end product of combining all of those choices. To do that I have to talk about you as a writer—about how you feel about your subject, your audience, and even yourself.

In good writing, the overall effects of all individual stylistic choices are *tone* and *voice*—tone is how the writing sounds, and voice is how the writer sounds. The two together give, or should give, the readers an image of the writer as a real person, speaking to them on a personal level. As with imagery in general, there is often a wrong-headed prejudice against coming across as a person in more practical writing; in fact, a bland, impersonal tone and voice are often equated with objectivity and encouraged in scientific or legal writing. The main stylistic tactic in creating the so-called objective voice is avoidance of the first-person pronoun *I*. The assumption, I suppose, is that if you don't talk about yourself, you aren't there, and if you aren't there, you can't be subjective. Writers who have been indoctrinated in this ostrich-like philosophy resort to strange constructions like "this reporter interviewed" or "this officer observed." Of course this doesn't make them any more objective. Human beings get involved, and the best anyone can do is be aware of the involvement and try not to let it overcome reason in writing. Pretending to possess robot-like objectivity does nothing more than deceive the most imperceptive readers and, worse yet, convince you that you are endowed with inhuman objectivity and allow your subjectivity to rule unchecked.

No, there is nothing wrong with being a person when you write, even if you are writing a business report or a legal brief. And there is plenty right about it. Writing is communication, and people communicate with people. The evidence of the need for people at both ends of the communicating process is all around you in your educational system. Obviously it would be much cheaper to tape record all the lectures, print up all the book lists, program the tests into the computers, and fire the expensive human teachers. But how would you like to go to the school that did? I wouldn't. I wouldn't want to show up for a seven-thirty class and find a tape recorder sitting at the front of the room, or a computer terminal. I'd want someone who knew what it was like to get up at six and fight the commuter traffic, someone who had struggled to learn the subject matter as I might have to struggle, and would understand my weaknesses and insecurities. I'd want someone I could like and trust up there in front of the classroom, and I suspect you would too.

So it is in reading as well. The printed page is only an intermediary, a link between people communicating, and there must be people on both ends.

THE WRITER AND THE MATERIAL

Tone is the result of your attitude toward your subject matter. Do you think it is important? Do you think it is funny? Does it anger you? Does it inspire you? Like tone of voice in speaking, tone in writing shows your honest response to the subject at hand. In the best writing, tone is apparent in the first paragraph. Look at the opening paragraphs of Kathleen Lynch's and Leif Lindseth's essays:

> First you were born. Then someone swathed in green surgical cloth suctioned the mucus from your nostrils and began a series of medical activities that ushered you into the world of air and light. Within your first hour on this planet, another figure loomed before you, also gowned and masked, and raised a small black rectangle in front of your face. With a sharp "click" and a sudden blast of light, you were born again, into the twentieth century, where the lines between image and reality often blur. Your passage was recorded by a camera. At that moment, you became one of us.

> Most of us don't have time, or at least our priorities won't allow us, to be as creative as we wish to be. We are so busy with our day-to-day business that we don't see the potential in the things around us. But, those of us who can apply our imagination to the situations and extra time we find ourselves in can significantly improve the world around us—like the man who turned a forgotten piece of land into a fantasy world of giant creatures and bizarre objects.

There is a basic similarity in tone here in that both writers seem serious about their topics, seem to believe that what they are writing about is significant. But there are important differences in their tones as well. Lynch's tone is one of awe at the magnitude of the phenomenon she is about to discuss, while Lindseth's signals a milder interest. Lynch sounds as if she's going to write about pressing, unavoidable issues, while Lindseth seems to present us with something more peripheral, more easily overlooked by the unthoughtful. Lynch seems to be drawing us into something potentially unpleasant, while Lindseth seems to have a treat in store for us. In each the tone is consistent, and in each it reflects the writer's honest response to the subject.

Tone can shift within a given essay as the writer responds differently to different parts of the subject, or as the writer's response evolves through the increasing familiarity with the subject and the feelings that writing provokes. Here are two more paragraphs from Wendy Hanabusa's essay:

As the writer approaches Angel Island:

> The secrets of the angels await discovery on a wonderful April morning. The clouds and early morning drizzle, dismissed by the sun, are urged by the gentle wind beyond the horizon. Fresh salted breezes play with the birds in light, care-free frolic. And, comforted by her sisters, the bay quietly consents to the intrusion of the ferry, delicately cradled in her bosom. The seaside town of Tiburon discreetly transforms into an enchanting watercolor as the ferry drifts from its shore

toward the droplet of foothills suspended in the bay, toward Angel Island. Much too quickly, the peaceful cruise draws to a close as the angels' white-washed pier extends it arms to the ferry, and the ferry, in turn, gracefully falls into the embrace and empties its precious cargo onto the island's shore.

And as she contemplates what she found there:

What is more important than dignity? National security? Quotas or economic protection? The first Asian immigrants came to give their children a chance at life, for success in this fertile land. We have fulfilled their dreams. My family nurtured an attorney, a CPA, a nurse, businessmen and women, and yes, even a self-made millionaire. But how high was the cost? Could I make that sacrifice for mine? Would I hold my anguish in, rather than demanding rightful dues from my offspring? The questions without answers seem to circle the room and I run out into the sunlight and toward the sea.

You can see the mechanical differences that account for the tone, the difference in the length of sentences and the use of figurative language. But what accounts for the differences is the change in the writer's attitude, from innocent expectation of a holiday outing to the uncomfortable thoughts provoked by the sight of the old incarceration barracks. Both are honest responses to the subject.

THE WRITER AND THE READER

Voice is a result of who you think you are and who you think your readers are. And of course you're not always the same person, so your voice changes as you don different hats. Look at the following response to an in-class exercise I sometimes ask my students to do to illustrate how voice can change:

February 7, 1985

President Gail Fullerton
Tower Hall
San Jose State University
San Jose Ca. 95112

President Fullerton:

I would like to bring to your attention a problem with the Spartan Marching Band. Due to lack of funding, the band couldn't go to the University of California, Berkeley, football game in November, 1984. Many fans of San Jose State were disappointed because the band was not in attendance. I also, being a fan of San Jose State, was disappointed.

I believe the band is an important part of a football game. They should not be forced to miss any of the San Jose State football games because the funds are not there. I ask that extra consideration be given to the band. Our marching band is an excellent one, and we should be proud to show it off.

Sincerely,
Perry Eggleston

February 7, 1985

Dear Tanya,

How's it going down in Bakersfield? I hope your senior year is going well. I heard you want to go to this school next year. Great! San Jose State has much to offer. Even the band is good.

The people at the football games like to watch the band. I love to sit back and listen to some really good music. The only problem is they don't get to go to all the football games. Other schools in the state can't afford marching bands. The football game gets pretty dull if the band isn't there. I hope the school decides to get some more money to them for next year. The school should try to show the band off, since the football team isn't so good.

Got to go now, Tanya, maybe I'll see you at one of the games next year.

See you later,
Perry

The exercise is a simple one; I ask the students to write a letter to the president of the university, bringing to her attention some problem they have encountered. Then I have them write a note to a friend about the same topic. As Perry did, they usually end up sounding like two different people. This doesn't mean that they're two-faced, just that everyone is many critters in the same hide, and everyone tries to let the most appropriate side of his or her personality show in any given situation. Here are some paragraphs from one of my favorite examples of how a writer can establish a relationship with an audience:

All of the Japanese-made pickups and most of the current American ones are wide-bed. These have a cargo space five and a half feet wide (American) or four and a half feet (Japanese). Obviously you can carry a lot more cargo. On the other hand, the rear wheel housings stick in on each side, which is sometimes inconvenient. (I will say they are handy for children to sit on.) And on many wide-beds you get a fancy one-handed tailgate, like a station wagon's, which won't drop down unless you disconnect the hinges. It's not difficult, it's just tedious. And when you want to close the tailgate, you have to reconnect them.

Which style is better? Myself, I used to have a narrow-bed and now have a wide-bed. I think the advantages and disadvantages of the two models just about balance. So on my current truck, I made the choice on esthetic grounds. The narrow-bed lost. Properly designed, it is the truest of trucks, the very platonic essence of a truck. But in the last five years Ford, Dodge, Chevrolet, Jeep, and

International Harvester (a GMC pickup is just a relabeled Chevrolet)—all have moved to such enormously wide cabs that a new narrow-bed looks hydrocephalic. Wide-bed is now the handsomer truck.

Noel Perrin

The relationship here is more host and guests than writer and readers. The whole book from which the paragraph comes, *First Person Rural*, is equally friendly, equally pleasant to read. Perrin is candid about his own subjectivity, very aware of his audience, a real person talking to real people. The key to achieving this kind of voice lies in picturing your audience as you write. I mean picturing a real, live, specific audience. Obviously I've never seen you, but as I write, I picture an audience of your peers. The students whose essays are included in this book are in that audience, and other students who have been particularly eager to learn over the years. Sometimes I picture them in a group in the classroom, and sometimes I picture one of them individually in my office or walking beside me down the hall away from class, where I find myself most frequently asked the questions I'm trying to answer in this book. This imagining of audiences (I hope) will make you feel as you read that you are being more talked *to* than talked *at*. Make up your own audiences as you write, and you'll find yourself making accurate stylistic choices more often on the first try, and you'll find that your voice is more like that of a real person, talking to real people.

THE WRITER AND THE SELF

Of course, sometimes writers who don't pay any attention to how they come across can put the wrong face forward. A young man who was training to be a pilot once wrote an essay for my class about how he had crash-landed a small plane. We were peer-editing the essays in pairs, and his partner was a very attractive young woman. Hoping to impress her, he wrote "With eyes like Steve Austin, the six-million-dollar man, I scanned the desert below for a place to put it down." She underlined the sentence and wrote in the margin "GIMME A BREAK!" Vanity doesn't impress anyone.

Of course he wasn't guilty of anything that you or I haven't been guilty of. Vanity is a universal human condition, and the people who don't *seem* vain are usually trying not to let the vain part of themselves show. In writing, as in life, you try to put your best self forward, to be the best person you can be. The effect on voice is immense. I can think of no better example than E. B. White, commenting on a journal he kept as a young (and recently fired) newsreporter in Seattle:

You might suppose that the next few entries in my journal, covering the days when I must have been winding up my affairs and getting ready to sail on a long voyage of discovery, would offer a few crumbs of solid information. Not at all. From Friday morning, when I announced that I would soon be off, until the

departure of the *Buford*, several days later, my journal contains no helpful re-
marks, no hint of preparation, no facts about clothes, money, friends, family,
anything. A few aphorisms; a long, serious poem to the girl on Lake Union ("Those
countless, dim, immeasurable years," it begins); a Morley clipping from the "Bowl-
ing Green" about writing ("A child writes well, and a highly trained and long-
suffering performer may sometimes write with intelligence. It is the middle stages
that are appalling . . ."); a short effort in *vers libre* written on Sunday morning
and describing my boardinghouse slatting around in the doldrums of a summer
Sabbath—that is all I find in these tantalizing pages. Mr. Morley was right; the
middle stages are appalling. As a diarist, I was a master of suspense, leaving to
the reader's imagination everything pertinent to the action of my play. I operated,
generally, on too high a level for routine reporting, and had not at that time
discovered the eloquence of facts. I can see why the *Times* fired me. A youth
who persisted in rising above facts must have been a headache to a city editor.

Few people have more right to be vain about their wisdom and writing
ability than White, America's premier essayist, and yet here we find him
making fun of himself. It is this self-effacing quality that I like best about
White's voice, a humility that seems to come from his respect for both his
audience and his topic. It is the voice, simply put, of wisdom. Perhaps, as
White suggests in his quotation of Morley, some aspects of style are inac-
cessible without the advent of age and wisdom; but I think that by being
aware of the face you put forward to your readers, you can attain some of
White's graciousness, even before your hairs grow grey.

Situations and Style

If you're really aware of all of the facets of style I've discussed here, you
don't have *a* style—you have the potential for a variety of styles, and the
trick is to use the appropriate style for the writing occasion. It is easy to
fall into the trap of generalization about writing situations: Journalists, influenced by the format of newspapers and their ethical commitment to
report factually, tend toward short sentences and extreme objectivity. Technical writers, because accuracy is extremely important to them, value precise word choice and clarity of sentence structure, and they are inclined
to do things with format like creating lists, tables, and diagrams to aid
comprehension. Business writers assume that their readers are serious,
busy people, so they value a brief, no-nonsense style.

All of these generalizations are sensible ones that arise out of real involvement in writing activities, but all generalizations are perpetually in
danger of becoming oversimplifications. Whatever you do, don't reduce
style to formulae. Often an imaginative comparison is just the thing to get
the point across in technical writing, and the right metaphor in a business

memo can inspire the work force to make the extra effort that gets the job done. It is best to look at every separate writing task as unique, having its own topic, its own audience, and its own special problems that govern your stylistic choices.

Examples of Student Writing

I've discussed tools in this chapter—tools that can accomplish a variety of different purposes. The variety is infinite; there are choices enough to create combinations enough so that style can always be tailored to the audience, the topic, and the occasion. Here are some essays in which writers have chosen among the available tools to achieve their desired effects.

The Emeryville Crescent
Leif Lindseth

Remember what I said about avoiding the white wall syndrome? Your readers have the ability to envision what is not actually in front of their eyes, as long as you bring the imaging capacities of their minds into play. Here Leif Lindseth has an abstract idea to get across, having to do with human nature, but he communicates it by creating images, setting a rich and varied scene in front of us.

Most of us don't have time, or at least our priorities won't allow us, to be as creative as we wish to be. We are so busy with our day-to-day business that we don't see the potential in the things around us. But, those of us who can apply our imagination to the situations and extra time we find ourselves in can significantly improve the world around us—like the man who turned a forgotten piece of land into a fantasy world of giant creatures and bizarre objects.

The Emeryville Crescent is a strip of mud flats perhaps 200 feet wide and half a mile long. It is bounded on the west by the San Francisco Bay, on the east by Interstate 80, and it stretches between the Emeryville Peninsula and the San Francisco Bay Bridge toll plaza. It is a soggy piece of land with low lying pickleweed and cordgrass growing between the puddles. Its only inhabitants are birds and the insects they eat. In places, the tide has washed up great piles of driftwood, logs, boards, plywood, sticks, and other smaller scraps of wood. It is also a place that collects trash. From the Interstate come the usual beer cans, paper wrappers, cigarette butts, pieces of tires, broken trim, and the larger objects that have blown out of trucks, such as boxes and mattresses.

Most of us wouldn't even notice this piece of land; we see San Francisco across the bay, or we see the bay itself as we drive by; or maybe we see Angel Island or Alcatraz, the bridges that span the bay, or the boats and ships that sail upon it. We may look the other way to the Berkeley hills, or maybe we see the multi-story hotels and office buildings of Emeryville. To us the mud flats would be just a bit of drab green before the mostly greys and blues of the scene beyond. But someone saw more and created a world that we do see.

Somebody, for whatever reason, found himself with some extra time and took a walk along the mudflats. He saw the piles of trash and drift-wood, and he saw his audience whizzing by on the interstate and started to build. I don't know what he built there, but other people liked the idea and started doing the same. Today there are scores of sculptures rising from the mud. Some are very simple, just a couple of logs rising from a tangled base of boards and pointing into the sky, or a platform of broken plywood raised ten feet off the ground on top of a pole; and some are quite elaborate, like the three-masted sailing ship a full 30 feet long and 25 feet high. There is an incredible variety of creatures and objects. There is a horse with a plywood body and shaggy mane of shredded plastic. A twenty-foot elk is poised to leap across one of the many puddles, and across another someone has built a bridge consisting of two parallel boards covered with planks, and a railing sticking out of the mud. A bespectacled giraffe with yellow legs and brown polka dots watches the cars go by on the freeway. And what freeway would be complete without billboards? There are three of them here; one is rather standard—a piece of plywood painted with a rainbow—while the other two have plywood cut-outs tacked up on their open frameworks. One shows the sun in several positions in its trip across the sky, while the other shows a bird flying just below the sun. There is a tee-pee made of sticks and old canvas that, if you walk around to the other side, becomes Opus the penguin.

Everywhere, the old pieces of wood have been dabbed with color. There is a man whose legs have been painted with blue and red stripes, wearing a yellow bucket for a hat, signaling to the planes that fly over with red flags in his hands. Another man with a four foot red and white striped nose has a yellow peace sign painted on his chest.

Much of the color is found in the messages scrawled everywhere; for instance, there is an outhouse haunted by ghosts and goblins and raised ten feet off the ground, proclaiming "R.I.P. Reagan." Elsewhere, someone has written "We love Fae," and somebody is urging us to "be as active as a swamp," while another cries "I loved you." A lion with tears streaming from its eyes points to a curious pile of wood, but if you walk to the other side of the pile you see what has him so upset: the pile is actually sup-porting a large green missile aimed in the direction of Mt. Tamalpais. Nearby, a buglike green tank appears to be rolling across the mud on its twelve wheels. In making their statements, the builders have utilized materials other than wood. One of many scarecrows has a toilet seat for a head, a two-foot cube of styrofoam has been suspended between two sculptures, and someone has brought out a lifesize paper mache crucifix emblazoned with the words, "Art is dead."

Who of us would have the time or inclination to walk out on a forgotten strip of land like this? That first person probably was lonely or had some things to think over, or more probably, he wasn't alone. To originate the idea of building a spur of the moment driftwood sculpture may take more than one person, and it may take the encouragement of others to keep the project going. Anyway, the world they started there lured me out of my car 50 miles from home to take a walk out on the mud flats. As I walked out along a path not more than 20 feet from the cars racing by on the freeway, I ran into an old bum. He wore the usual shabby old clothes, the trenchcoat, and a wide-brimmed hat. His hair and his long beard were white. His nose had swollen to twice its normal size, and his teeth were chipped and brown. He spoke to me of the things you could find along the freeway. "You'd be surprised at what people throw away," he said. He talked about the weather, a ball game, and some other things I couldn't make out. We were separated by a chain link fence. I was glad it was there. As he spoke, I thought of how I was there because I had some free time and some curiosity, while he was there out of necessity, looking for, perhaps, half-smoked cigarettes or bottles that hadn't been quite emptied. I wonder what he saw in that strip of land, or if he realized just how well he fit in with those sculptures.

I saw in that old bum much of what was in the sculptures. The clothes he wore were cast-offs, possibly pulled from a Goodwill bin or trash can. The few things he carried with him had been picked up in back alleys or along the highway. He himself was a cast-off from society, his features as weathered and his skin as grey as that driftwood lying about. And then, seeing what had been created on a forgotten piece of land out of driftwood and garbage, simply because someone had found the time to do something, I wondered, what else are we passing over? In what other areas do we fail to see or realize potential because our priorities won't allow it? What can be made of an old bum perhaps?

Verses of Promise
Wendy Ichimaru Hanabusa

Like Lindseth's essay, this one engages the imaging capacities of the brain. One of the main ways in which it does is through the frequent use of figurative language. Figurative language can create pictures, but it can do more. It can affect the emotions of the readers and it can convey value judgements that writers make about their topics. Here Wendy Hanabusa explains her re-

sponses to and attitudes about Angel Island, once an incarceration camp for Asian immigrants. As you can see from the number of times I've alluded to this essay in this chapter, it exemplifies many different aspects of good style, but its use of figurative language is particularly effective.

The secrets of the angels await discovery on a wonderful April morning. The clouds and early morning drizzle, dismissed by the sun, are urged by the gentle wind beyond the horizon. Fresh salted breezes play with the birds in light, carefree frolic. And, comforted by her sisters, the bay quietly consents to the intrusion of the ferry, delicately cradled in her bosom. The seaside town of Tiburon discreetly transforms into an enchanting water-color as the ferry drifts from its shore toward the droplet of foothills suspended in the bay, toward Angel Island. Much too quickly, the peaceful cruise draws to a close as the angels' white-washed pier extends its arms to the ferry, and the ferry, in turn, gracefully falls into the embrace and empties its precious cargo onto the island's shore.

Indeed, Angel Island is a beautiful sight, a peaceful playground surrounded by blue, nestled between the Peninsula and the East Bay. Serenity abounds as two young boys send delicate threads into the unsuspecting blue-green shallows; couples amble down manicured paths, drinking in the sun and making the breeze laugh with their passing. A quaint building, lush green carpet at its feet, plays host to feasting families at the white wooden tables before it. Smiling rangers greet the new arrivals, their island charge clean and composed. But it is the blackened road that we choose to follow, and we are carried lazily up the hillside into the trees and fragrant folliage. The birds and deer take cover as we humans pass, the fauna stepping aside to share their quiet home. The island reveals its vistas, each view a treasure to behold. The hillside crevices whisper with mystery, though the blackened earth leads us silently onward.

Obediently we follow the trail, absorbing nature's gifts in a slow, simple pace, until another path startles our spirits and beckons our souls. It is a steep, uncaring road that takes us back to the sea. Crumbling foundations lie by its side behind futile warnings although only a quick glance and a passing thought are granted to the cold cement steps and ruins, the day much too wonderful to dwell on their meaning, the grade too steep for ponder. Mercifully, the road levels to twist among dilapidated buildings that seem to call, thirsting to be explored. The road does not betray us, for it contains a wealth of history unlike any other, its buildings of dubious distinction from a time almost forgotten. Each step draws us deeper into the buildings toward their thresholds, toward their hearts and away from the sun and the sea. We are engulfed in old, moldy wood and the haunting memories of yesterday.

The yellowing wood forms barren rooms, save the displays that unlock their story, a tale of promise and lost hope, of broken men and pressing dreams. Corroding poles, in stark formation, gaze mindlessly at the walls; their arms, now mercifully gone, once held hundreds of men in their close confines. The mute, musky tomb once bulged with life, its barred windows offering glimpses of the sea. And from behind the bars' cruel grin, the Chinese saw the water they had just crossed to escape China's desperation and to enter a brave, new world. They touched this golden land of opportunity and thanked their gods for their safe passage only to be herded into these prison walls, to await their fate. And indeed they waited. Day by day, week to week, month after month for the final verdict, freedom or extradition, prosperity or poverty. Confined in the poles' cold arms, with no space to move freely, their fingers traced the verses of promise upward on the walls. Line by line, each man added to the saga, perhaps to lend a breath of life to the monotony, surely to express frustration and fear. The poems circle the rooms, edging up the doors' frames and across window sills, searching for cracks that will bring them closer to the sun.

The poems, like Chinese spiders, scatter as the layers of paint peel only to release more of their somber siblings. The sorrow and desperation of their confusing incarceration crawl from the depths and meet the fresh sea air, their creators long since gone. The salted breeze picks up the tiny, spindly legs and breathes life once more into the spiders' beings, lifting them onto its back to gently land on our very souls and tug on the sinews of our hearts.

The ancient arachnids arouse painful empathy for my Asian kindred, though my ancestors were not the cattle of this pen. But the feeling does not compare to the pain in my breast and the emptiness surrounding me, for my family can understand this angels' home. My grandfather would never come here by choice, for he was one of the unfortunate few, kidnapped from his home, shanghai'd across the Pacific when the world went to war with itself a second time. Snatched from his family, he was seen as a threat to his adopted nation. The quiet fisherman was brought to a very different island paradise to spend his days and hollow hours, to gaze longingly at the ocean waters that were as precious to him as his life's blood.

Surely words could not express his pain and fear that were shared by the Chinese before him. I would never know how he suffered or how he felt, his grief encased in silent sorrow. He was deprived of his rightful station; his children strengthened in his absence. He returned to his family to be stripped of his parental responsibilities and now, viewed as a parasite in his grandchildrens' eyes, as an infant man to be led and coddled. Seemingly wasting away the hours on the beaches of Hawaii, he still struggles for his identity in stubborn disobedience to his all-knowing children.

What is more important than dignity? National security? Quotas or economic protection? The first Asian immigrants came to give their children a chance at life, for success in this fertile land. We have fulfilled their dreams. My family nurtured an attorney, a CPA, a nurse, businessmen and women, and yes, even a self-made millionaire. But how high was the cost? Could I make that sacrifice for mine? Would I hold my anguish in, rather than demanding rightful dues from my offspring? The questions without answers seem to circle the room and I run out into the sunlight and toward the sea.

With the sun calming my spirit, I lean against a bell frame's rough legs and look up at its prize. The bell which once rang for each new boatload of immigrants is now, in sweet irony, the Chinese Liberty Bell; this island their Plymouth Rock. It sounds in a clear, unforeboding tone. The bell is awakened into life by the hand of its guardian, a Chinese-American, proud of his heritage, steadfastly protecting this domain, determined that this history be known. His silhouette against the island's beauty lends truth to its serene existence. The Chinese souls and my grandfather's tears are in the very soil beneath my feet, enriching the earth and sustaining the flora. Nature and the heavens are kind to this island because of the forgotten sorrow witnessed by their angels, and celebrate the retelling of the tale. The island, indeed, flourishes in splendor.

Seeing Ourselves
Kathleen Lynch

Pace, rhythm, and emphasis—all can be controlled by controlling sentence variation. In the following essay Kathleen Lynch uses parallelism, alliteration, repetition of important words, emphatic short sentences, and a variety of other syntactical techniques to orchestrate her sentences so that they do more than communicate her ideas clearly—they communicate powerfully.

First you were born. Then someone swathed in green surgical cloth suctioned the mucous from your nostrils and began a series of medical activities that ushered you into the world of air and light. Within your first hour on this planet, another figure loomed before you, also gowned and masked, and raised a small black rectangle in front of your face. With a sharp "click" and a sudden blast of light, you were born again, into the twentieth century, where the lines between image and reality often blur. Your passage was recorded by a camera. At that moment, you became one of us.

Photography itself is really an infant, as technological innovations go. Invented in 1839, the camera has been in human possession only 146 years—not a very large part of our two million year history as a species. But the power and proliferation of photographic images have changed us forever. The word "photography" has its roots in the Greek language, and means, literally, "writing with light." If photography is a form of writing, then, implied in that idea, it speaks to us; it is equivalent in some way to words. The camera becomes another tool we use to tell each other what it means to be human. It helps us apprehend and comprehend the earth on which we dwell and the vast, black territory of our far-flung universe. In her ambitious text *On Photography* Susan Sontag writes, "In teaching us a new visual code, photographs alter and enlarge our notions of what is worth looking at and what we have a right to observe. They are a grammar, and even more importantly, an ethics of seeing" (Sontag 3).

It is this "ethics of seeing" which I want to explore in this essay. I will examine how camera images affect the way we respond to the plight of others, concentrating on still images, basically those found in a journalistic context. I believe the number and context of these images have a dual impact: they can inspire us to care and act on behalf of others, and they can numb us so that we could not care less.

Let me start with the dark side: the vast body of photographs that injure, stun and deaden our sensitivity. They focus on the horrific and show us a part of ourselves we are reluctant to live with. We see that we are killers. We see our sons in a news tabloid beaming at the camera, revealing forever the momentary elation of conquest, the severed ears of Vietnamese sons dangling from their bayonet tips, pinned to their shirts, and held aloft like small flags. And long after the deaths of these survivors, the image of them will continue, showing them as young and alive, proud of their trophies. And we are ashamed. We also don't know what to do about it—about us—so something in us shuts down, protecting us from the pain of seeing ourselves this way. Such photographs document a reality we would like to deny. A proliferation of painful images can induce a psychic denial of the reality they portray. For years the camera sent us thousands of images of ourselves battling in Vietnam, but most of us could hardly bear to admit or accept the fact that we were at war. Even those whose brothers and sons came home to Travis Air Force Base in black zippered sacks were unsure of what was going on. Though the majority of those war photographs are documentary, they seemed to be records of an alien event in a place we had never heard of. They had the power to hurt and confuse us, and to make us feel helpless. So we shut our hearts to them.

It is the same with pornography. Our first view of a pornographic image may indeed shock and excite us, but if we look at a second, third, hundredth and thousandth image, that same part of our hearts must shut down if we are to bear the shame of seeing ourselves that way. Cruelty is inherent to pornography. In these images of sexual jeopardy, confusion and loathing, the victims are human beings, usually women and children. The pornographic camera documents their humiliation: they are tethered, punished, subjugated, gagged, beaten, mastered and sometimes even murdered. In order to "enjoy" pornography, the viewer must psychically deny or "forget" that the people in such images are real, that they have feelings, that they suffer. The images of the dark side of our nature that transfix us, can also anesthetize us. Sontag says:

> The shock of photographed atrocities wears off with repeated viewings, just as the surprise and bemusement felt the first time one sees a pornographic movie wears off after one sees a few more. . . . The vast catalogue of misery and injustice throughout the world has given everyone a certain familiarity with atrocity, making the horrible seem more ordinary—making it appear familiar, remote ("it's only a photograph"), inevitable. (Sontag 20-21)

So how can a photographic image arouse conciousness, inspire empathy and encourage actions? It seems it must stake out a territory in our psyche which has not been walled off by the stunning inundation of images we take in every day. Photographer Cornell Cape states, "We are exposed to so much of commonplace photography that it needs a greater imagery, a greater subtlety, a greater anything to engage us" (Danziger 69). Sontag says, "Photographs shock insofar as they show something novel. Unfortunately, the ante keeps getting raised, partly through the very proliferation of such images of horror" (Sontag 19). And if there is a proliferation of images of horror, then there are actual horrors which are being played out before the lens. For the camera, without passion or dispassion, opens and closes its glass eye on the scene we put before it. And then it gives us back to ourselves in images, whether we like them or not.

In 1963, it gave us an image of Reverend Quang Duc's death. And though most of us who saw the photograph will not recall his name, we will never forget the vivid image of the man sitting on the asphalt of the main street in his home town. His robes were soaked with gasoline and he prayed, then lit the match he held and burst into flame. In the picture one can see the shock of pain on his face, the flames eating the cloth on his torso and the flesh on his right cheek. You can see the parked cars behind him, the onlookers and the soldiers. Though I was only nineteen when I saw that picture, it worked on me in a profound and terrifying way. I began to seriously consider the question of American responsibility, and my own, for the first time. The "ante" was definitely raised by the image of a monk burning himself to death on a Saigon street. His death took only minutes. His charred body shuddered in a final spasm and fell back; the fire flickered and died out. But because the camera gave us Quang Duc in flames, he will burn anew every time that image is viewed in the future. And the photograph will register his protest over and over, and it will show us what kind of beings we sometimes become.

Sontag says that all photographs are *memento mori*. She claims, "They are a way to participate in another person's . . . mortality, vulnerability, mutability" (Sontag 15). In her discussion of how war images stimulate the moral impulse, she cites a particular event recorded by a cameraman in South Vietnam: "Photographs like the one that made the front page of most newspapers in the world in 1972—a naked South Vietnamese child just sprayed by American napalm, running down a highway toward the camera, her arms open, screaming with pain—probably did more to increase the public revulsion against the war than a hundred hours of televised barbarities" (Sontag 18). And the ante was raised again.

Then came a Vietnam era picture we could not turn away from. A young woman, her arms thrown wide and her mouth open in horror and shock, knelt over the body of a young man who lay dead at her knees. The asphalt darkened by his draining blood was not on a street in Saigon or any other Vietnamese city. It was on a path in the quad at Kent State University. The war had finally, and irrevocably, come home. That was our son shot to death on his own ground for protesting against the war. And it was our daughter's grief that registered forever as an image in our brains. And in the background of the photo, another son of ours stood, stunned, his rifle barrel still hot from the passage of the bullet into the body of the dead boy. After Kent State, colleges were shut down across the country, and antiwar activism reached a peak that was not to subside until we, the people, and our government, got out of Vietnam.

Besides the direct impact of such emotionally stirring images, pictures have the power to work on us subliminally. We know that the brain records everything we ever see. Even the images we would repress or deny, once seen, become permanent reference material in the depths of our conciousness. In *Pornography and Silence* Susan Griffin explores the subliminal nature of images. She says, "One cannot overestimate the effect of images on our lives . . . The human mind has a capacity beyond our conscious understanding to take in and imitate what it sees . . . And no image we have ever seen leaves our minds. What we see does become part of us" (Griffin 108).

I want to use as personal examples two images that became a part of me. In the past months, we have all seen hundreds of pictures of the devastating famine in Ethiopia. They disturbed me and they made me feel helpless. The scope of the problem seemed overwhelming. Besides making me feel powerless, they made me feel guilty. I was usually preparing dinner when the television screen flashed the faces of countless humans who had eaten less food in a month than the amount I was readying for our table. It became easy to disregard these faces, simply by not looking, or by turning off the set. But already, I knew they were there. In the morning the faces were back. Through the fragrant mist of fresh coffee and the buttery burst of steam from my croissant, I saw them staring at me from the newspaper page. One was of a four-year-old girl lying on her side. She could no longer brush away the flies that clustered at the corners of her eyes and mouth. Even if I could defy the laws of logic and physics and reach through my world into the world in which her image was captured, even if I could reach through and offer her my bread, she was too weak to grasp or to chew it. She was already Death's child. And I was changed. I thought about her all day. The next morning there was another photo from Ethiopia. This time, instead of turning the page, I cut it out and taped it to the wall in my kitchen. By changing its context, I gave the image the opportunity to work on me in new ways.

The picture I hung in my kitchen is enigmatic. In the foreground a figure lies face down in the shade. It is an adult and the upper part of the body is swathed in a loose white garment. The legs extend from it, bare and very thin. In the distance there is a row of tents. Without captions, one could imagine several possible interpretations of the picture. It could be a tired traveler resting in the shade as he journeys through the countryside. Or it could be one of the lost souls of downtown San Jose, still sleeping off a drunk while more enterprising citizens set up tents in the background for the annual crafts fair. But I knew what it really was. It was a man who died of starvation only a few yards from the medical tents set up to aid refugees. He was one of the many thousands of Ethiopians who starved to death in 1984.

I began to think of the picture as "the man with the legs." I saw it many times a day and after a few weeks it seemed that when I saw it, I didn't really see it. That is, I didn't see it in the same way any more. For a while, I saw his legs and thought of table legs, because we have a semi-abstract silkscreen print in our kitchen called "Table Legs." I noted the connection between dining at a table and having nothing to eat. More weeks passed. I can hardly remember seeing it at all during that time. Then one evening as I rose from the table I caught the picture out of the corner of my eye and was stunned by what I saw. The picture had finally revealed itself to me: the legs belonged to my father. In a flash I recalled the night before he died. My sisters and I were in the "back bedroom" of our family home, helping our mother change his sickbed and bathe him. It was astonishing to see a man who had once been so big, so full of life and noise, lying mute and weak and shrunken. He was dying of starvation, as many cancer victims do. The man lying on the ground in the photo had also been full of life. And in the moment that the image finally came home to me, I realized that there was a connection between that man's loss of life and my own father's death. And just as I am a part of my father, I became a part of the man with the legs. The image moved into the realm of intuitional reality, and changed me. Since then, I have participated in famine relief efforts, because I finally see the connection.

Of course the associations I made with the image are very personal. But images have the potential to work on each of us in a similar manner. I am not the only American to respond to the plight of people so far away, so seemingly foreign. Consider the enormous popularity of the record album produced to aid in the Ethiopian famine relief effort. Listen to the lyrics: "We are the world, we are the children. We are the ones who make a better day, so let's start giving. There's a choice we're making; we're saving our own lives." *Our* own lives! My father and me and the man with the legs and you! It's hard to imagine that such an outpouring of empathy and support could take place if none of us had ever seen a visual image of the suffering in Africa.

The camera brought our human relatives in Africa into our homes. Photographer Helmut Gernsheim says, "Photography is the only 'language' understood in all parts of the world, and bridging all natures and cultures, it links the family of man . . . It reflects . . . life and events, allows us to share in the hopes and despair of others, and illuminates political and social conditions. We become eye-witnesses of the humanity and inhumanity of mankind" (Sontag 192). Like a technological mirror, the camera keeps holding its images up to our faces, saying, "Here, just look at yourselves!" Last week's *San Jose Mercury* reported that Pacific Gas and Electric will begin publishing photographs of missing children in the monthly statements. And last month many milk companies began printing photographs of disappeared children on their cartons. The images will exist in a new context. They will be given the opportunity to work on us in a new way. Already two of the children have been found. Without the camera, this outreach would be impossible. Like the airplane, the computer, and the nuclear warhead, the camera is the product of a technology that is catapulting us into the twenty-first century. It has become a basic tool in our communication with the world. Its images are a natural part of our evolution, just as the cave drawings of bison and antelopes were natural images to our ancient brothers and sisters. And whether or not its shutter opens and shuts on the lethal billowing form of a mushroom cloud, or on the squinting, squirming face of newborn child, is entirely up to us.

Works Cited

Danziger, James. *Interviews with Master Photographers*. New York, 1977.
Griffin, Susan. *Pornography and Silence*. New York. 1981.
Sontag, Susan. *On Photography*. New York. 1977.
San Jose Mercury News. April 4, 1985. p. B1.
San Jose Mercury News. January 2, 1986. p. 10A.

Lasers in the Modern Hospital
David Leonard

In manipulating style, clarity is your first objective, and one of the most difficult undertakings is to write about a complicated technical topic clearly. The following essay is part of a larger report on lasers. In order to communicate clearly, the writer has kept jargon to a minimum, controlled the length and shape of his sentences, used literal comparisons to help the readers envision the equipment and processes he describes, and employed graphic devices such as illustrations and subheadings. The result is a "user friendly" report—a report that makes difficult concepts accessible to the readers.

2.1 The Surgical Laser

2.1.1 *Surgical Lasers Defined*

Surgical lasers are medical instruments which use radiant energy to vaporize, coagulate, or photoradiate tissue. Consequently, the general term "laser surgery" involves any of these three laser applications.

Using a laser to vaporize tissue is specifically called laser surgery. In this application, a very fine, dense beam of radiant energy is converted to intense heat at the target tissue. The response is identical to water boiling; intracellular liquid vaporizes. Directing the beam along a path produces a fine line of vaporized cells: an incision. In this case, the surgical laser is like a scalpel except the blade is made of light instead of steel.

Using a laser to coagulate tissue is called photocoagulation. The process is similar to vaporization except that the thermal response is not as intense in photocoagulation. Before liquids can vaporize, protein rearrangements cause clotting. The same process occurs on a larger scale when an egg is cooked.

Using a laser in photoradiation is quite different from either vaporization or photocoagulation. Photoradiation therapy is a cancer treatment in which a nontoxic chemical (a hematoporphyrin derivative) acts selectively on malignant cells. Laser radiation reaching the chemical stimulates a toxic product (singlet oxygen). Thus, the laser treats a specific area with a local toxin.

Surgical lasers, then, are the tools that make possible these invaluable medical procedures.

2.1.2 Surgical Lasers Explained (process of laser action)

A surgeon wants a tool that will cut and ablate tissue structures, coagulate vessels, and simultaneously sterilize the process. The laser, because of three special qualities, meets the surgeon's requirements. The three qualities that differentiate laser radiation from conventional radiation sources are listed below and illustrated in Figure 1.

1. Single FREQUENCY. All laser radiation has the same frequency. This makes visible laser light MONOCHROMATIC. Some lasers produce invisible radiation; nevertheless, the beam is pure.

2. Temporal Coherence. All the wave fronts in a laser beam are in phase.

3. Spatial Coherence. The distance between waves in a laser beam remains virtually constant. This produces directed, or COLLIMATED, light as opposed to dispersed light.

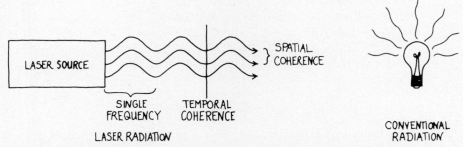

Figure 1. Special Qualities of Laser Radiation Are Not Found in Conventional Sources.

Pure frequency allows the surgeon to act on specific tissues. Temporal coherence allows the surgeon to deliver constant energy to the target tissue. Spatial coherence allows the surgeon to accurately focus the beam.

The process of laser action gives the laser these qualities. Although the laser beam is generated automatically within the laser device when it is turned on, a basic understanding of the process should give the surgeon added skill and confidence.

The basic process of laser action involves four steps:

1. Excitation

2. Spontaneous Emission

3. Stimulated Emission

4. Amplification

These steps all occur within the laser mechanism.

Step 1: Excitation

The first step is initiated when power is supplied. It is based on fundamental properties of matter.

In a normal state atoms exist as minute particles of matter, each with a nucleus and a specific number of electrons. These electrons assume definite energy levels. In the absence of external energy, the electrons assume the lowest possible energy level. However, when energy is supplied, electrons can take higher energy levels. The energy absorbed must exactly equal the difference in energy between levels; there are no partial steps. Electrons in elevated energy levels are called excited electrons. Thus, pumping energy into atoms excites electrons and initiates the excitation step.

Step 2: Spontaneous Emission

Usually within one-hundredth of a MICROSECOND an excited electron will regain a lower energy level. Since the atom has less energy after the transition than before, energy must have been released. The released energy is exactly equal to the energy gained during excitation. The energy is given off as a PHOTON, a minute particle of light. This process is called spontaneous emission.

All the photons spontaneously emitted by similar atoms have the same frequency. They travel in all directions, however. Therefore, spontaneous emission alone will not create a collimated beam.

Step 3: Stimulated Emission

The step most crucial to laser beam generation is stimulated emission. In this step a photon strikes an electron that is already excited. When this happens, the energy of the photon is not absorbed by the atom as in excitation. Instead, the atom simultaneously releases the energy of the photon and the energy it would have released by spontaneous emission. The result is two photons with equal frequency. Not only do they have equal frequencies, but they also travel in the same direction.

Step 4: Amplification

As photons produced by stimulated emission travel, they can strike other excited electrons. If the process continues, the number of photons traveling in the same direction with indentical frequency amplifies until a beam is produced.

Unless certain conditions exist, however, amplification cannot occur. Because excited electrons are very short-lived, a photon normally has little chance of striking one. The laser mechanism provides the necessary conditions.

Three basic components of the mechanism involved in the process of laser action are illustrated in Figure 2.

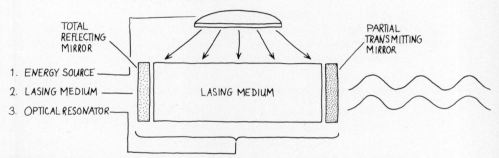

Figure 2. Three Basic Components of the Laser Mechanism Are Responsible for Laser Production.

The energy source pumps energy into the LASING MEDIUM and excites electrons. Enough energy must be supplied to keep more electrons excited than unexcited. This condition is called a POPULATION INVERSION.

With abundant excited electrons, amplification can proceed. Photons traveling along the axis of the optical resonator are reflected by the mirrors at each end. Then they travel back through the inverted population, amplifying the beam in their direction.

After sufficient amplification, part of the collimated beam passes through the partially reflecting mirror at one end of the optical resonator. The reflected beam travels back through the medium, stimulating enough photons to make up for the beam leaving the resonator. Thus, a sustained laser beam is produced.

Summary of Laser Action

To bring all the steps together, the process of laser action occurs as follows. The energy source pumps energy into the lasing medium. Electrons within the medium become excited and they form a population inversion. At this stage conditions for stimulated emission exist, and a beam amplifies along the axis of the optical resonator. Part of this beam passes through the partially reflecting mirror and is available to the surgeon. The process is described by the word *laser*; it is the acronym of Light Amplification by Stimulated Emission of Radiation.

That's Mr. Dills to You, Buddy!
Paul Anderson

Paul Anderson draws a cartoon strip for The Spartan Daily, *the student newspaper at San Jose State University. The following essay is his attempt to create a cartoon character. It is an exercise in which his attitude toward his subject and his relationship with his audience are extremely important; he must make fun of the character without being contemptuous, and cause the audience to be amused by the character while still making them like and respect him. His success in this exercise shows up in the tone and voice of the piece. The tone is light, wry, bemused, appropriate for that state of mind people are in when they read the newspaper comics, and the voice is self-effacing, the writer (cartoonist) in the background to such an extent that at points the voice actually becomes that of the character, Burse Dills.*

Burse Dills is a man, a big, big man, 285 pounds worth. Burse was born in, raised in, and is still one of the major pillars of Mazeville, Oklahoma (famous for Broomcorn). He reaches close to 6' 6" when standing up straight, with a thin crop of reddish-brown hair capping his always sunburned face and neck. He sports a dark brown mustache, the size and shape of a Baby Ruth bar, and has a jaw that sort of sweeps to one side, giving him the often prophetic look of a man who's about to inflict serious pain on one or more people. Burse is aware of how he looks to people in much the same way a large watch dog gets used to the respect he's treated with due to his mobility, mean looks, and mass; and Burse loves it. It's true respect, indeed, the respect he deserves. In actuality, Burse rarely gets into fights, but when he does, it's never really more than about 45 seconds of aerobics for him, partly because of his devastating strength, and partly because of his great arm span, which makes it almost impossible for whomever Burse doesn't like to even touch him. Sometimes he feels guilty about dislodging someone's bicuspids . . . till he remembers some Sunday school lesson which ended in a chorus of "Onward Christian Soldiers" or an old Popeye cartoon, and he feels better about the action; then he'll order another Lonestar in a bottle, always—hell, you can't break a can.

Burse is always seen driving his '71 Chevy Cheyenne 3/4 ton, purchased after his 9th grade graduation from Stillwater Chevrolet. He liked it because it was Sooner Crimson, and because he associated the name Cheyenne with the day his best friend got a driver's license and they drove to the World's Biggest Rodeo, in Cheyenne, Wyoming. This truck reminded Burse of long, high-speed, alcohol-induced excursions, so he bought it, cash, then installed a gun rack and the Magnavox "Auto 10" 8-track, which is the constant home of Merle Haggard's Hits, Vol. II; in fact, he's never pulled the half dusty, half shiny tape from the player; it just stops when he shuts off the ignition. Burse likes to drive around town, to work, and to bars in L-1 on the transmission gear selector; it really makes that big V8 scream and pop, especially when he slows down and the back pressure builds up and combusts in the Glass-pac mufflers, which are in fact anything but mufflers.

Once every two weeks, Burse goes to the Piggly Wiggly Supermarket, after he gets his haircut, to pick up any sundries not sold at Jay's Liquor. 15 Pop-n-fresh buttermilk biscuits in the tubes that pop when hit, and 15 tins of assorted gravies to ride on top for breakfast. Burse always eats biscuits and gravy for breakfast and always has; he's never asked himself if he really even likes 'em—he just eats 'em and knows he doesn't like oatmeal. Also in the brown grocery bag will be razor blades, shaving soap, T. P., canned corn meat, Home Pride split-top white bread, and always hidden in the bottom, 2 half gallons of pineapple sherbet, to be eaten a quart at a time. (For some reason he's always called it SHUR-BURT.)

Burse Dills lives in an old, one room farm house that he got when the company he works for, Ralston Purina, bought out the old farm which used to produce stock feeding corn (Broomcorn) and arranged a credit deal so Burse could purchase the house from them. It's a nice little place, good plumbing, and it has its own well, and an oversized sewer tank. To this day it's never filled. He touched up the place himself. Over the fireplace is an old oil painting of Chief Joseph, left there when he moved in and nearly taken down, but instead Burse hung below it his neon Falstaff light, which he got from a bar when they stopped serving it and started serving Olympia instead. The neon light gives the savage face a ghostly glow; that glow, Burse tells neighbor kids, is an omen. Also in the living room/bedroom, hangs Burse's trout net and an American Savings calendar from the previous owner's better days. On the calendar are egg-shaped pictures of the Presidents, from Washington to Johnson. On the end table, next to the sleeper sofa, on top of the C. B. scanner, is a "Good to the Last Drop" can with a grayish colored marijuana plant growing in it. Burse doesn't smoke pot, nor do his close friends, but he couldn't resist the fun of having it under his roof, thereby breaking the law by really not doing anything. The arrangements for the house were made by the Southwestern States Feed Division manager of Ralston Purina, a good friend of Burse's, so he doesn't even have to make payments. They're automatically taken from one of his pay checks each month, no fuss.

Burse's job at Ralston Purina entails lifting 130 pound bales of hay onto flatbed trucks or box cars during the spring, summer, and fall, and then during the winter he works a grain dryer; in the winter Burse often will gain as much as 30 pounds, but he quickly loses it again come the warm months. You might think a job of this nature would leave Burse with a low man on the totem pole or groundling status with his fellow employees, but instead, he's held quite highly in esteem—it's hard work; it needs to be done; and Burse does it well without complaining. Once for lunch he drank 9 pitchers of beer; by the time Burse returned, he was a bit intoxicated and accidently missed the truck with a hay bale, hitting a fellow worker, breaking a collar bone and three ribs. Other than that, Burse has a spotless record of employment and thus brings home a good wage.

Burse, like most people, thinks he has or could come up with the answers to most problems facing the world. A year ago he was seeing a girl whom he liked okay; and being a gentleman, he'd often bring her gifts, Whitman candies, flowers, Mrs. Renfro's Chili-Chow-Chow, and such. When he found out she was flirting around with some funny-boy where she worked, he was hard pressed to do something, but what? His friends told him this kind of problem had faced people in love since the beginning of time, and that there's no rational solution short of crackin' the guy a good shot up-side the head—course that went without saying, but what about her? It took a while, but just like he thought he would, Burse came up with a solution! He sent her a beautifully wrapped package special delivery so that she would think herself the object of an affection bidding war; inside that package, which cost him almost $10.00 to send just across town, was a 25-pound salt lick he'd gotten from work. He delighted in his triumph in the ending of the relationship, and reinforced his own faith in himself as a great problem solver.

A long time ago, Burse saw an episode of Wild Kindgom in which Marlin and Jim were working with sharks. Marlin said something to the effect of sharks being unchanged for 72 million years, then something about how man, unlike the shark, needs protection. This ultimately ended in an insurance ad, but the blurb about the sharks stuck with Burse. He views himself as Marlin views sharks, "an animal perfectly suited for its environment."

Now at the end of a long day of good, hard work, a ghostly Indian chief stares out across the great plains, across the living room/bedroom of the roughest man in Mazeville, who's toying with a battle against sleep—listening to the evening news and farm report but not hearing it; Burse Dills thinks to himself how different the world would be if he were in charge. How right it'd be. He peers down at the large, thick salad bowl whose insides are coated with the cool, white remnants of a Burse-sized helping (seven servings according to the box) of pineapple shur-burt. He thinks to himself that it looks like a snow-filled valley, and in the summer that snow would melt and eventually make it to the ocean . . . and there waiting for 72 million years, unchanged, the man in charge, the shark waits. "The Burse Dills of the water world" he says to himself.

Then, just prior to slipping off to sleep, he looks up at Chief Joseph and growls "That's Mr. Dills to you, buddy."

EXERCISES:

1. Here's your chance to write like Ernest Hemingway, in one easy lesson.

The following passage is the beginning of his short story, "In Another Country."

> In the fall the war was always there, but we did not go to it anymore. It was cold in the fall in Milan and the dark came very early. Then the electric lights came on, and it was pleasant along the streets looking in the windows. There was much game hanging outside the shops, and the snow powdered in the fur of the foxes and the wind blew their tails. The deer hung stiff and heavy and empty, and small birds blew in the wind and the wind turned their feathers. It was a cold fall and the wind came down from the mountains.
>
> We were all at the hospital every afternoon, and there were different ways of walking across town through the dusk to the hospital. Two of the ways were alongside canals, but they were very long. Always, though, you crossed a bridge across a canal to enter the hospital. There was a choice of three bridges. On one of them a woman sold chestnuts. It was warm, standing in front of her charcoal fire, and the chestnuts were warm afterward in your pocket. The hospital was very old and very beautiful, and you entered through a gate and walked across a courtyard and out a gate on the other side. There were usually funerals starting from the courtyard. Beyond the old hospital were the new brick pavilions, and there we met every afternoon and were all very polite and interested in what was the matter, and sat in the machines that were to make so much difference.

Do a close imitation of this passage, changing the topic to a scene with which you are familiar, but keeping the structure of each sentence as similar as you can to the sentences in the passage. For instance, your imitation might begin: "In the morning the rain was always there, but we had to go out in it anyway. It was wet in the morning in Seattle and the rain came down constantly. Then the engines of the cars came to life . . ." Get the idea? After you have finished your passage, read it aloud. Does it reproduce the tone and voice of the Hemingway passage? What effect has the form had on your selection of detail?

2. Now let's try Chandler, only this time see if you can apply abstract principles and reproduce the style without so much guidance. Write a descriptive sketch at least one page long in the voice of the hard-boiled private eye. Remember, some of the characteristics of the voice are first-person narration; use of "you" to bring the readers into the scene; short, matter-of-fact sentences and fragments; detailed description; exaggerated similes that call up images of the gritty side of life like smoky pool halls and cigarette butts on the floor. Make your character tough, cynical, worldly wise, with a wry, self-deprecating sense of humor. After you have finished your paragraph, read it aloud. Does it sound tough enough? What effect has your attempt to recreate the voice had on your selection of detail?

3. Take a medium length sentence from your own writing, around ten to 15 words long. Choose a sentence if possible that is awkward or unclear, one that you're pretty sure can be improved. Write 25 different variations of the sentence, trying to keep the content and the word choice

as unchanged as you can while varying the order of elements, the ways they are combined, and the grammatical forms they take. The example on pages 142–143 will give you a better idea of how to proceed. After you have written all 25 sentences, answer the following:

    a. Which has the slowest pace?

    b. Which has the fastest pace?

    c. Which has the most regular rhythm?

    d. Which has the most irregular rhythm?

    e. Which variations are most clear? Are any unclear?

    f. Which fits best in the piece of writing you took it from?

4. Now experiment with variations of diction. Write a sentence, 15 to 20 words long, in the jargon of some professional or recreational group with which you are familiar. Use as much jargon as possible, and assume that the audience for the sentence is composed of insiders who understand the jargon.

    a. Rewrite the sentence so that it says the same thing but the jargon is completely eliminated.

    b. Write the sentence again, including as much of the jargon as you can while still making the meaning clear to outsiders.

    c. Write the most abstract version of the sentence *and* the most concrete one that you can write.

    d. Write the most general version of the sentence *and* the most specific one that you can write.

5. Describe an ordinary object like a pencil sharpener or a typewriter. Assume that your readers have never seen or heard of the object before, but are otherwise fully informed about your culture. Use as many comparisons with familiar objects as you can to help the audience envision what you are describing.

6. Complete the following sentences with vivid, imaginative comparisons. Complete each sentence three or four different ways:

    a. If the frightened elephant came our way, we'd have about as much chance as . . .

    b. The shell of the burned mansion loomed up out of the dark like . . .

    c. Her laughter rose above the chatter of the party like . . .

    d. He paused just inside the door as if . . .

    e. The rain tore at her exposed hands and face like . . .

f. He leered at the waitresses like . . .

g. The car sat in the tall weeds behind the barn like . . .

h. In the twilight, the lights of the city came on one by one as if . . .

What additional imagery do your comparisons bring into the sentences. How might these images affect the readers' emotions? Which version of each sentence is your best? Why?

Chapter Six

Mechanics

In this chapter, I want to review the mechanics of sentences. "Mechanics" may seem a strange word to apply to something as natural as language, but consider the sense in which we more commonly use the word—to name people who repair mechanisms, especially automobiles. When a mechanic repairs a car, she puts the parts back in working order so that each part does its separate job and all parts work together smoothly. Well, sentences, too, are made up of parts, and if a sentence is to work efficiently the parts must be assembled correctly and kept in good repair. Thus, at some point in the writing process, all writers must become mechanics, tinkering with the machinery that conveys their ideas.

To help you become a more confident and competent mechanic, I am going to look first at the basic parts from which all sentences are built; then at some of the devices that connect these parts; and finally at some of the more common ways sentences can break down. Let me start with the most basic parts.

A Short Course in Sentence Structure

Sentences are complicated things. I cannot hope to explain, and I cannot expect you to learn, all there is to know about them in a few pages. Really mastering the complexities of sentences requires either a long and repeated exposure to good writing, or much rigorous practice in analyzing their parts and practicing how to assemble them. What I can offer you here, though, is a refresher course in the things that are most important to know—particularly in the terms that name basic parts of sentences. You have probably learned many of these terms at one time or another, but cobwebs may have grown over your memories of just what some mean. I want to take a little time to dust some of them off.

First, consider the core, the engine, of any sentence. A sentence *is* a sentence because it combines two essential parts—a *subject* and a *verb*. The subject is the main person, place, or thing the sentence says something about. The verb makes a statement about that subject; it does the saying. Many sentences also contain a third basic part, a *complement*. Complements are nouns or adjectives that complete the statement made by the verb. Other parts of the sentence may add information about these parts, or connect parts, but these three, and especially the subject and verb, convey the essential message.

Consider these sentences. I've underlined the subjects once and the verbs twice to help identify them:

> Melissa, smiling slyly, stole into the pantry.
> She grabbed a cabbage, and then she hurried into the kitchen with it.
> When the odor of cooking cabbage wafted into the next room, Brenda finally abandoned the television and left the house.
> Melissa loves cabbage and hates television.

As you can see, a subject may have several verbs, and a verb several subjects, though one of each is all that is required.

Subjects and verbs are combined to form two larger parts: *independent clauses* and *dependent clauses*. All sentences are made out of some arrangement of these two larger structures. If you're not already famliar with these terms, study the definitions below carefully before you go on. If you understand these, I promise that everything else having to do with grammar will be much easier.

An *independent clause* is a group of words containing one subject-verb relationship and making a complete statement by itself.

Examples:

> The crows have arrived.
> They circle the pine tree, cawing loudly, and land.
> In the rain, they are black and shiny.

A *dependent clause* also has one complete subject-verb relationship, but unlike an independent clause it cannot stand by itself. Instead, a dependent clause must be connected to an independent clause.

Examples:

> when the crows leave
> if they do not nest
> as they swoop and swirl around the tree

Dependent clauses are recognizable because they begin with *subordinators*, among which these are the most common:

as	if	because
when	since	although
while	who	that
where	how	until
why	though	whenever

Of course, both kinds of clauses usually contain more than just their subjects, verbs, and complements. If we could work only with those three elements, we'd have to make a whole new statement for every little piece of information we wanted to convey. We'd have to say: "Malcolm is mean." "Malcolm dislikes me." "Malcolm's dislike is intense." "Malcolm is a cat." "Emily owns Malcolm." "Malcolm is grey." Instead, of course, we simply say: "Emily's grey cat, Malcolm, dislikes me intensely." What we've done when we write or speak this last sentence is to take one independent clause, "Malcolm dislikes me," and add *modifiers* to include all the other information we'd like to get across.

Modifiers may be single words, phrases, or whole new dependent clauses. They attach to a sentence in order to add meaning to the basic statement made by a clause. To illustrate, let me begin with a simple, independent clause and add different types of modifiers to it, gradually building up a more elaborate structure as I go. Here's a beginning:

The fire danced.

It's not much of a sentence, is it? Reading it, we don't know anything about the fire, or the dancing. To begin modifying the sentence and making it more meaningful, I can add single word modifiers: *adjectives* and *adverbs*. Adjectives modify nouns in the clause; adverbs modify anything else, including verbs. I'll add one of each:

The *flickering* fire danced *lazily*.

"Flickering" modifies "fire"—it is an adjective. "Lazily" modifies "danced"—it is an adverb.

But we still don't know much about the fire, and we need more than just single word modifiers to build up a more interesting and informative statement. Most sentences include larger structures, the phrase modifiers: *prepositional phrases*, *participial phrases* and, more rarely, *infinitive phrases*. Please bear with me through a few more definitions; they are the last I'll have to impose on you for a while:

Prepositional Phrases combine a preposition, one or more nouns, and any adjectives that may modify the nouns. Examples: *in* the book, *around* the corner, *through* the long night, *behind* the barn, *with* his consent, *out of* order.

Participial Phrases are built around participles—"ing," "ed," or "en" words that come from verbs, and look like verbs, but are really adjectives. These phrases may themselves have other modifers, including both of the other kinds of phrases, imbedded within them. Examples: *arriving* late, *scared* silly, *seeming* pleased, slowly *twisting* in the wind, *sunken* in the sand.

Infinitive Phrases get their name from the infinitive form of verbs, the "to" form—to eat, to dream, to rejoice, and so on. But infinitives and the phrases built around them are modifiers or nouns, not verbs. Examples: *to get* some rest, *to understand* her point, suddenly *to realize* the truth, *to satisfy* her curiosity.

Using phrase modifiers, I can generate a more informative and interesting sentence. I'll add one phrase modifier of each type.

Moving slowly to gather strength, the flickering fire danced lazily *along the roof-tops*.

Now the sentence begins to build real meaning. The first addition is a participial phrase, the second an infinitive phrase, the third a prepositional phrase. Prepositional phrases are particularly valuable building blocks, by far the most common type of phrase in most sentences. Let me add two more to illustrate:

Moving slowly to gather strength, the flickering fire danced lazily along the roof-tops, *down narrow alleys, around empty courtyards*.

Fully-developed sentences often contain another kind of modifier, whole dependent clauses. Dependent clauses, often containing smaller modifiers themselves, may act as adjectives or adverbs, modifying some part of an independent clause or another dependent clause. So far, my on-going example has only one, heavily modified, independent clause. I'll modify it further by adding a dependent clause:

Moving slowly to gather strength, the flickering fire danced lazily along the roof-tops, down narrow alleys, around empty courtyards, *while Nero stood, with fiddle in hand, on Palatine Hill*.

The dependent clause, beginning with the subordinator "while," acts as an adverb, modifying the verb in the independent clause, "danced." Taken together as a unit, the clause adds information about when and under what conditions the dancing took place. Notice that the dependent clause itself contains several prepositional phrases.

There are more parts to sentences, parts I have not mentioned—articles, coordinating conjunctions, and so on. But if you understand the elements I've discussed so far you should have no trouble with the things I'd like to tell you about punctuation and mechanical errors in this chapter. If I need to bring up any new terms, I'll pause to define them as I go along. If you do still feel uncertain, though, about terms such as "dependent clause" or "prepositional phrase," you may want to consult a larger handbook or your instructor for a more thorough review before you go on.

A Short Course in Punctuation

In Chapter Four, I talked about "ducks and blazes," the trailmarkers experienced writers use to guide their readers through and between paragraphs. Punctuation marks provide another set of guideposts, sometimes signaling the division between one sentence and another, sometimes forging the links between the elements of a single sentence, always flashing signals to the readers about how one part relates to another. Some punctuation marks link whole sentences; some work within sentences; some do both. I'll start by discussing those that can stand between complete sentences.

PUNCTUATION BETWEEN SENTENCES

The period: The surest, most reliable, and most obvious way to start and stop sentences is, of course, simply to plop a period down in front of your readers. From the readers' perspective, a period is something like a stop sign—final, absolute, insistant. But encountering periods too often, readers may feel like drivers coming to a new stop sign at every corner. They may want to get on with things. They may grow weary. They may become annoyed. They may stop reading. My advice is to avoid annoying them with too many periods in too short a passage; find alternative ways to link your ideas if you find that periods are popping up like prairie dogs in your prose.

The exclamation point: If a period is a stop sign, an exclamation point is a flashing, clanging railroad sign. It simply calls too much attention to itself to be useful very often.

I am often tempted to slap an exclamation point at the end of a sentence in which I've expressed some strong emotion. By the end of such a sentence I'm often angry, or ecstatic, or otherwise worked up about my subject. But later, when I revise, I almost always forgo the exclamation point, recalling that exclamation points have the effect of raising one's voice to the yelling point and that nobody likes to be yelled at.

If you want to find more subtle ways to express strong emotions, look back at Chapter Five. Careful choice of words—taking their connotations especially into consideration—and deliberate use of other stylistic devices such as repetition and parallelism are far more effective than exclamation points for moving readers without insulting them.

The semicolon: Like periods, semicolons usually stand between complete sentences. But they are more like yield signs than stop signs; they allow readers to glide into the next sentence after a pause, without quite stopping.

Because of this softer effect, semicolons are wonderfully useful, and many novice writers become infatuated with them, peppering their papers with them indiscriminately. Unfortunately, like all punctuation marks, semicolons lose their effectiveness if over used. I would reserve semicolons for three situations between sentences:

1. When the idea in the second sentence is closely related to the idea in the first sentence and you want to knit the two ideas together rather than separating them as a period would:

It is an illusion to think that there is anything fragile about the life of the earth; surely this is the toughest membrane imaginable in the universe, opaque to probability, impermeable to death.

Lewis Thomas

The cat walks quietly at all times; she seems to think her life depends on it.

Often, when we watch a comedy, we laugh at the characters' foolishness; nearly as often, we are laughing at ourselves.

2. When you want to balance two opposing ideas, using the semicolon like the apex a teeter-totter totters on. You can accentuate the balancing effect by expressing both sentences in parallel structures:

She was in essence a lady; she was in influence a leader.

Wilma Dykeman

3. When you begin the second sentence with a *conjunctive adverb*, such as "however," "nevertheless," "consequently," "therefore," "moreover," "thus," or "then":

The governor slashed the budget; therefore, there will be fewer services this year.

The colon: A colon makes a promise: it reassures readers that some kind of explanation or elaboration lies just ahead. Coming across a colon, readers will interpret it to mean, "Hold on a moment; I'm about to clarify what I've said here." Colons are particularly useful in academic writing, where they often signal the movement from a general or abstract statement to a more specific, clarifying statement. Notice that you need not capitalize (though you may) the first word of a sentence that follows a colon:

The cost of redevelopment would be too high: even at current prices the project budget would exceed seventy million dollars.

We should credit the sky for what it is: for sheer size and perfection of function, it is far and away the grandest product of collaboration in all of nature.

Lewis Thomas

Faulkner's sentences are more than just long: They are intricate and convoluted, recreating the disjointed, piecemeal way in which we experience the world.

In formal, academic writing the colon may also introduce a quotation—especially a longer passage—or any piece of writing used as an example. Here, for economy's sake, is a shorter quote. Notice that you *do* capitalize if the quotation begins a sentence:

Goethe said something I keep close to my heart: "It is the property of true genius to disturb all settled ideas."

The dash: We English teachers often fret when our students join sentences with dashes. I suppose our objections come partly from a suspicion that students who resort to dashes simply don't know of a more legitimate way to connect certain kinds of sentences. Then, too, a dash between two sentences is often imprecise: It doesn't really signal very clearly how the first sentence relates to the second. Still, you should know that at times nothing works quite so well as a dash to lead from a long, complex sentence, like this one, into a short emphatic one—it just seems natural.

PUNCTUATION WITHIN SENTENCES

The comma: Inexperienced writers often take the comma to be a sort of all-purpose punctuation mark, something to put down whenever something seems needed. The result, unfortunately, is prose that is so halting, so plagued by small pauses, that getting through it is like driving down a street with too many speed bumps.

I recommend that you foster a conservative attitude where commas are concerned; save them for occasions when you know of a particular reason for using them. There are fewer such occasions than you might suspect. Only six situations call absolutely for commas.

1. *Between Items in a Series.* Most people naturally separate the parts of a list or series with commas, but many wonder whether they need to tack on the final item with "and" or whether they need to put one last comma before that "and." The answer to both questions is, "It's up to you." Usually, the best practice—to preclude confusion on your readers' part—is to provide the "and," complete with a comma. To give you a sense of the options, though, I've included some examples here that omit one or the other for stylistic reasons.

> He is an honorable, obstinate, truthful, high-spirited, intensely prejudiced, perfectly unreasonable man.
>
> *Charles Dickens*

> In the blue light ships were blue dark images, masked men, men with silvery faces, men with blue stars for eyes, men with carved golden ears, men with tinfoil cheeks and ruby-studded lips, men with arms folded, men following him, Martian men.
>
> *Ray Bradbury*

> Is she beautiful, clever, rich, splendid, universally intelligent and unprecedentedly virtuous? It's only on those conditions that I care to make her acquaintance.
>
> *Henry James*

> I knew that she would be there, that she would be happy, and that she would want to buy me dinner.

> The elephant rose steadily, silently.

Notice in the last example that the series consists of only two parts, two separate adverbs. A series is born the moment you place two or more equal structures next to each other.

2. *After Introductory Phrases or Clauses.* A comma after introductory re-marks has the effect of telling your readers: "Everything up to this point has been preparatory; pay attention now to the main idea in my inde-pendent clause." If the introductory phrasing is very short, you might omit the comma, but as the introduction grows longer the need for the comma grows greater. Sometimes you may want to pile a series of phrases or clauses up in front of your main idea—the first commas separating the items in the series, the last announcing the end of the introduction.

> Setting out in this world, a child feels so indelible.
>
> *Eudora Welty*

> If he had been a smaller man and more quietly dressed, I might have thought he was going to pull a stick-up.
>
> *Raymond Chandler*

> On Sunday afternoon, when the prune orchard was dotted with people from the city who had come down to pick their own fruit, and Tom and the boys were out distributing ladders and pails and weighing up baskets and keeping the unpracticed pickers from breaking down limbs, Janet took a cool limeade in to Grandma and found her gone.
>
> *Wallace Stegner.*

3. *Before a Coordinating Conjunction That Joins Two Independent Clauses.* The coordinating conjunctions are few and easily recognizable:

for	but
and	or
nor	yet
	so

When a conjunction stands between complete sentences, each with its own independent clause, it is preceded by a comma. Readers react to the com-bination of a comma and a conjunction as they would to a period: They take what has come before to be one sentence and expect another to com-mence at this point. Only if both sentences are so short that the readers can take them in with a glance should you consider omitting the comma.

> On the porch stood one lonely wooden rocker, and the afternoon breeze made the unpruned shoots of last year's poinsettias tap-tap against the cracked stucco wall.
>
> *Raymond Chandler*

> My first real friend was a girl who lived down the street, and no two such opposite girls were ever so close.
>
> *Wendy Hanabusa*

> Every thinking person fears nuclear war, and every technological state plans for it. Everyone knows it is madness, and every nation has an excuse.
>
> *Carl Sagan*

Have you seen Cody at work this week, or has he begun his vacation to California and Oregon?

Notice in the last example that the final conjunction, "and," joins two nouns, not two independent clauses, so it takes no comma.

4. *Around Nonessential Interrupters.* In general, any kind of phrasing that intrudes into the structure of a sentence, like this for example, ought to be set off with a comma before and after the interruption. Example:

> The awful fight for money, into which we are all forced, hurts our good nature more than we can bear.
>
> *D. H. Lawrence*

The first comma announces the beginning of an interruption; the second announces the ending. Unfortunately, though, punctuating interrupters isn't quite that easy.

What I didn't tell you about modifiers earlier, in "A Short Course in Sentence Structure," is that—whether they are single words, phrases, or whole dependent clauses—modifiers come in two varieties: *essential* and *nonessential*. If the information a modifier adds to the sentence is necessary to define something in the larger sentence, it is essential and cannot be set off with commas; but if the information is not necessary to define some other term in the sentence, the modifier is nonessential and can be set off with commas. Consider some more examples. I've italicized the modifiers in both sentences.

Essential:
The woman *wearing a frumpy hat* stepped onto the dance floor.

Nonessential:
Thelma, *wearing a frumpy hat*, stepped onto the dance floor.

In the first sentence, the information "wearing a frumpy hat" defines whom the writer means by "the woman"; it identifies one particular woman out of many. To put commas around it would imply that the information was nonessential, that it could be removed from the sentence. But if it were removed, we could not know what woman was meant, and so there can be no commas even though the phrase interrupts the sentence.

In the second sentence, the modifying phrase merely adds extra information about an element that has already been adequately defined, "Thelma." Since the phrase could be removed without changing the essential meaning of the sentence, and since it is an interrupter, commas are in order.

Here are some more nonessential interrupters, some of them containing internal commas to separate parts of a series:

> And the children, silent and white, with a kind of locked obstinancy, in sheepskins and lumberjackets, stood beside her.
>
> *Saul Bellow*

Her bicycle, which had stood in the rain all winter, grew a red coat of rust.

One half of the Earthworm, looking like a great, thick, juicy, pink sausage, lay innocently in the sun for all to see.

Roald Dahl

5. *To Add on Deliberate Afterthoughts.* Often you will want to string a sentence out, adding more modifiers as you develop your idea, elaborating the main point. So long as the new elements are not whole new sentences and do not contain essential, defining information, you can attach these additions with commas. Though commas are not absolutely required here, they are useful for slowing your readers down and parceling out your information:

There was still daylight, shining softly and with a tarnish, like the lining of a shell.

James Agee

John Chapman was sitting alone in the bank, peeling an apple carefully, the unbroken spiral hanging like a shaving as he turned the fruit.

Wallace Stegner

Often, the information will form a series of items:

Don Antonio was a large man, heavy, full at the waist, a trifle bald, and very slow at speech.

Willa Cather

I was in heaven among the other campers, spending time mucking out stalls, cooking over wood fires, taking ice-cold showers under a garden hose in a little clearing draped with canvas for privacy, and sharing a tent for four with six other girls.

Karen Smail

6. *To Attach Short or Informal Quotations to Your Own Sentence.* In formal writing, quotations—especially long ones—are sometimes introduced with a colon, but a comma will suffice in most other situations. In everyday dialogue, the comma moves readers both into and out of quoted material:

She stared in amazement and gasped, "How *could* you?"

Kathleen Lynch

"*Bandidos*," she said with a surly, unnecessary vigor.

Truman Capote

"You must not tell anyone," my mother said, "what I am about to tell you."

Maxine Hong Kingston

The semicolon: Semicolons ordinarily join two complete sentences; they are seldom found within a single sentence. But there are, in fact, at least two situations in which a semicolon has a legitimate place inside a sentence. Remembering that semicolons are not simply strong commas; that they, like periods, will at first glance seem to your readers to mark the end of the sentence; and that you ought, therefore, to use them within sentences only very cautiously, consider these options for using semicolons within sentences:

1. *Before a Coordinating Conjunction, to Provide a More Emphatic Break between Two Independent Clauses Than a Comma and Conjunction Would Produce but a Less Emphatic Break Than a Period.* The effect is to slow down but not quite stop your readers, and in doing so to call unusual attention to the conjunction.

> Pure poetry is pure experiment; and it is not strange that nine-tenths of it should be pure failure.
>
> *George Santayana*

2. *To Separate Items in a List When the Items Themselves Contain Internal Commas.* If you were to connect parts containing commas with still more commas, the readers might well become confused about which commas worked within an item and which separated the items.

> I do not mean that there are not significant wrongs to be righted; law suits to be pressed; programs to be funded; laws to be passed, changed, or implemented; amendments to be ratified.
>
> *Nancy Heifferon*

> Now that I can have her only in memory, I see my grandmother in the several postures that were peculiar to her: standing at the wood stove on a winter morning and turning meat in a great iron skillet; sitting at the south window, bent above her beadwork, and afterwards, when her vision failed, looking down for a long time into the fold of her hands; going out upon a cane, very slowly as she did when the weight of age came upon her; praying.
>
> *N. Scott Momaday*

The colon: A colon, as we've seen, always signals some kind of explanation or elaboration to come, but that explanation or elaboration does not always take the form of a complete sentence. The beauty, in fact, of the colon is that it can attach any sort of illuminating material onto the end of a sentence: a list, a phrase, a dependent clause, or some combination of these. Here are some of the more common uses of the colon within sentences. To some extent, you'll find that they overlap:

1. *To Introduce a List.*

> Street sounds were those of human voices: criers of news and official announcements, shopkeepers in their doorways and itinerant vendors crying fresh eggs, charcoal at a penny a sack, candlewicks "brighter than the stars," cakes and waffles, mushrooms, hot baths.
>
> *Barbara Tuchman*

2. *To Introduce Examples.*

Thinking clearly is a conscious act that the writer must force upon himself, just as if he were embarking on any other project that requires logic: adding up a laundry list or doing an algebra problem.

William Zinsser

3. *To Add a Definition or Clarification.*

Spenser's *The Shepheardes Calendar* consists of a series of eclogues: formal pastoral poems in the Greek tradition.

The parenthesis: Parentheses wedge information suddenly and rather conspicuously into a sentence. Like the commas surrounding an interrupter, they announce that the sentence has been suspended (by the first parenthesis) until further notice (from the second). Parentheses, though, call more attention to themselves and the interruptions they enclose than do commas, and because of this, I suggest you use them sparingly; they will distract and confuse your readers if allowed to disrupt too many sentences.

Parentheses may set off a short definition, a lengthy explanation, several examples, a casual aside, an emotional response, an informal footnote, or nearly anything else you might want to interject in a sentence. They may enclose only a single word or several sentences, and this sometimes leads to confusion about how to use other kinds of punctuation within and around them. Don't put any sort of punctuation immediately before the opening parenthesis. Instead, place whatever punctuation you might need to end a clause behind and outside the parentheses (like the semicolon here); on the other hand, if the parentheses contain one or more whole sentences, place any punctuation applying to the sentence(s) inside the parentheses. (Let's see. How can I illustrate this?)

The examples below should give you some idea of the range of possibilities opened by parentheses:

1. *For a Definition.*

The historian has the comfort of knowing that man (meaning, here and hereafter, the species, not the sex) is always capable of his worst; has indulged in it, painfully struggled up from it, slid back, and gone on again.

Barbara Tuchman

2. *For Examples.*

Yet we do find writers of real stature writing literature in any category: spy and detective novels (Chandler), murder mysteries (Robbe-Grillet), gothic romances (Murdoch), fantasies (Calvino), fairy tales (Barth), and science fiction (Barth).

Annie Dillard

3. *For an Explanation*

I had brought the clothesline thinking I'd have to tie him (the pig weighed more than a hundred pounds), but we never used it.

E. B. White

4. *For an Aside.*

In his new role the old person will find that he is tempted by new vices, that he receives new compensations (not so widely known), and that he may possibly achieve new virtues.

Malcolm Cowley

5. *For an Informal Reference Note.*

He has joined a select minority that numbers, in this country, 4,842,000 persons (according to Census Bureau estimates for 1977), or about two percent of the American population.

Malcolm Cowley

The dash: The dash often seems to be the mockingbird of punctuation marks, imitating at various times the colon, the parenthesis, and the comma. But it is louder and bolder than any of these, always drawing extraordinary attention to the words it sets off from the rest of a sentence. It also tends to be slightly chatty, lightening the tone and lessening the formality of your prose.

Dashes—which are typed by placing two hyphens back to back—are most useful in three situations that may arise within sentences:

1. *Around Interrupters, Especially Those Containing Commas or Those That Break Dramatically into Your Sentence.* Dashes generally offer a better choice than either commas or parentheses for punctuating interruptions if the interrupting element itself contains commas or if it represents a radical intrusion into your sentence.

The manager—a fat, loose-lipped man—guffawed.

Virginia Woolf

One of the boys, a gleaming, curly-haired, golden-brown type—the color of his mother's fried chicken—is carrying a guitar.

James Baldwin

In all the arts, coherence in a work means that the relationship among parts—the jointed framework of the whole—is actual, solid, nailed down.

Annie Dillard

2. *Before a Summation, Restatement, or Clarification.* Here the dash acts like an informal colon—attaching an explanation of some kind to the end of a sentence.

He has never been able to understand the monumental purity of the Winstead's hamburger—no seeds planted on the buns, no strong sauce that might keep the exquisite flavor of the meat from dominating, no showy meat-thickness that is the downfall of most hamburgers.

Calvin Trillin

Many animals, for reasons having nothing to do with the inspiration of affection in humans, possess some features also shared by human babies but not by human adults—large eyes and a bulging forehead with retreating chin, in particular.

Steven Jay Gould

3. *Before a Final Point, to Underscore It.* At times you may want to save an important piece of information until the end of sentence and drop it there suddenly. A dash leading into the last part of any sentence, and particularly a long sentence, will focus your readers' attention on whatever you say there and dramatize the ending—providing the proverbial bombshell.

The Manhattan Telephone Directory has 776,300 names, of which 3,316 are Smith, 2,835 are Brown, 2,444 are Williams, 2,070 are Cohen—and one is Mike Krasilovsky.

Gay Talese

The quotation mark: Quotation marks themselves are easy enough to use. They allow you to inject the wording of another writer into your own writing, indicating where that other writer's words begin and end. The only problem you might encounter using quotation marks would have to do with distinguishing between direct and indirect quotations. The first require quotation marks, but the second don't. Let me illustrate:

1. *A Direct Quotation:*

According to Professor Waugmump: "The image, in all its intricate detail, expresses the poet's deep longing for a return to a pre-natal state."

2. *An Indirect Quotation:*

Professor Waugmump argues that the image conveys the poet's desire to return to the womb.

In the first instance, the good professor's exact—and rather pompous—wording is brought to the page, and so it must be acknowledged with the quotation marks; in the second, the writer has simply reported the essence of the idea, paraphrasing the quotation but not using Waugmump's wording, so there is no need for quotation marks.

A more frequent source of confusion has to do with how to combine other sorts of punctuation marks with quotation marks. What do you do, for instance, if you want to interrupt your own sentence with a quotation and then resume the original thought? Where do you put a period at the end of a quotation, inside the quotation marks or outside? What if the quote is a statement, but your own sentence asks a question? There are really only two kinds of problems here: how to get into a quote, and how to get back out.

Getting into a quotation. If a quotation is short, and the writing situation is informal, you may be able simply to introduce the quotation with an expression such as "he said" or "the writer concludes." If the expression leads grammatically into the quote you don't need any punctuation at all; if it doesn't, use a comma.

> *Newsweek* reports that ". . . education in America, despite many obstacles, seems to be making a comeback."
>
> According to *Newsweek*, ". . . education in America, despite many obstacles, seems to be making a comeback."

If the quote is longer than a single sentence, however, or if the writing situation is especially formal, use a colon. With a colon serving as introduction, you need not worry about whether your own sentence leads grammatically into the quotation:

> In 1985, the senator assured us that the economy would continue to prosper throughout the 1980's: "Inflation will subside, interest rates will remain moderate, and the GNP will grow at a steady pace until after 1992. . . ."

Notice that in the *Newsweek* examples the quotation begins with an *ellipsis*, three dots to show that the quoted sentence has been picked up in midstream; the ellipsis stands in for the words that have been omitted from the beginning of the sentence. In the last example, you'll find another ellipsis at the end of the sentence, indicating that the remainder of the sentence has been omitted from the quote. But if you look more closely, you'll find four dots this time. The first is the period ending the sentence.

In the case of still longer quotations—opinions vary as to how much longer, but let's say more than two typed lines of verse or four of prose—you will want to do something quite different. Instead of enclosing the quoted material in quotation marks, *offset* it from the rest of your text in the following way:

1. End your own text with a colon.

2. Triple-space (instead of the usual double-spacing) to leave white space before the quotation.

3. Indent the entire passage 10 spaces from the left margin. If the passage consists of more than one paragraph, indent the first line of each new paragraph an additional three spaces.

4. Type the passage double-spaced, without enclosing it in quotation marks.

5. Triple-space again to leave more white space and return to the original left margin before your own text resumes.

Getting out of a quotation. In the case of an offset quote, simply conclude the quote with whatever punctuation ends the original passage (or with an ellipsis if you want to omit part of the last sentence), return to your original margins, and continue with your essay.

In the case of shorter quotes, however, there is more potential for confusion. The following, rather elaborate, set of rules has evolved for punctuating within and around quotation marks. If you find the rules annoyingly complex, rest assured that many generations of college writers have shared (and I, too, share) your sentiments:

1. Always place any necessary *periods* and *commas inside* closing quotation marks, whether they are part of the original quote or not.

   Emerson tells us that "Nothing is at last sacred but the integrity of your own mind," but many would argue that his view puts too much emphasis on the self.

   "Nothing," according to Emerson, "is at last sacred but the integrity of your own mind."

2. Place *semicolons* and *colons outside* quotation marks.

   Emerson writes, "Nothing is at last sacred but the integrity of your own mind"; many, though, disagree.

3. Place *question marks* and *exclamation points inside* the quotation marks if they are part of the quotation, *outside* if they apply to your own sentence.

   Can we agree with Emerson when he tells us that "Nothing is at last sacred but the the integrity of your own mind"?

   Sheila's response reminded me of a line by Dorothy Parker: "Where's the man could ease a heart / Like a satin gown?"

As capricious as these rules may seem, they are binding nevertheless on anyone who intends to write formal, college papers; and so you will do well to keep them in mind, or at hand, when you find yourself quoting sources.

One last observation. You'll notice a slash in the middle of my last example, the quotation from Dorothy Parker. It indicates a break between two lines of her verse. This is the usual convention for representing line breaks in poetry, unless the quotation is long enough to be offset. In the latter case, you may simply use spacing to recreate the line breaks as they appear in the original poem.

Repairing Errors

Even the best writers' sentences sometimes break down. In the excitement of invention, parts are likely to get put together in ways that turn out not to work so well in the end. Mistakes, it seems, are simply the price anyone has to pay for the rewards of making something truly new.

But mistakes are also an avenue to finding out what does work. I certainly don't encourage my students to make errors in their writing, but I do encourage them to be bold and inventive when working with language, to take some chances, to reach out and embrace words and structures they have never tried using before. I try to get them to look upon whatever errors result in their papers as resources to be tapped in future writing. Knowing what doesn't work, they are that much closer to knowing what does work.

What follows is a short catalogue of common errors. Some errors that trouble you may not be represented here, but the most serious ones probably are. By referring to the "User's Guide to Mechanics" at the end of this chapter as you review your instructor's comments on your papers, you will be able to find discussions here that will allow you to convert many of your own errors into resources.

I've arranged this catalogue to cover three main types of errors, in this order: 1) those that obscure your meaning, 2) those that violate your readers' expectations, and 3) those that simply undermine your credibility as someone worth listening to. To some extent, these categories overlap. Any error that obscures your meaning, for instance, is bound also to violate your readers' expectations and reflect badly on you as a person worth listening to. The general movement here is from the more important and damaging errors to the less important, so give first priority to eliminating those errors that you find earliest on the list.

ERRORS THAT OBSCURE MEANING

The most serious kinds of writing errors are those that keep your readers from understanding what you mean to say. All of these, in one way or another, can stop readers cold in their tracks, leave them casting around for your point, re-reading sentences with pained, prune-like looks on their faces. These, above all, you want to avoid.

Run-together sentences (R.T.S.): Run-togethers occur whenever a writer places two or more sentences next to one another without indicating a full stop between them. They are the very deadliest of sentence errors. Moving through a run-together, readers can have no idea where one idea ends and the next begins, let alone how the two ideas relate to one another.

If you are prone to writing run-together sentences, I suggest you get in the habit of reading through your rough drafts to yourself, *aloud*. You may feel a little silly, but you'll probably hear very pronounced pauses where each sentence should end. Having in this way found the breaks between sentences, you can then revise out any run-togethers, inserting the appropriate punctuation (usually a period or semicolon) or connecting word (either a coordinating conjunction preceded by a comma or a subordinator) between the sentences. If need be, re-read my comments on "Punctuation between Sentences" in this chapter before attempting the revision. Here are some examples to consider:

Run-together:
The butler did it with help from the cook and the maid and the chauffeur proved innocent.

Revision:
The butler did it with help from the cook, and the maid and the chauffeur proved innocent.

Revision:
The butler did it with help from the cook and the maid, and the chauffeur proved innocent.

Run-together:
Although I have not seen her in seven months, I do expect to talk with Brenda when I get to Bora Bora I will call her.

Revision:
Although I have not seen her in seven months, I do expect to talk with Brenda. When I get to Bora Bora, I will call her.

Revision:
Although I have not seen her in seven months, I do expect to talk with Brenda when I get to Bora Bora. I will call her.

Revision:
Although I have not seen her in seven months, I do expect to talk with Brenda; when I get to Bora Bora, I will call her.

Revision:
Although I have not seen her in seven months, I do expect to talk with Brenda, for when I get to Bora Bora, I will call her.

Revision:
Although I have not seen her in seven months, I do expect to talk with Brenda: when I get to Bora Bora, I will call her.

Revision:
Although I have not seen her in seven months, I do expect to talk with Brenda— when I get to Bora Bora, I will call her.

Obviously, there are many ways to revise a run-together. Don't assume that a period between sentences is your only option. On the other hand, some of the connectors used above might not work in other sentences. The colon and the dash in the last two revisions, for instance, can join these sentences only because the second sentence explains what the first means.

Comma splices (C.S.): Commas splices are close cousins to run-togethers; the only difference is that here the writer puts a comma (instead of nothing) between the two sentences. The problem, of course, is that a comma by itself can't join sentences, and the effect is usually to befuddle the readers as badly as a run-together does.

Two situations might prompt you to write a comma splice. Sometimes two ideas may seem so closely related that you will want to connect them more closely than a period will allow. A comma may seem a way to glide from one idea into the next, tying them together. But readers, when they encounter a comma alone, will not expect to enter another sentence and will therefore not understand the following group of words to *be* a sentence. A much better choice here is a semicolon, which does stop one sentence and start another, but which also ties the two ideas together. The other situation that might lure you into writing a comma splice occurs when you join two sentences with a *conjunctive adverb* like "then," "thus," "however," or "therefore." These words seem to be connectors, and you may mistake them for conjunctions—which can, indeed, join sentences when preceded by a comma. The conjunctive adverbs, though, cannot; thus, they need a semicolon or a period before them to do the connecting.

Revise a comma splice as you would a run-together:

Comma Splice:
Brooke Shields tells us that nothing comes between her and her jeans, in a flash cash registers begin to ring.

Revision:
Brooke Shields tells us that nothing comes between her and her jeans, and in a flash cash registers begin to ring.

Revision:
Brooke Shields tells us that nothing comes between her and her jeans; in a flash cash registers begin to ring.

Comma Splice:
When we get out of this canyon, I'll buy you all a beer, then I'm going home to sleep for a week.

Revision:
When we get out of this canyon, I'll buy you all a beer; then, I'm going home to sleep for a week.

Revision:
When we get out of this canyon, I'll buy you all a beer, but then I'm going home to sleep for a week.

On rare occasions—when the two sentences are short and clear and you are sure there is no potential for confusing your readers—you may want to write an intentional comma splice, for stylistic purposes. Used this way, a comma splice can fuse two ideas or images together into one unit. When you do this, though, you might want to provide an informal footnote for your instructor, explaining the effect you are trying to create with the comma splice.

Sentence fragments (Frag.): Fragments occur when a writer breaks one part of a sentence off from the rest, punctuating the part as if it were a complete sentence itself, or when a writer mistakes for a sentence any group of words that does not contain an independent clause. If you tend to write fragments, you will want to proofread very carefully, making sure that any chunk of words you end with a period, semicolon, question mark, or exclamation point really does make a complete statement or ask a complete question. Reading your prose aloud should help in finding any lurking fragments, as it does in finding run-togethers.

Once you've found them, you can eliminate fragments either by recombining them with the sentence they have been broken off from, or by recasting them as independent sentences, with their own complete subject-verb combinations.

The fragments here are italicized:

Fragment:
Arthur saved the lady in the green gown from the black knight of Winchester. *Who had taken her jewels but not her heart.*

Revision:
Arthur saved the lady in the green gown from the black knight of Winchester, who had taken her jewels but not her heart.

Revision:
Arthur saved the lady in the green gown from the black knight of Winchester. The black knight had taken her jewels but not her heart.

Note that fragments are not neccessarily short. Mere length does not a sentence make:

Fragment:
The second half of the movie seeming to drag on forever, especially the scene in which one of the Martians falls in love with a fire hydrant and launches into a five minute proposal of marriage, in Martian, without subtitles. We finally got up and walked out.

Revision:
The second half of the movie seemed to drag on forever, especially the scene in which one of the Martians falls in love with a fire hydrant and launches into a five minute proposal of marriage, in Martian, without subtitles. We finally got up and walked out.

Revision:
With the second half of the movie seeming to drag on forever—especially the scene in which one of the Martians falls in love with a fire hydrant and launches into a five minute proposal of marriage, in Martian, without subtitles—we finally got up and walked out.

As with comma splices, there are stylistic purposes to which you might occasionally want to put fragments. They may, for instance, prove useful in writing descriptions or narratives, where they can create the effect of disconnected impressions or events. Again, though, if you use fragments deliberately to create an effect, provide a footnote so your instructor can see exactly where and why you are doing so.

Muddled modifiers (M. M.): In the "Short Course in Sentence Structure" earlier in this chapter, I pointed out that words, phrases, or even whole clauses often modify a sentence, adding information to it.

Be sure to place any chunk of language that acts as a modifier strategically close to the object of its affections. Placed between two terms it might reasonably describe, a modifier may seem to describe both of those terms; placed too far from what it describes, it may seem to describe the wrong term or nothing at all. Either way your readers are likely to misconstrue your meaning. Be particularly careful about clauses beginning with "which." They offer the most abundant opportunities to get confused and to confuse others. I've italicized the modifiers in question in each of these examples:

> *Muddled Modifier:*
> In the chair, *like a great, white, bloated oyster,* Maxwell sank deeper into thoughts about the sea.

You can see the problem here; we cannot tell from the sentence whether the modifying phrase applies to Maxwell, or to the chair, or to the sinking. To fix the problem, we would have to rearrange the phrasing so it could not be misread:

> *Revision:*
> In the chair, Maxwell sank, *like a great, white, bloated oyster,* deeper into thoughts about the sea.

> *Revision:*
> In the chair, Maxwell—*who looked like a great, white, bloated, oyster*—sank deeper into thoughts about the sea.

> *Revision:*
> In the chair, *which was like a great, white, bloated oyster,* Maxwell sank deeper into thoughts about the sea.

Each revision alters the meaning; but each more clearly says what it sets out to say than the original.

Here are a few more muddled modifiers. I'll leave the revising to you:

> *Muddled Modifier:*
> *Darting into the street suddenly,* my car nearly hit the frolicsome young puppy.

> *Muddled Modifier:*
> *Rumbling and sputtering loudly,* Maurice pulled away from the Last Chance Cafe in his old Chevy.

> *Muddled Modifier:*
> I tossed a slice of prime beef to my dog, *which was delicious.*

Muddled Modifier:
Slipping through my hands, the branch hits him in his face, *which is frightening.*

Vague pronoun references (Ref.): Pronouns refer back to nouns that have come earlier in your sentence or paragraph. On encountering a pronoun, your readers must be able to see immediately and precisely what earlier term it stands in for. If a pronoun is placed too far from the term it refers to, or if there are several earlier terms it might reasonably refer to, or if there isn't anything for it to refer to, chances are your readers will be unable to follow the thread of your meaning and will have to cast back through the sentence trying to figure out the puzzle.

It's hard to spot and remedy vague pronoun references in the early stages of the writing process. After all, you will know what you mean when you say "it," or "him," or "their" as you write. But your readers can't read your mind, only what's before them on the page. You'll find it easier to identify vague pronouns during the revision stage of writing. After you've put the paper aside and come back to it, you may find that you've forgotten yourself what some of those pronouns refer to. Here are some examples to give you an idea of what to look for:

Vague Reference:
After *he* robbed the stagecoach, Shorty gave Slim the slip.

Revision:
After Shorty robbed the stagecoach, he gave Slim the slip.

Revision:
After Slim robbed the stagecoach, Shorty gave him the slip.

Vague Reference:
Wilma Flintstone and Betty Rubble arrived at the party driving *her* new dinosaur.

Revision:
Wilma Flintstone and Betty Rubble arrived at the party driving Betty's new dinosaur.

Vague Reference:
She has spent too many years worrying about her bank account. *It* has diverted her attention from the people she cares for.

Revision:
She has spent too many years worrying about her bank account, and that worrying has diverted her attention from the people she cares for.

ERRORS THAT VIOLATE THE READERS' EXPECTATIONS

Like those in the first group above, errors in this second category may also confuse your readers and obscure your meaning—especially if they occur in large numbers or in combination with other errors. But these are more likely simply to cause a momentary distraction and provoke annoyance than to completely undermine the sense of what you wish to say. All of them in one way or another violate expectations your readers will bring to your pages—expectations of consistency, logic, and correctness. Since you probably don't want your readers to be either distracted or annoyed, all of these are errors you should try to weed out of your prose.

Faulty pronoun agreement (Pro. Agr.): Pronouns must *agree in number* with the words for which they stand; that is, only a singular pronoun can refer back to a singular noun, only a plural pronoun to a plural noun. Notice in my examples that some pronouns such as "every," "everyone," "either," and "neither"—which might at first glance seem to be plural—are actually singular. In each example, I've italicized both the pronoun in question and the word it refers back to earlier in the sentence:

Faulty Agreement:
You'll need to choose *one* of the new women—Marilyn, or Prudence, or Rebecca—and assign *them* the job.

Revision:
You'll need to choose *one* of the new women—Marilyn, or Prudence, or Rebecca—and assign *her* the job.

Faulty Agreement:
It's clear that *neither* of these poets has yet truly found *their* Muse.

Revision:
It's clear that *neither* of these poets has yet truly found *his* Muse.

Faulty Agreement:
It's time for *everybody* to get *their* things together for the trip.

Revision:
It's time for *everybody* to get *his* or *her* things together for the trip.

Notice that in revising these sentences I've had to come to grips with the thorny question of sex and the single pronoun—of whether to make my singular pronoun references masculine or feminine when I don't know the gender of the person being referred to. I have no one answer to the question. I sometimes use "he," "his," "him" throughout a piece of writing; other times I stick with "she," "her," "her"; and sometimes I alternate back and forth, giving equal time to both sexes. I only occasionally resort to the "he or she," "his or her," "him or her" solution, because this form begins to seem awkward and self-conscious if used too often. The only solution I repudiate entirely is the slash solution: "he/she," "his/her," and so on. These forms go beyond mere awkwardness to achieve the status of genuine eyesores, guaranteed to inject an element of ugliness into your prose, and I strongly recommend against them.

Faulty subject-verb agreement (SVA): Like pronouns and the nouns they refer to, subjects and their verbs must agree in number: singular subjects must have singular verbs; plural subjects, plural verbs. Three situations might lead you into writing the wrong form of a verb. Let me take them in turn:

If the subject and verb are far removed from one another in the sentence, with many intervening phrases or clauses, you may confuse another noun, closer to the verb, with the subject.

Faulty Agreement:
She assured us that the *books* on the reading list for the course *is going* to be fun.

Revision:
She assured us that the *books* on the reading list for the course *are going* to be fun.

Faulty Agreement:
The last I heard, *Roberto*, whom I met in Chicago last summer while I was visiting with my old school friends, *are coming* to California in the spring.

Revision:
The last I heard, *Roberto*, whom I met in Chicago last summer while I was visiting with my old school friends, *is coming* to California in the spring.

If the subject is a pronoun—such as "everybody," "everyone," "each," "either," "neither," etc.—it may seem to be plural when in fact it is singular.

Faulty Agreement:
Belinda insists vehemently that *neither* of her children *eat* "like slavering oinkers," as Marcia reported after the birthday party.

Revision:
Belinda insists vehemently that *neither* of her children *eats* "like slavering oinkers," as Marcia reported after the birthday party.

Faulty Agreement:
Each of his vices *are* readily apparent.

Revision:
Each of his vices *is* readily apparent.

If the subject comes after the verb in the sentence, you may have a hard time recognizing it. This is most likely in the case of verbs that are part of an *expletive pattern*: sentences that begin with "There is," "There are," "There was," and so on; or "Here is," "Here are," "Here was," and the like. In such sentences, the subject will ordinarily be the first noun or pronoun *after* the verb and not in a prepositional phrase.

Faulty Agreement:
There *was* three *armadillos* on the porch this morning.

Revision:
There *were* three *armadillos* on the porch this morning.

Faulty Agreement:
Here in Frost's fourth stanza *is* an *image* of eternal life *and*, later, a *symbol* of rebirth.

Revision:
Here in Frost's fourth stanza *are* an *image* of eternal life *and*, later, a *symbol* of rebirth.

In the last example, the verb must be plural because two singular subjects are joined with "and." On the other hand, when two or more singular subjects are joined with "or," "but," or "nor," the verb remains singular.

Tense shift (T.S.): Often, of course, you will need to move your readers from one tense to another—from the present to the past, from the past to the more distant past, and so on. The movement from one tense to another is natural and inevitable in any sort of sophisticated writing. But some writers are prone to shifting tenses without any apparent reason. If you are among them, you may find yourself writing at one moment in the present tense, at the next in the past, and at the next in the present again. The result, I'm afraid, is probably much confusion among your readers.

If you are afflicted by this tendency, I suggest that you not worry about it too much until it comes time to revise your paper. You don't want your concern for verb tenses to stand in the way of getting your ideas out onto a piece of paper. Once you have a rough draft, though, take a close look at where and why you've changed tenses. If the content of the writing demands a change, don't hesitate to step from one tense into another. But at any point where you find yourself flip-flopping between two tenses erratically, revise for consistency. Here's an example with the tense shifts italicized:

Tense Shift:
When we got to Monterey, the fog was creeping in off the bay and foghorns were moaning beyond the wharf. We *walk* briskly along Cannery Row, smelling caramel corn and cotton candy and sardines and kelp. We *don't want* to linger and look into the shops because the cold air *is clinging* to us like a blanket now. Finally we got to the new Monterey Bay Aquarium, where we *spend* three hours studying the local marine life. The exhibit is well worth the trip, and we will be going back again soon.

This paragraph could as easily be cast in the present tense or the past, but it cannot shift back and forth as it does without annoying us. In the revision below, I've made the past tense the controlling tense of the passage, but notice that the last sentence can still contain a present tense and a future tense verb because the content clearly calls for the changes:

Revision:
When we got to Monterey, the fog was creeping in off the bay and foghorns were moaning beyond the wharf. We *walked* briskly along Cannery Row, smelling caramel corn and cotton candy and sardines and kelp. We *didn't want* to linger and look into the shops because the cold air *was clinging* to us like a blanket now. Finally we got to the new Monterey Bay Aquarium, where we *spent* three hours studying the local marine life. The exhibit is well worth the trip, and we will be going back again soon.

Unfounded commas (Un. C.): In the "Short Course in Punctuation" section of this chapter, I pointed out that commas are really only necessary in six situations. I suggested that you not allow yourself to use a comma until you find yourself in one of those situations. Another way of approaching the same topic is to consider that there are several places where you should never put a comma, where a comma will at the very least irk your readers and at most confound them entirely. Such commas are unfounded.

1. *Don't put a lone comma between a subject and its verb:*

   Unfounded Comma:
   The usually invulnerable Brewster Morgan, crumbled like a stale graham cracker as he gazed into Bonnie's dark and limpid eyes.

   Revision:
   The usually invulnerable Brewster Morgan crumbled like a stale graham cracker as he gazed into Bonnie's dark and limpid eyes.

   You should, however, put a pair of commas around a nonessential interrupter between a subject and verb:

   Revision:
   The usually invulnerable Brewster Morgan, ace playboy of the Westchester Tennis Club, crumbled like a stale graham cracker as he gazed into Bonnie's dark and limpid eyes.

2. *Don't—except for emphasis—put a comma before a conjunction unless the conjunction joins complete sentences or adds a final item to a series.* Readers encountering a comma followed by a conjunction will ordinarily expect either a new sentence or the last item in a series to follow the combination:

   Unfounded Comma:
   It was well known that Lombardo Torin could sing, and dance all night 'when inspired by the presence of a comely young lady.

   Revision:
   It was well known that Lombardo Torin could sing and dance all night when inspired by the presence of a comely young lady.

3. *Don't put commas between an essential modifier and whatever it modifies.* Commas around a modifier imply that it can be removed from

the sentence. Consider how taking the modifying "who" clause out of this sentence would change its meaning:

Unfounded Commas:
Any student, *who completes the work*, will get credit in the class.

Since the writer means that only those students who complete the work will get credit, the information conveyed by the modifier is essential and can't be separated from the sentence by commas.

Revision:
Any student who completes the work will get credit in the class.

Errors That Reflect Badly on the Writer

The errors I've assembled in this third grouping will seldom obscure your meaning and only occasionally violate expectations your readers develop as they move through your sentences. But all of them are important for what they say about you. Any one of them—and especially large numbers of them—will undermine your credibility as a person worth paying serious attention to. Errors of this sort weaken what the Greek rhetoricians called "ethical appeal."

The Greek idea was that whenever we speak or write we inevitably present an "ethos," a personality, to our audience, and that if we want the audience seriously to consider what we say, we must make sure the personality is one our audience will respect. Writers who subject their readers to large numbers of small errors of the sorts I'm about to discuss weaken their ethical appeals because, in essence, they say to their readers: "I don't care enough about what I am saying or about you as an audience to look up the spelling of these words or proofread this paper." Writers who take care with the small details of their language, on the other hand, transmit the opposite message. They say: "Yes. This is me speaking. I am committed to what I am saying and am honestly concerned that you understand and believe me."

Capitalization (Cap./No Cap.): Nothing looks sillier—to anyone who knows better—than a word that is capitalized if it shouldn't be or isn't capitalized if it should be. Unfortunately, the conventions of capitalization in English are complex and erratic. I'll try to simplify them below by listing the most common situations in which you should and shouldn't capitalize.

Do Capitalize:

1. Names of specific people or organizations and titles that form part of a person's name: Merlin, The Xerox Corporation, Ms. Brautley, Doctor Lee.

2. Names of specific places and adjectives derived from those names: Armenia, Texas, Calistoga, the South; Armenian, Texan, Calistogan, Southerner.

3. Names of languages, nationalities, and races: Japanese, French, Caucasian, Asian.

4. Days of the week, months, holidays, historical events: Wednesday, May, Fourth of July, Labor Day, the Vietnam War.

5. The first word of a title and all subsequent words except articles (a, an, the), conjunctions, and short prepositions: *A Farewell to Arms*, "The Owl and the Pussy-Cat," *Writing the Natural Way*.

6. The titles of major, national, public officials: the Secretary of State, the President, the Congresswoman from Ohio.

7. Religious terms held sacred by you or your readers: God, the Torah, the Crucifixion, Allah.

Do Not Capitalize:

1. Words simply in order to emphasize them or because they seem important to you. Although high school may recently have been an important part of your life, and college is now, neither "high school" nor "college" is capitalized unless you are referring to the name of a specific school such as "Awalt High."

2. Directions: "Go east three blocks." "When I am done with business school, I'm heading south."

3. Family relationships, unless they are being used as a substitute for or part of an individual's name: " I think my father is much like my uncle." But, "I think Father is much like Uncle Waldo."

4. Academic subjects, unless they are also the name of a language or you are referring to the title of a specific course: "I will major in psychology and also take courses in genetic engineering." But, "I will begin by taking German and Psychology 112."

Apostrophe errors (Ap./No Ap.): I have long felt that apostrophes are mostly useless and that we'd all be better off if we could simply dump them from the language. After all, if I write, "Dont go into the womens room unless youre a woman," you will know what I mean, even though I have left out three apostrophes. Of course you'd also know what I meant if I wrote, "Don go inta the wimins room less your a womin," but you probably wouldn't think much of me or my language skills if I did. The fact is that most apostrophe errors don't have a thing to do with whether or not your readers understand you, but they have a great deal to do with how literate you appear to be. And that in itself makes them worth a quick review.

Apostrophes, of course, do two things: They mark the place where letters have been taken out of contracted words, and they signal possession. You're unlikely to have any trouble with the first use: Simply remember that the apostrophe stands in for the missing letter(s) in contractions and should be inserted where any letters have been omitted, not where two words may have been stuck together. Write "don't"; don't write "do'nt."

The second use of apostrophes may cause more trouble. When you use an apostrophe to signal possession follow this formula:

1. If the possessive word—naming whoever or whatever possesses something else—already ends in "s," simply add an apostrophe after the "s."

2. If the possessive word does not end in "s," add an apostrophe followed by an "s."

Let's apply the formula to one sample sentence with two possessives:

Incorrect:
Marylou Whites dog, Rambo, slept fitfully as a coalition of neighborhood cats crept into the Whites yard, seeking revenge.

Two words need apostrophes here: "Whites," and "Whites." But they can't be punctuated in the same way. In the first case the possessor is not "Whites," but "White." Rambo belongs not to "Marylou Whites" but to "Marylou White"; since "White" does not end in "s," we must add both an apostrophe and an "s." In the second case, "Whites" is in fact the possessor; the yard belongs to "the Whites," which already ends in "s," and so we can simply add the apostrophe at the end of the word.

Revision:
Marylou White's dog, Rambo, slept fitfully as a coalition of neighborhood cats crept into the Whites' yard, seeking revenge.

Spelling (Sp.): If spelling errors plague you—and they plague most of us who write English—I can offer only this advice. First, a general suggestion: Don't expect to overcome your problems with spelling in a single week or in a single course. The vagaries of English spelling are many, and to master them you will have to sustain your efforts over a period of time and seize opportunities to learn new words wherever they present themselves, whether in an English class, or at a business seminar, or on the front page of the morning paper.

More specifically, you can:

1. Keep a dictionary on your desk and another in your bookbag, purse, or briefcase. Usually, you'll get an uncomfortable feeling when writing a word you are not sure how to spell. Learn to recognize the feeling and to reach for a dictionary in response.

2. Maintain an on-going list of words you have trouble spelling. Add to the list any word you find corrected on a paper or have to look up

while writing. Study this list regularly, and don't scratch off any entries until you are sure you've learned them.

Wrong word (W.W.): A friend of mine—a bright, articulate, young woman upset about an invitation she had received from another friend—came up to me in the hall recently and said, emphatically, "I don't think bringing gifts to a going-away party should be compulsive!" She stood there for a moment, looking righteously indignant until she saw a smile creeping across my face and guessed that perhaps something was amiss. She had meant "compulsory," of course. I explained, and her righteousness turned slowly to chagrin. Her ethical appeal had evaporated.

Wrong words in writing aren't always as spectacular as my friend's mistake. But since writers have more time to select their words than speakers do, readers expect more precision than listeners do. Choosing even slightly inaccurate or inappropriate words can undo your best efforts to come across as a person worth reading. If you have trouble choosing appropriate words, I urge you first to consult the "Diction" section of Chapter Five. Then consider several more suggestions:

1. In general, avoid the temptation to pump your prose full of jargon, technical terms, or "big words" in order to sound academic. You will communicate best, and avoid potential disasters, if you use language you are already comfortable with.

2. Keep a dictionary at hand and use it to check definitions whenever you do need to use unfamiliar words—especially if you are reaching for language that is more formal or technical than you ordinarily use.

3. If you use a thesaurus to find new words, look for terms that have the right connotations (see page 140) for the context in which you will use them. Just because one word is technically a synonym for another doesn't mean both will bring the same emotional associations to your readers' minds, and a word with the wrong connotations can be just as unfortunate as one with the wrong dictionary meaning.

4. Be cautious in using terms you have heard used but never seen in print. You would not want to find yourself, as one student did, writing: "She was looking for me everywhere, and in the mean wild I was waiting for her."

EXERCISES

1. In each sentence in the following paragraph, first underline the subject once and place an "S" above it. Then underline the verb twice and place a "V" above it. Be sure to underline all parts of multiple subjects and verbs. Finally, circle each phrase modifier you find. Be prepared to explain what kind of phrase each is—prepositional, participial, or infinitive.

The unrelenting rain beat down. San Carlos Street was transformed by the deluge. There was water everywhere. Water dripped from the phone lines, beaded on the windows of parked cars, and collected in puddles in the street. In the gutters along the curbs ran grey rivulets of water. The rain plastered pages of the newspaper flat on the glistening sidewalks. The curtains of rain gave the campus a misty, secretive look. Unhappy students, soaked to the skin, tired to death of bad weather, tried to keep their books dry. Splashing through puddles, peering from beneath umbrellas, they hurried to and from class. The street itself was one huge traffic jam. City buses, delivery trucks, and students' cars plowed on through the rain. Their wipers thrashing furiously, their lights gleaming feebly, cars crept past the Ed Building and McQuarrie Hall. The drivers cursed.

2. Expand each of these core sentences by adding to it one prepositional phrase, one participial phrase, and one infinitive phrase.

   a. The driver slows.

   b. George groaned loudly.

   c. She arrives.

   d. The poet spoke.

3. Add *two* dependent clauses to each of the following independent clauses.

   a. You will prevail.

   b. Silence falls.

   c. The mountain loomed.

   d. The waves crash.

4. Punctuate each of the following sentences with whichever is most appropriate: a period, a semicolon, a question mark, a colon, a dash, or an exclamation point. In some sentences several options are available, so be prepared to defend the choice you make.

   a. It seems unlikely that Sarah will want to spend any more money she just bought a car last week.

   b. The costs of building in this town have continued to rise therefore further development seems unlikely.

   c. Will you let us know when the leaves begin to turn color we'd like to come to New England this year.

   d. Forget it you don't have a chance of dating her.

   e. Everyone keeps asking me if I feel well I do.

   f. First you'll want to get into law school then you can start wondering about running for the Senate.

   g. Her apartment is lovely her furniture is shabby.

5. Insert any *necessary* commas in the following sentences.

   a. My wife who usually fixes the family car is out of town so I won't be able to drive anywhere until next week.

   b. As soon as the thunder starts my sister-in-law gets into bed and pulls the sheets over her head.

   c. The last time I saw him he had acquired a long white scar on his chin but I don't know how he got it.

   d. She speaks well writes better and thinks superbly.

   e. The town seemed a sad lonesome place a place to get away from.

   f. After a long and dusty ride across the Dakota badlands it was nice to drink an ice-cold sarsaparilla in the cool darkness of Miss Mae's front parlor.

   g. It was Aristotle who said " Poverty is the parent of revolution and crime."

   h. Politics it is generally assumed has more to do with money than with honor.

   i. Seattle which is at sea level does not often get snow.

   j. Now however it is most certainly snowing.

6. Referring to the "Errors" section of the "User's Guide to Mechanics" on page 220, find the correction symbol that identifies each of the following sentence errors. Write down the marking symbol followed by a *corrected* version of each sentence.

   a. _____ Her first shot went into the lake then the next went into the woods.

   b. _____ Meet me at macy's on friday and we'll do some shopping for our trip South.

   c. _____ The best meet in the shop was the flank stake.

   d. _____ The Klamath River being about 25 yards wide, very deep, and painfully cold in the winter months.

   e. _____ When the picture was taken I have a big smile on my face.

   f. _____ Alfonsos car breaks down with alarming regularity.

   g. _____ The computer, that she wants, costs more money than my car did.

   h. _____ Each of the new species of insects discovered in the last five years are catalogued in her new book.

   i. _____ By selling sex appeal along with their products, encouraging us to valu the former and buy the latter, many in the advertising world have built personal fortuns.

j. ____ The macho image has returned, from the era of the sensitive hippie, we have moved to the hairy-chested, tough-as-nails, quiche-phobic hunk.

k. ____ Lake Tahoe is the most beautiful lake in the mountains that I've seen.

l. ____ Neither of the women has found their baggage yet.

m.____ The bicycle smacked into the car, but it wasn't damaged.

A User's Guide to Mechanics

This chart will help you use Chapter Six as a reference tool when you revise or edit drafts of your writing. It will also help you to interpret and make good use of your instructor's marks and comments on corrected papers. The chart refers you to discussions of any aspect of mechanics you might want to review.

The Parts of Sentences

Punctuation

Errors

ERRORS THAT OBSCURE MEANING

ERRORS THAT VIOLATE THE READERS' EXPECTATIONS

ERRORS THAT REFLECT BADLY ON THE WRITER

Index